Letters and Literar

Samuel J. Tilden,

(Volume II)

Samuel J. Tilden

Alpha Editions

This edition published in 2022

ISBN : 9789356718708

Design and Setting By
Alpha Editions
www.alphaedis.com
Email - info@alphaedis.com

Contents

DAVID A. WELLS TO TILDEN

"NORWICH, CONN, *Jan'y 6th, 1876.*

"MY DEAR GOVERNOR,—I do not know as I can testify of my admiration of your message better than by saying that I want you to send me an early copy in pamphlet form for more careful reading and preservation.

"When the novel which Mr. Sherman and I have been writing (now in press) comes out, in a week or two, please see how curiously prices worked on our imaginary island, where the people used something for currency which had no value as a commodity.

"Very truly yours,
"DAVID A. WELLS."

Answered January 10, 1876, by the Governor, that he desired to submit some of the messages to Mr. Wells, but it was a race against time. The tables were not completed until the discussion was in the proof-reading. "Even I was surprised at the surplus of currency which they evince."

CHARLES O'CONOR TO TILDEN

"FORT WASHINGTON, *Jan'y 12, 1876.*

"MY DEAR GOVERNOR TILDEN,—In this form I will say nothing of the proceedings, surprising to me, as they must have been to you, which have marked the movements toward trying the Tweed civil cases. I have neither seen nor heard from the present chief of the 'bureau of municipal correction' since the newspapers began to regale us with its recent fortunes.

"My object in addressing you is to submit certain suggestions for consideration.

"When the present leading counsel for Tweed fell into a line of practice which, steadily pursued for years as it has been, might well have led to his being dubbed Attorney-General for Rascals, it was my lot to be much in professional antagonism to him. I found him to be neither wise, learned, nor, properly speaking, able, but essentially a trickster. He seems capable of being very troublesome, and to a *negligent* or unskilful adversary he may be regarded as dangerous.

"In dealing with his class, one will generally find a central device around which all their series of tricks revolve, and from which all their force and effectiveness are drawn. This man's course and career furnish an admirable illustration of this fact.

"Our multitude of judges, with equal powers, were perceived by him to furnish a hopeful quarry. One wicked, weak, or manageable could be found somewhere. The next item in his scheme for making judicial proceedings do the work which a bolder thief might seek to accomplish by piracy, highway robbery, or counterfeiting was to engage himself in quarrels where an unlimited number of separate suits by separate plaintiffs might be brought before different judges—all aimed at the same substantial object. This enabled him to make almost at random all sorts of harassing movements against the same parties. Slap-dash, hit or miss, he poured his shot upon the selected victims, the loss of a suit or failure of a movement troubling him not, the number of strings to his bow making this of no more consequence to him than the loss of a single soldier to the general of an army.

"You are aware that any single stockholder in a private or trading corporation may file a bill in equity against the corporation itself, its managing officers, and any one else suggesting malversation, and, of course, such a suit has all the usual incidents of receivership, injunctions, etc., etc.

With a desperate Wall Street swindler for plaintiff, an utterly unscrupulous legal practitioner to direct it, and an unprincipled or manageable judge, the blackmailing capabilities of such a suit are not slight. And when you consider that the stock is always in the market, and that five shares, or, indeed, a single share, may be sufficient to qualify a plaintiff, you see the readiness with which a lot of these suits, like a swarm of insects in summer, may harass. It was with this single scrap of technical knowledge that the Attorney-General for Scoundrels qualified himself for his office. In a very large degree he has lived upon it ever since.

"It was in analogy to this right of the stockholder of a private corporation that some well-intentioned persons devised the scheme of judicially restraining municipal and other public officers from improper action. I believe the history of the rise and fall of this idea may be found in a long argument of mine reported in 'Wetmore *v.* Story,' *22* or *23 Barbour.* You have read it and spoken of it to me. There is no analogy between the cases, and no basis in our common-law or customary jurisprudence for the pretended right of a taxpayer thus to intervene. The inconveniences of such a practice would be enormous. It should not be permitted.

"Using a noted and life-long corruptionist, Charles Devlin, one of Tweed's bail, the Scoundrel's Attorney-General has brought a suit of this kind intended to perplex the Ring prosecutions and aid in misleading the thoughtless readers of their partisan journals.

"I have said that such a suit is wholly without warrant in the common law, and the claim to sustain it thereby has been by the highest authority, in every form, judicially exploded; but in two statutes it may find some color at least of support, and I write in the hope that these may be at once repealed.

"The first of these is S. 3 of the city tax levy of 1864, ch. 405, p. 945. It was obtained by Nathaniel Sands, the then leader of reform, as actuary or general agent of Peter Cooper's Citizens' Association. His subsequent history is known to you. The other is ch. 161 of the laws of 1872, p. 467. You were then in the Legislature, and may have favored its passage; it is not impossible that I may have failed to condemn it when spoken to, but I never believed in the utility of such a remedy. A reluctance to throw cold water on the efforts of our friends sometimes dictates a prudent silence. But whatever might be said at that time, the law of 1875, establishing the right of the State, has superseded the use of any such private taxpayer's action, and this inexpressibly impudent suit of Devlin shows that the privilege tends to mischief. I hope you will get some real and earnest reformer belonging to the Republican party to bring in and push through a bill for the repeal of both these enactments.

"Another subject may seem to demand attention, and that speedily. In Polly Bodine's case, some years ago, it was found that the public journals had so thoroughly imbued the minds of the people with information or reports and ideas concerning the facts of the case that under the existing common law touching challenges to the favor it was hardly possible to get a jury. This must be so in Tweed's cases. The Legislature then altered the law, but I am told that the change is confined in its terms to criminal cases. It ought, by supplemental legislation, to be extended to all cases.

Yours faithfully,
"CH. O'CONOR."

BONAMY PRICE TO TILDEN

"2 NORHAM GARDENS, OXFORD, *Jan'y 31, 1876.*

"MY DEAR SIR,—I hope that the great kindness which you showed me at New York will be allowed to plead my excuse with you for trespassing on your time with a few lines.

"I am anxious to tell you of the deep sympathy and interest with which I have closely watched your public career since I had the honor of becoming acquainted with you in America, as well as the strong admiration which it excited in me.

"Never did a man deserve better of his country; and I fervently hope that the new year will bring the amplest recognition of this fact from your fellow-countrymen.

"Yours truly,
"BONAMY PRICE."

THOMAS COTTMAN TO TILDEN

"NEW YORK, *Feb'y 6th, 1876.*

"DEAR SIR,—I see by the papers this morning that Senator Francis Kernan had taken steps to reconcile the discordant elements of the Democratic party of this city. I am convinced of the unpracticability of the effort without your active interposition. Success with Tammany as at present organized is entirely out of the question. John Kelly, as chief, with Ned Gale, Tom Boize, Frank Spinola, Billy Boyd, and the like as chief counsel, will inevitably bring disaster upon the party and turn the State over to the Republicans in the fall. I would in no wise depreciate Mr. Kelly, whom I regard as a very estimable gentleman. But he has been most unfortunate in selecting his '*entourage*.' There is no lack of efficient material in this city for constructing a capital to the Democratic edifice and insure harmony in all its proportions. As at present constituted, it is an incongruous mass, ready to disintegrate and form other affinities. Without some decided action on your part, there will most certainly be two delegations from this city to the convention, and the bad blood thus generated will outcrop in the fall election to the detriment of the party. I shall leave home to-morrow night for Washington, where I expect to remain a short time to confer with my Democratic friends from the different sections of the country. There being quite a number of my acquaintances representing different constituencies in Congress, the dissensions of the New York Democracy are certain to form the leading topic of conversation and the topic upon which the least satisfaction can be vouchsafed—and the entire responsibility laid at your door. Your personal friendship for Andrew H. Green might have been so evinced as not to have provoked antagonism to yourself, and might have availed by its influence to have kept him from exciting the wrath of a majority of the voting community. Wickham is weaker than Green in the popular estimation. Wickham is looked upon as milk and water, whilst Green is regarded as gall and wormwood, whilst Kelly is so encumbered with *barnacles* as to be impervious to the popular demand for a more democratic form of government than that now run exclusively for the benefit of favorites.

Very respectfully yours,
"THOMAS COTTMAN."

A. E. SILLIMAN TO TILDEN

"Please do not trouble yourself to read until at entire leisure.

"56 CLINTON ST., BROOKLYN, *Feb. 14, '76.*

"MY DEAR SIR,—I am indebted to some kind friend for a copy of your Message for 1876 (secluded among my books, I do not know whom); but recollecting your conversations with Mr. Bennett and myself some years since at Delmonico's, I am fain to believe that I am one of a number to whom you may have directed it to be sent; but in the uncertainty deem it more decorous to address you *personally* in my recognition of the favor. I read the Message at the time of its appearance with much interest, and was particularly struck with the strong clearness and distinctness of that portion of it pertaining to financial affairs, which perhaps is the 'part of the schooner' I am (or rather ought to be) more particularly conversant with. We are much indebted to Mr. Chase for the present state of things—his refusal to recognize the banks as government depositors, and have a clearing-house for the daily settlement of its debt, with *enormous* resulting economy of its *physical* features (for instance, the issue of legal-tender notes under such circumstances need not have exceeded one hundred million)—but mainly for setting loose under his national bank system a thousand *new* inflating-machines, called banks, practically unmuzzling the old banks which he cowed in under its flag. Admitting other causes, in my opinion it is mainly[1] the bank inflation which has caused the state of things *culminating* in 1873; and which crisis, opening the eyes of the community to its truths on the one side, shows them the terrors of contraction on the other, and the natural apprehension of a sudden contraction to a specie basis produces thus, of course, almost paralysis in all business movement beyond the *immediate* present. I do not think that the plan for *arbitrary* resumption in 1879 will be attended with happy effect. 'There is no royal road to learning,' and assuredly none to specie resumption. We have slid down the hill with intense velocity; we have got *slowly* to trudge up the hill again through the snow if we would have another slide. I think that if ten years ago we had commenced destroying the legal tender at the rate of 5 per cent. per annum we would have avoided *1873*, and have been paying specie now; and I think if we commence[2] now in that ratio we shall in ten years arrive at the desired result, relieving the business community from the bugbear of rapid contraction. The destruction of *20* million legal-tender would carry with it *80* million bank credit—say, an annual contraction of *100* million. This, if the country is let alone, with a decent attention to the economy you suggest, it could have from the increasing receipts of its industry. In *1873*, as a matter of *curiosity*, I examined into the statistics of finance for the periods stated, and it is from them I draw my conclusions above expressed. I annex a copy, as perhaps your experienced eye will take in at a glance the gravity of the record. Now, my dear sir, I hope you will excuse my troubling you with this long note, and not trouble yourself to answer it. With hopes that you may be blessed in health, and remain long as the head of your State, I am

"Very truly your friend and servant,
"A. E. SILLIMAN.

CAUSE OF FINANCIAL CRISIS IN 1873

1862.

Total *liability* of all the banks in the United States	$1024 mills.
Increase of *capital* in the preceding nine years	117 mills.
Increase of *liability* in the same nine years	248 mills.

1872.

Total *liability* of national banks, including the *State* banks *only*, of the city of New York	$1759 mills.
Increase of *liability* in said ten years $717 mills.	
Increase of *bank capital* in said ten years $78 mills (!)	
Add legal-tender notes and fractional c.	400 mills.
Total	$2159 mills.

"*Showing*

"Money means in the hands of the community in excess of that of 1862, *$1117* mills. And this *$2,159,000,000* is the *hub* of the wheel from which radiates the *individual* debt of the community, until it reaches the apple-woman at the corner.

"Perhaps the above may vary, more or less, *20 or 30 mills.*

In 1854 the number was		1208
In 1873 the number was		1945
Nineteen years an increase of	738	
In 1862 the number was		1492
In 1873 the number was		1946
Eleven years an increase of	454	

New banks with an increase of capital only of *$78 mills.*

"In considering the position, the banks are recognized *as part of the public* in their representations of their stockholders, and it is not intended to dissect out of their liabilities their *individual* status."

CHARLES O'CONOR TO TILDEN

"FORT WASHINGTON, *March 16th, 1876.*

"MY DEAR GOVERNOR,—I had the honor of addressing you some time ago concerning the expediency of repealing a section of 1864 and an act of 1867, both of which most absurdly recognized a right of action in tax-payers for maladministration by public corporations.

"My reason for urging the step at this time is an action by one Charles Devlin, Tweed's bail, against the Attorney-General and others, seeking the appointment of a receiver and the transfer of the Ring suits to the control of the Tweed faction. Tweed's attorneys are attorneys for the plaintiff in this action, and for their motions they select as judge Charles Donohue, who, by the order for a bill of particulars, showed his fidelity to Tweed principles.

"It is ridiculous that such a suit should be permitted to harass us and bring our movements under the control of Donohue.

"I have supposed that a real reformer of the Republican party should be enlisted to push this repeal through, and if you select such an one I am willing, if put in communication with him, to aid him in any way that I can, and, if need be, I will go to Albany to co-operate with him.

"The relations of D. D. Field and Judge Peabody are such that the latter, though a very correct and honorable man, ought not to be drawn into this affair. Of course, his son, the member of Assembly, is subject to the same remark. And as young Mr. Fish and he are *very* intimate, and reside together in private joint lodgings, I would advise that Mr. Fish be not included in any movement on this subject.

"Yours truly,
"CH. O'CONOR."

WHEELER H. PECKHAM TO S. J. TILDEN

"NEW YORK, *April 15th, 1876.*

"DEAR SIR,—I enclose draft of a bill appropriating twenty-five thousand dollars for expenses prosecuting the ring suits.

"The last appropriation was in 1874, ch. 359, laws of that year—$25,000.

"Of the sum then appropriated but about $8000 are left. The expenses of the last civil trial of Tweed will more than exhaust this. The disbursements of that trial are about $3000, and Mr. Carter's very moderate bill is $5000. That exhausts the appropriation without any bill for my own services.

"The trial was protracted and expensive beyond expectation. It consumed the two months of January and February and part of March. The deft. Tweed is making a case and will appeal, and consequently further expense must be incurred. The case vs. Sweeney is also ready for trial, and we expect to try it in May. Active proceedings are pending against others, which must result in the collection of very considerable sums of money. Over half a million of dollars has already been realized and paid over to the city treasury. Under the circumstances, it seems to me that there should be no hesitation on the part of the Legislature in passing the bill.

"Of course, the force of my opinion must be weighed in the light of my own interest. On that account it is proper to add that I have submitted this proposed law to your consideration at the request of Mr. O'Conor.

"Yours truly,
"WHEELER H. PECKHAM."

"Mr. O'Conor's name is left out of the act by his special request.—W. H. P."

CHARLES O'CONOR TO GOVERNOR TILDEN

"NEW YORK, *May 1st, 1876.*

"MY DEAR SIR,—I write to remind you that great trouble and inconvenience are likely to result if the repealing acts sent up and handed to Senator Robertson are not pressed.

"Yours truly,
"CH. O'CONOR."

D. A. WELLS TO TILDEN

"NORWICH, CONN., *May 5th, 1876.*

"MY DEAR GOVERNOR,—I have canvassed the political situation in this State since I last saw you, and think there is no doubt of your receiving the unanimous support of Connecticut at St. Louis. Indeed, there is no diversity of sentiment, so far as I can hear, Loomis, of New London, being the only one of the delegates whom I should regard as doubtful. Dick Hubbard, of Hartford, who heads the delegation; Waller, of New London, the Speaker of the House (who will probably go as a substitute); and Hunter, of Willimantic, are all to be relied on as warm supporters, and they will control the delegation if it should need controlling. Barr, of Hartford, is a tricky fellow, and if you could bring some influence to bear on him it may be as well, though I am advised that it is not necessary.

"There is one element of the future that I do not like, and that is the probable election of Barnum to the Senate from this State in place of English. Barnum is so unfit, so much of the Tweed order of men, and a pig-iron protectionist into the bargain, that the effect of his election will be bad, not only in the State, but throughout the country. It will be cited everywhere as a proof that the professions of the party do not amount to anything; I do not, however, know what you can do about it, or whether it would be advisable to exert an influence if you could; but it is an event that is likely to disgust the free-trade element intensely, and also those who have a deep conviction of the necessity of political reform. Eaton is probably more responsible for this movement than any other man, except Barnum.

"Do you think I had better go to the 18th of May conference? I see nothing antagonistic in it to your interest; neither do I think it will amount to much. I know the Republican managers have a most profound contempt for the whole movement, and haven't an idea of allowing to Bristow to be nominated.

"Command me for any service I can render.

"Truly yours,
"DAVID A. WELLS."

"*Hon. S. J. Tilden.*"

Shortly after the inauguration of Mr. Tilden as Governor, in January, 1875, he sent to the Legislature a special message setting forth his convictions of the corrupt management of the canals of the State. This message abounded with specific details of fraud of so infamous a character that even friends of the implicated contractors in the Legislature felt constrained to grant the request of the Governor, and by a concurrent resolution, adopted on the 31st day of March, 1875, authorized him to appoint a committee of four "to investigate the affairs of the canals of the State, and especially the matters embraced in the special message of the Governor, communicated to Legislature on the 19th of March, 1875."

In compliance with this authority, the Governor appointed four gentlemen, whose names are signed to the following report, two theretofore having acted with the Republican party and two with the Democratic. The Governor's commissioners organized at Albany on the 12th of April following; but before they began to take testimony the friends of the canal jobbers in the Assembly managed to pass a resolution appointing a commission of that body also to make a similar investigation, but naming in the resolution commissioners satisfactory to those who constituted what was known as the "Canal Ring."

This commission met two or three times, and then offered to the Governor's commission, under pretext of saving time and expense, to join them, so that the two commissions should constitute but one body. Of course this proffer was promptly declined, and the legislative commission took no more testimony, and was never heard of again.

The interval between the organization of the Governor's commission, in April, and the time for the introduction of water into the canals, near the end of May, was devoted exclusively to an examination of the most important works in progress or recently completed in the prism of the canals.

Between the 31st day of July of that year, when the commission submitted its first report, and the 14th of February, when it submitted its final report, it issued twelve reports. That which follows gives a summary of the facts developed by the investigation which confirm in every detail the charges made in the Governor's message, besides adding very much to the total amount of confirming testimony. The reason for this confirmation being so complete was that the Governor, almost immediately after his election, employed privately, and at his own expense, an engineer in whose professional training and experience he could place entire confidence, the late Mr. Elkanah Sweet, to make an investigation of the recent canal work, gave him authority to take down any portion of the work to ascertain how far and in what way it was not in conformity with the contract, and gave him also authority to inspect all the canal contracts in the archives of the Canal Board and compare them with his observations. Upon his report the facts presented in the Governor's canal message were based. Mr. Sweet, therefore, was naturally employed by the Governor's commission to make the yet more thorough and elaborate investigation required of them.

The Governor's canal message, with this incontestable confirmation of all its allegations, gave him a national fame, and contributed more than anything he had previously done to make his nomination to the Presidency a political necessity for the Democratic party.

Several previous efforts to investigate frauds in the operation of the State canals had been made by the Legislature, but all had theretofore proved abortive. One reason which contributed largely to prevent the investigation of the Governor's commission sharing the same fate was the exclusion of reporters from the meetings of the board during the examination of witnesses. By this means nothing of its work was given to the public until the testimony was digested into an intelligible report of what had been proved. The testimony was necessarily so largely technical that if given to the press day by day, as received, the public would have soon tired of the subject, and, what was worse, the witnesses would have been tempted to shape their testimony rather to its effects upon the newspaper public than upon the commissioners. The consequence was that when the reports appeared they were read, and their impact upon the public was proportionately prompt, instructive, and penetrating.

CANAL INVESTIGATING COMMISSION

FIRST REPORT TO THE GOVERNOR[3]

"*To his Excellency the Governor, and to the Honorable the Legislature of the State of New York*:

"The undersigned commissioners, appointed by the Governor, with the advice and consent of the Senate, under a concurrent resolution of the Legislature adopted on the 31st day of March last, 'to investigate the affairs of the canals of the States, and especially the matters embraced in the special message of the Governor, communicated to the Legislature on the 19th day of March, 1875,' have the honor to submit the following report of the progress of their investigations:

"Your commissioners, assembled at the capitol, qualified and organized on the 12th day of April, 1875. The interval between that time and the opening of the canals, a period of about six weeks, was devoted exclusively to an examination of the most important works in progress, or recently completed in the prism of the canals. When this examination was interrupted by the introduction of water, near the end of May, your commission returned to the capitol and proceeded to supplement and enlarge the area of their information by the examination of witnesses.

"In this work they were unexpectedly embarrassed by a decision of one of the judges of this district, at Special Term, denying to them a power, which they supposed to have been conferred upon them by the legislative authorities, to require the production before them of the books and papers of witnesses. They directed an appeal to be taken from this decision, and it was finally reversed at the General Term, but not until late in the month of November, till when your commission was obliged to contend with all the inconveniences resulting from the privation of such a necessary and indispensable prerogative. The opinion of Justice Learned at the Special Term, and that of Justice James at the General Term, are annexed to this report.

"On the 31st of July the commission submitted their first annual report to the Governor. It relates to a contract for substituting slope and vertical for bench wall between Port Schuyler and the lower Mohawk aqueduct. This report was followed at intervals by eleven others, entitled, respectively, as follows:

"Second report.—H. D. Denison's contract east of the city of Utica.

"Third report.—Hulser's bridge contract.

"Fourth report.—Willard Johnson's lower side cut lock contract at West Troy.

"Fifth report.—Buffalo contracts and legislative awards.

"Sixth report.—Champlain enlargement; Bullard's bend contract.

"Seventh report.—Buffalo contracts and State officers.

"Eighth report.—The Baxter award.

"Ninth report.—Contract of E. W. Williams for building vertical wall at Rome.

"Tenth report.—Flagler & Reilley's pending contract at Fort Plain.

"Eleventh report.—Jordan level contracts.

"Twelfth report.—The auditor's traffic in canal certificates.

"A copy of these several reports, together with the testimony taken before the commission, covering together 2927 pages, are submitted with this report.

"Several other reports are in course of preparation. One on the Glen's Fall feeder, a second on the Canal Appraiser's ice awards at Rochester in 187 , and a third on the W. C. Stevens contract assigned to Denison, Belden & Co., for dredging the Albany basin, dated December 31, 1866, will be submitted at an early day.

"Though we have given this investigation our most unremitting and exclusive attention, we not only have not exhausted the subject, but there are many matters falling within the range of our inquiry which we have only been able to touch incidentally. Among these we regret that the subjects of 'ordinary repairs,' the lateral canals, and the present system of appraising canal damages are included.

"As we have been able to examine only a limited portion of the work done on the canals since 1868, of course we have found it impossible to extend our inquiries beyond that year, though we have abundant evidence that the mismanagement of the canals dates from a much earlier period. But the results of our investigation—incomplete as any investigation made in so short a time must necessarily have been—will, we think, suffice to indicate with tolerable distinctness what have been the more mischievous errors in the management of our canals, and some of their more obvious correctives.

"We propose to-day to submit to you such of the conclusions as we have reached, with all the testimony we have taken, reserving for a later day some further recommendations which are under consideration.

"Introductory to such conclusions as we are now prepared to submit to you, it is proper that we first invite your attention to the character of our canal property as an investment, and show precisely how it stands upon the books of the State.

The total revenues from our system of canals at the close of the last fiscal year, including gains resulting from the management of the sinking fund, amounted to	$138,507,129.91
Total payments for canal purposes up to same period, including construction	167,003,357.91
Excess of cost over earnings	$28,496,228.00

"This sum of $28,000,000 and upwards represents the premium which the people of this State have paid in taxes during the last fifty-odd years to secure and encourage the use of these waterways for purposes of transportation, the equivalent of an annual subsidy of over $560,000.

The tolls received from all the canals during the fiscal year ending September 30, 1875, amounted to	$1,902,990.64	
There were expended for repairs and maintenance during the same period	$2,247,297.01	
Damages during the same period	305,796.68	
		2,553,093.69
Balance against the State		$650,103.05

"If to this be added the interest on the canal debt, the cost of collection, and the difference between miscellaneous expenses and receipts, as set forth in detail in Exhibit B, the loss to the State from the canals during the last fiscal year will be found to amount to the enormous sum of $1,412,470.79.

"The cost of repairs and maintenance is so obviously out of all proportion with the necessities of a system of completed structures like our canals, which have little that is complicated or perishable about them, that we are forced to seek the explanation of it in their administration.

"Our investigation was not long in revealing the fact that the canals have not been managed upon the principles which would govern any man in the administration of his private estate. The interests of the public have been systematically disregarded. The precautions with which the Legislature has attempted to defend this property from peculation and fraud, and secure for it faithful and efficient service, have been deliberately and persistently disregarded; while the responsibility of its agents has been so divided and distributed as to leave the State comparatively remediless and at the mercy of the predatory classes, who have been, if they do not continue to be, a formidable political power.

"The more conspicuous evidences of mismanagement which our investigation has disclosed may be divided into three categories:

"*First*, as to the modes of letting contracts.

"*Second*, as to the modes of measuring and estimating work to the contractors.

"*Third*, as to the facilities for procuring legislative relief.

"*First*, as to the mode of letting the contracts:

"It seems to have been the practice for years to let contracts upon conditions which exclude honest contractors and confine this business, at least as to what are termed 'extraordinary repairs,' almost exclusively to large capitalists. The large deposits required from contractors discouraged bidders with small means, while the encouragement offered to unbalanced bidding, by a neglect to enforce the faithful performance of the provisions of the contract, have a tendency to exclude all who bid fair prices, with the honest intention of giving the State fair work for them. Till since the commencement of this investigation we do not know of a single instance in which any forfeiture of his deposit had been enforced against any contractor; while we believe we do no one any injustice in saying that no contract has been let since 1868 the provisions of which have been properly complied with.

"There has been a corresponding disregard of all the provisions of law regulating the letting of the contracts. The law wisely required a preliminary survey, with maps, specifications, and estimates to be made by the division engineer, approved by the State Engineer and by the Canal Board, before a contract could be let. The purpose of these precautions was to ascertain the amount and probable cost of the work as a means of determining the relative merits of the respective bids, and to serve as a protection against false or erroneous estimates of engineers. These precautions have been almost universally neglected. The result has been that the amount of work and materials required in the actual construction varied so widely from the quantities let that in nearly every instance the person receiving the contract proved in the end to have been the highest instead of the lowest bidder;[4] and we cannot resist the conclusion that these precautions in many instances were neglected with the intent to afford greater facilities for defrauding the State. These evils have been greatly aggravated by the frequent changes of the engineers on the canals and the loss of knowledge as to work done, which the removed engineers carried away with them.

"*Second*, as to the mode of measuring and estimating work to the contractors:

"This responsible duty, involving, as it should, a perfect familiarity with the terms of the contract and with the character of the work in progress, has been devolved, not by law, but in practice, entirely upon assistants who are not sworn; who, but in few instances, have been found to possess a competent knowledge of engineering; and who, in most cases, appear to owe their positions, and therefore to have been in a greater or less degree dependent upon the political favor and influence of the contracting class. It will be hardly a matter of surprise, therefore, that in not more than a single instance that has come under our scrutiny have we found the work faithfully measured, or a single contract closed, under which the contractor has not received more than he was entitled to.

"Under these influences, operating in favor of the contractor and to the prejudice of the State, a system of fraudulent estimates and measurements has become so established that though in direct and flagrant violation of the very language of the contract, it is deliberately defended by those who profit by it, on the ground that it has been sanctioned by long usage. For example: it has been a practice of the engineers to allow the contractor for excavating behind vertical wall, on a slope of one to one, without regard to the necessity for such excavation, and whether the excavation was made or not.

"As nearly all vertical wall is constructed in the winter or early spring, and when the banks are frozen, the cut is usually vertical or nearly so, and any charge for such excavation is a fraud upon the State. The contracts also uniformly provide that the contractor shall be allowed nothing for the filling in of the place supposed to be excavated behind the walls, if such filling is from earth already paid for as excavation, unless he is obliged to draw his material more than 200 feet on the line of the canal. This provision has also come to be treated as obsolete, and the State seems to have been uniformly charged not only for excavation which had not been made, but for filling up the assumed excavation which, had it been made, the State was not bound to pay for. The profits derived in this indirect way through the fraudulent connivance of the agents of the State, has led to an enormous expenditure for works wholly unnecessary, and which to keep in repair must continue to subject the State to a very considerable yearly expense.

"One of the principal expenditures upon the canals since 1868 for extraordinary repairs has been made in the construction of vertical and slope walls which have been, as we think, very unwisely substituted for the old walls, the capacity of the canals before their removal having been ample for all their business.

"Between the 1st of January, 1868, and the 1st of July, 1875, there have been built forty-three and one-third miles, linear measure, of vertical wall, at a total cost, including the removal of bench walls which they displaced, of $1,589,885, the cost per linear foot averaging $6.95.

"These walls, besides costing four or five times as much as the slope walls, are less durable, much more expensive to keep in repair, and possess no substantial advantage except in large towns, the commerce of which requires special facilities for docking. But of the forty-three and one-third miles built since 1868, it cannot be pretended that so many as three were needed to meet such exigencies.

"Without stopping at present to inquire if the business of the canal justified the removal of the old bench walls at all, it is very certain that a good slope wall would have been preferable throughout nine-tenths, at least, of the entire extent upon which vertical wall has been constructed; and, at the rate paid for slope wall during this period, would have resulted in an economy to the State of not less than $1,300,000, or nearly $200,000 a year.

"An important item in the cost of this vertical wall was made up of the fictitious estimates to which we have already alluded. Assuming that the State was uniformly charged with fictitious excavation and embankment along the entire length of this vertical wall—and we have no satisfactory proof that a single rod of it was entitled to be excepted—the loss to the State from this source alone cannot be estimated at less than $230,000.

"We have found all the other more important provisions of these contracts as uniformly disregarded. We have torn down and carefully examined the work under more than forty contracts; and we cannot name one in which the work comes up, even approximately, to the specifications. The contracts define with great precision the size and character of the stone to be used, the mode of their disposition, the thickness and other dimensions of the wall, the character of the cement and sand, the quality of lining, and what else is needed to insure durability and a capacity to resist the shocks from loaded boats to which the walls of canals are constantly subjected. In no one of the forty-odd contracts that we examined did we find the stone either in size or disposition; the dimensions of the wall; the quality of the sand, lime, cement, and gravel, to correspond with the specifications. The consequences to the State are not only that it has been called upon to pay for a higher class of work than it has received, but that it is exposed to a large annual expenditure to keep these ill-constructed and for the most part worthless walls in repair. It has been a not uncommon circumstance for the superintendent to be called upon to repair the earlier work under a vertical wall contract while other portions of the structure were still in progress. To keep this class of walls in repair promises to be one of the principal sources of expense for the future maintenance of our canals.[5]

"Nor is this system of fictitious estimates confined to vertical wall. Since 1868 fifty-three and two-thirds miles of slope wall have been built. By the terms of the contracts these walls should have had an average thickness of at least fifteen inches, measured perpendicularly to the slope. None of the stone composing it should have been less than twelve inches in length at right angles to the face, and the rear of the wall was to rest on a base of clean, hard gravel nine inches thick. The engineers have uniformly estimated these walls at the specified thickness of fifteen inches, while in point of fact we have not found on any of our canals a single stretch of slope wall, constructed since 1868, that would average over ten inches. Of course, the stones are usually smaller than the minimum size required by the specifications, and we did not find a single specimen of the clean, hard gravel lining required by the contract; so that the State has been made to pay, throughout the whole forty-three and two-thirds miles of slope wall, for one-third more of constructed wall than it has received—full prices for a very inferior quality of stone—and for lining the whole work, though not a single yard of the required quality appears to have been ever furnished.

"To confirm our own judgments, and to be sure that we were not applying an erroneous standard to the work done in the prism of the canals, we invited Professors Peter S. Michie and J. B. Wheeler, of the United States Military Academy at West Point, to go over a large proportion of what we had already visited and to give us the benefit of their judgment about it. Their report is annexed, and will be found to accord in all substantial particulars with the opinions we have felt it our duty to express in our previous report to his Excellency the Governor, and in this communication, in reference to all the contract work on the canals that has fallen under our observation.

"*Third*, as to the facilities afforded by the Legislature to contractors for procuring legislative relief:

"These facilities appear to have been grossly and corruptly abused under the discretionary power conferred upon the Canal Board by the Legislature. Numbers of contracts have been cancelled when such portions of the work as were let on terms profitable to the contractor had been executed, while those portions of the work that were let upon terms more advantageous to the State were left unexecuted. In such cases it not unfrequently happened that this remaining work was let to the same parties, under a new contract, at much higher rates. When the Canal Board was found to turn a deaf ear to such appeals, these applications for relief would be addressed directly to the Legislature, where the fear of doing injustice, and the want of the time and familiarity with the subject necessary for investigating its details, often permitted the allowance of awards conceived in fraud and without a single legal or equitable merit.

"An illustration of this class of abuses will be found in the fifth and seventh reports of this commission to the Governor. For one of them—the case of the award for the relief of John Hand—George D. Lord, a member of the Assembly which made the award, is now under indictment, it appearing that the claim made in his behalf was altogether fraudulent and the alleged proofs fictitious. Another award was also made to George D. Lord of $119,000 for alleged losses under contracts with the State for work in Buffalo harbor. This was, to all appearances, as much greater an abuse of legislative credulity, as the amount exceeded that which was realized under the award to John Hand. The limited technical knowledge of canal administration possessed by a large majority of State legislators, and the claims of other important business upon their attention, make it impossible for them to properly scrutinize appeals of this character, which are usually pressed by designing men, perfectly familiar with all the resources for deception which our complicated canal system afforded, prior to the constitutional amendment of 1874.

"In view of the systematic infidelity of the agents of the State which this investigation has disclosed, is it surprising that the expenditures for extraordinary repairs alone on our canals have amounted, since 1867, to $8,444,827.24, or to nearly as much as the whole of our canal debt, less the sinking fund, which on the 30th of September, 1875, was $8,638,314.49? Of these expenditures for extraordinary repairs it is our belief that fully seventy per cent. have been inconsiderate, unwise, and unprofitable to the State.[6]

"The facts which have been brought to light in the course of this investigation have constrained us already to recommend rigorous proceedings to be taken against the following parties:

"First.—Against Denison, Belden & Co. for the recovery of large sums of money which they appear to have received unlawfully under their contracts for work between Port Schuyler and the lower Mohawk aqueduct, and for work east of the city of Utica, both on the Erie Canal. The claims of the State against these parties are fully set forth in the first and second reports of this commission to the Governor, and suits are in progress.

"Second.—George D. Lord has been indicted by a grand jury of Erie County, upon the facts disclosed by this commission, for bribery in procuring an act of the Legislature for the relief of one John Hand. The history of this case will be found in the fifth report of this commission to the Governor.

"Third.—Thaddeus C. Davis, late member of the Board of Canal Appraisers, has also been indicted for a conspiracy to cheat the State. The circumstances which made him amenable to the criminal courts are set forth in the fifth, seventh, and eighth reports of this commission to the Governor.

"A civil suit has also been instituted against Davis to recover moneys fraudulently obtained from the State by himself in conjunction with George D. Lord.

"Fourth.—Indictments have also been found upon the testimony furnished by the commission against the following other high officials: Alexander Barkley, ex-canal commissioner; John Kelly, late superintendent of section No. 12 of the Erie Canal; J. Frederick Behn, division engineer of the western section; and D. Clinton Welch, ex-superintendent of section No. 12.

"Fifth.—Upon testimony furnished by this commission, the commissioners of the canal fund made a requisition upon the Governor for the removal of Francis S. Thayer, late Auditor of the Canal Department, and on the twenty-eighth day of December last Mr. Thayer was suspended upon charges of unlawfully trafficking in canal certificates and violating his duty as auditor 'in respect to the public moneys in his charge and subject to his draft.' The charges preferred by the commission upon which the commissioners of the canal fund and the Governor acted, together with their proceedings thereon, respectively, are hereunto annexed.[7] The testimony by which these charges were established will be found in volume three of the accompanying testimony, at pages 1140, 2070, 2156, 2162, 2180, 2215, 2226, 2239, 2256, 2305, 2347, 2379, 2381, 2382, 2383, 2385,

2389, 2407, 2414, 2417, 2420, 2422, 2426, 2445, 2460, 2461, 2534, 2560, 2585, 2587.

"The following sums in cash, or evidences of indebtedness, obtained from the State through fraud, have already been reclaimed by and restored through the commission to the treasury:

Canal Commissioner's certificates of indebtedness, issued on account of the second John Hand award:

No. 179, dated Feb. 10, 1875	$2,500 00	
No. 181, dated Feb. 10, 1875	9,355 00	
No. 182, dated Feb. 10, 1875	4,000 00	
No. 183, dated Feb. 10, 1875	1,000 00	
No. 185, dated Feb. 10, 1875	2,000 00	
[Nos. 179, 181, 182, and 185 were returned by Lewis J. Bennett;		
No. 183 was returned by Wm. H. Bowman, Esq.]		
Returned in cash by Lewis J. Bennett, on account of the first John Hand award	3,199 50	
Cash returned by Ellis Webster and Son, on account of money received on false vouchers	582 68	
Forward		$22,637 18

Carried forward		$22,637 18
Plenary authority conferred upon the Commission by the parties interested, to cancel the Canal Commissioner's certificates of Feb. 10th, 1875, issued on account of the second John Hand award, delivered as a gift by Lewis H. Bennett to Thad. C. Davis, then Canal Appraiser; by Davis given to ex-Canal Commissioner Alexander Barkley, who claims to have mailed it to Lewis H. Bennett, though it appears from the evidence before us that, if mailed, it never reached him	2,000 00	2,000 00
Canal Commissioner's certificate, No. 184, issued Feb. 10th, 1875, under the second John Hand award, to Lewis J. Bennett, for $16,000, by him delivered under an agreement to the agent of Geo. D. Lord, and rendered void through testimony elicited by the Commission	16,000 00	16,000 00
		$40,637 18
Accrued interest to February 14, 1876		2,259 21
Total		$42,896 39

"The following sums are shown by the reports of this commission to the Executive to have been estimated to the contractors for work that was never performed, or was improperly paid for through erroneous classification, and for which the receivers should be required to make restitution:

Denison, Belden & Co.:

Port Schuyler to lower Mohawk aqueduct	$157,337

	02
Denison, Belden & Co.:	
East of the city of Utica	16,121 35
Willard Johnson:	
Lower side-cut lock, West Troy	30,595 65
Denison, Belden & Co.:	
Bullard's Bend contract	85,547 62
E. W. Williams:	
Building vertical walls at Rome	3,041 08
Flagler & Reilley:	
Fort Plain contract	5,845 35
S. D. Keller:	
Jordan Level contract	36,568 39
N. S. Gere:	
Jordan Level contract	8,801 90
Thomas Gale:	
Jordan Level contract	6,667 94
Hiram Candee:	
Jordan Level contract	17,567 33
	$368,093 63
Add to this the balance yet due for money paid under the first John Hand award	30,782 36
Total	$398,875

"Large as these sums appear, we are fully impressed with the belief that they form but a fraction of the amount that is due to the State from similar sources.

"For the purpose of ascertaining more precisely the extent of this class of liabilities, and to protect the State in future from the irregularities and improvidence out of which they have arisen, we recommend that the Canal Board be clothed with ample powers and authority for taking testimony.

"A perusal of the testimony and the reports to the Executive herewith submitted clearly establish the fact that our canals are a burden to the States less, perhaps, through the imperfection of our laws, than the mode in which they have been administered.

"Every appropriation for new work and extraordinary repairs on the canals for the six years from 1867 to 1873 contained a provision that no part or portion of the money therein appropriated 'for new work or work on change of plan' should be expended or paid, nor any contract involving such expenditure and payment be made on behalf of the States, until the maps, plans, and estimates of such new work had been submitted to and approved by the Canal Board.

"There has been a law on the statute-books since 1850, yet more stringent, which provides that 'before any work shall be contracted for on any canals of the State the division engineer shall cause to be ascertained, with all practical accuracy, the quantity of embankment, excavation, and masonry, and the quality and quantity of all materials to be used, and all other items of work to be placed under contract, a statement of which, together with maps, plans, and specifications corresponding with those adopted by the Canal Board, and on file in the office of the State Engineer and Surveyor, shall be publicly exhibited to persons proposing for work to be let.'

"These most explicit provisions of law have been very rarely observed. Contracts have not only been let without the preliminary surveys, maps, plans, and estimates, but one of the most familiar abuses on the canals of late years has been to change the plan of work after the contract is signed, by which the contractor gets relieved from the unprofitable portions of his work, and is furnished a pretext for establishing a new scale of prices, in connivance with the auditing officers. Illustrations of this method of defrauding the State may be found in several of the reports submitted to the Executive. The most costly one to the State is described in our first report. The contract for substituting slope and vertical wall for the bench wall between the Port Schuyler and the lower Mohawk aqueduct provided originally for 14,000 cubic yards of slope wall and only 9000 of vertical wall. As if distrustful of the influence of the contractor over its own agents, the Legislature, within six months after the time this work could have begun, in appropriating money to carry it on, absolutely prohibited the expenditure of more than five per cent. of the appropriation for vertical wall. Regardless, however, of this restriction, and regardless of the terms of the contract which provided for twice as much slope as vertical wall, nearly ninety-five per cent. of the cost of the work on that contract was incurred upon vertical wall and work incident to such construction, while not a single yard of slope wall was built; and as a consequence, an improvement which could have been readily and well done for the original appropriation of $84,645 has already cost the State about half a million for wretched work, and is still far from completion. No attention was ever paid to the provision of the act requiring the change of plan from slope to vertical wall, with the maps, plans, and estimates for such new work to be submitted to and approved by the Canal Board, and advertised and let to the lowest bidder.

"Nor does the infidelity of the State's agents appear to have stopped here. While the records of the canal commissioners and of the Canal Board certify that the preliminary surveys, maps, plans, specifications, estimates, etc., required by law were actually produced before them and approved by them and by the State Engineer; in point of fact, no such precautions for the protection of the State, so far as we have been able to ascertain, were actually taken.[8]

"It is obvious that the abuses to which we have invited your attention cannot be remedied except:

"*First*, by concentrating responsibility for the administration of the canals in fewer hands;

"*Second*, by lodging somewhere a more efficient power for the suspension or removal of offenders;

"*Third*, by providing more specific, complete, and efficient laws for preventing and punishing abuses when disclosed; and,

"*Fourth*, by providing for the vigorous prosecution and punishment of unfaithful servants.

"Under the present organization the responsibility for a non-compliance with the provisions of the laws for the repair and maintenance of the canals is so distributed between nine State officers, composing the Canal Board, and the auditor, the superintendents, the division, resident and assistant Engineers, that it is nearly impossible to bring any one of them to justice, unless all, or at least a large majority, are of accord in that purpose. Could one person be held responsible for the acts of all of his subordinates, the remedy would be simple and probably adequate. Should the people ratify the proposed amendment of the Constitution, which is designed to clothe a new officer, to be called Superintendent of Public Works, with the powers now vested in the canal commissioners, together with other powers necessary to his functions, this evil of divided responsibility will be greatly diminished. At present the powers of removal and suspension of unfaithful officers are altogether inadequate.

"We recommend, in addition, that the division and resident engineers, and such others engineers as it may be necessary, in the opinion of the State Engineer and Surveyor, to employ temporarily upon any particular work, should be appointed by the State Engineer and Surveyor, with the approval of the Canal Board, subject to removal by the State Engineer and Surveyor alone. In case of every such temporary employment, we would recommend that the rate of compensation be fixed by the Canal Board before such person employed enters upon duty; that he be required to file the usual oath of office, and that he be only paid by the auditor of the Canal Department upon his oath to the correctness of the items charged for expenses and time, and a certificate of the approval of the State Engineer and Surveyor attached.

"No modification of the Constitution or of the law, however, will ever work any substantial reform unless adequate provision is made in some way for a more vigorous prosecution of unfaithful servants. The law is no protection unless its penalties are enforced against those who violate it; the justice that sleeps might as well be dead. Had the laws been enforced promptly when they had been notoriously violated, our canals would not only now be out of debt, but a fruitful source of revenue to the State. It is our conviction that the Legislature will do well to see if this arm of the government ought not to be strengthened. The evidence here submitted will show that very large sums of money have been taken annually from the State by the fraudulent connivance of the State agents with contractors, which should be reclaimed and restored to the treasury and an example made of all the parties participating in the robberies. The preparation of the testimony in these prosecutions, covering, as it must in most cases, a series of years, the actions of a large number of public officers, and servants, and involving a scientific examination of great varieties of work and a familiarity with the principles of engineering and the field work of the engineers, and with the accounts preserved in our public archives, will involve an amount of labor and expense for which at present there is no adequate provision.

"The commission was occupied in the taking of testimony until after the present session of the Legislature had commenced. The testimony could not be written out by the stenographer and put into the hands of the printer until the latter part of the month of January. This will explain any apparent delay in the transmission of this report, there being obvious inconveniences in sending part in print and part in manuscript. There has been no delay in its preparation, except what was the natural and inevitable result of efforts of the commission to render its contents readily accessible to your Excellency and to the legislative bodies.

"For the expenses of the commission the sum of $30,000 was appropriated by the last Legislature. The expenses will exceed this sum about $5000, for which we respectfully ask an appropriation. For greater convenience in presenting the testimony taken, we had it printed at a cost of over $4000. This, together with the legal expenses growing out of the proceedings to establish the authority of the commission to compel the production of books and papers and the witnesses to testify, occasioned this deficiency.

"JOHN BIGELOW,
"D. MAGONE, JR.,
"A. E. ORR,
"JOHN D. VAN BUREN, JR.

"ALBANY, *February 14, 1876.*"

"EXHIBIT D.

"The commission to investigate the affairs of the canals of the State present to the honorable commissioners of the canal fund:

"That Hon. Francis S. Thayer, Auditor of the Canal Department, has violated his duty as such auditor 'in respect to the public moneys in his charge and subject to his draft':

"*First.*—In that, on the 21st day of July, 1874, he procured the passage of a resolution by the commissioners of the canal fund whereby $200,000 of the sinking fund was directed to be invested in the taxes to be levied pursuant to chapter 462 of the laws of 1874; and after procuring the passage of such resolution did set apart said sum in violation of the Constitution. That the auditor's motive was to benefit George D. Lord. That in carrying out such intent the auditor paid $120,497.02 of said sum of $200,000, so set apart, within two days thereafter to Thad. C. Davis, as the agent of George D. Lord. That this was a violation of the Constitution, see article seven, sections two and thirteen. That the auditor is responsible for this misapplication of money, see his testimony, pages 2544, 2546.

"*Second.*—In that, on or about the 1st day of December, 1874, there being money subject to the warrant of the auditor for that purpose, the said auditor refused payment to S. R. Wells, administrator, of an award in his favor for $5207.50 on the false pretence that he had no funds, and immediately after such refusal negotiated the purchase, and did purchase, the said award at about $200 less than it called for of principal and interest, and on the 9th day of February, 1875, audited the said claim at the sum of $5454.92, and drew his warrant therefor in favor of George A. Stone, as assignee.

"George A. Stone had no interest in the transaction, and the auditor testifies that it was purchased for his brother-in-law, E. J. McKie. As to the evidence of this charge, see testimony of S. R. Wells, page 37 (folio 513 to folio 517); testimony of D. Willers, Jr., page 42 (folios 571 and 572); testimony of the auditor, pages 2507-2511; that the profit went to the benefit of the auditor, see pages 2595.

"*Third.*—In that, on the 11th day of March, 1875, there being money subject to the warrant of the auditor for that purpose, the said auditor refused payment to George M. Case of an award in his favor for $9768.71, on the false pretence that he had no funds, and, immediately after such refusal, negotiated the purchase, and did purchase, the said award, including accrued interest, at $10,510.73, and did on the twentieth day of May thereafter audit said claim for the full amount thereof, including interest, to wit, $10,730.60, and drew his warrant therefor in favor of George A. Stone, assignee.

"George A. Stone had no interest in the purchase, as appeared by his testimony, pages 2160-2229, and the auditor testified that he made the purchase for his brother-in-law, E. J. McKie.

"As to the evidence, see testimony of Auditor Thayer, pages 2507, 2586, 2595.

"*Fourth.*—In that, on the 15th day of March, 1875, the auditor purchased a certificate in favor of E. H. French for $1184.26 at a discount of $24.64. It was paid May twentieth thereafter at its full face. As to evidence of this transaction, see testimony of Auditor Thayer, same pages and folios referred to above as to George M. Case's certificate.

"*Fifth.*—In that, on the 12th day of April, 1875, the auditor purchased sixteen canal commissioners' certificates, amounting in the aggregate to $29,962, from Nehemiah L. Osborne at a discount of seven per cent. per annum from the face thereof, but for what length of time the discount was made we are unable to ascertain, further than that the time was in excess of the time between the purchase and payment by the auditor.

"These certificates were paid May 20, 1875, to George A. Stone. That the auditor derived a personal advantage from this transaction, see testimony of George A. Stone and of Auditor Thayer, pages 2229, 2595.

"*Sixth.*—In that, on the 28th day of April, 1875, the auditor purchased from H. D. Denison five canal commissioners' certificates, of the aggregate amount of $49,610, at a discount of seven per cent. per annum, but for what time he discounted them we have not been able to ascertain, further than that it was in excess of the time between the purchase and payment. On the twentieth day of May thereafter the auditor audited said certificates and drew his warrant for the payment thereof in favor of George A. Stone, assignee, at $50,542.06, and the amount gained went to the personal advantage of the auditor. As to evidence of this transaction, see testimony of George A. Stone, page 2229; Francis S. Thayer, page 2476.

"*Seventh.*—In that, on the 29th day of April, 1875, the auditor purchased from H. D. Denison six canal commissioners' certificates, of the aggregate amount of $30,687, at a discount of seven per cent. per annum, but for what length of time he discounted them we have not been able to ascertain, further than that it was greater than the time between the purchase and payment; that on the twentieth day of May thereafter the auditor audited these certificates and drew his warrant therefor in favor of George A. Stone at $31,153.03. That the personal gain from this transaction went to the personal advantage of Francis S. Thayer, see his testimony, page 2595.

"*Eighth.*—That the auditor drew his warrant in payment for a canal commissioners' certificate, in favor of John D. Hamilton, for $38,000, on the 28th day of June, 1875, in violation of law in this: that he paid it without the sworn certificate of an engineer, as required by statute.

"*Ninth.*—In this, that the auditor, in June, 1875, purchased a canal commissioners' certificate, subject to his own audit, from James P. Buck, for $6496.28, at a discount of ten per cent. For the evidence of specification, see testimony of James P. Buck, page 2216.

"The auditor claims he made this purchase for his brother-in-law, E. J. McKie.

"*Tenth.*-In this, that on the 2d day of July, 1875, the auditor purchased canal commissioners' certificates, subject to his own audit, to the amount of $49,953.91, at a discount of eight per cent. and accrued interest, in favor of the purchaser. For evidence of this purchase, see testimony of Willard Johnson, page 2386; testimony of F. S. Thayer, page 2514.

"*Eleventh.*—In that, in addition to those above enumerated, the auditor purchased, between the 9th day of March and the 14th day of July, 1875, canal commissioners' drafts and certificates, subject to his own audit, to the amount of $64,959.81, all of which he afterward audited and drew his warrants in payment thereof. As to the evidence of these several transactions, see testimony of George A. Stone, page 2241; that the auditor derived a direct personal advantage from these transactions, see testimony of Francis S. Thayer, page 2595.

"JOHN BIGELOW,
"A. E. ORR,
"JOHN D. VAN BUREN, JR.,
"D. MAGONE, JR.,

"*Commissioners.*"

"EXHIBIT E
"COPY OF THE REQUISITION OF THE COMMISSIONERS OF THE CANAL FUND

"The undersigned hereby certify that, at a meeting of the commissioners of the canal fund, held at the Canal Department, in the city of Albany, on the 28th day of December, 1875, at 10 o'clock A. M.,

"Present—William Dorsheimer, Lieutenant-Governor; Diedrich Willers, Jr., Secretary of State; Nelson K. Hopkins, Comptroller; Thomas Raines, Treasurer; Daniel Pratt, Attorney-General,

"The following proceedings were had:

"On motion of the Attorney-General, it was

"*Resolved*, That a requisition is made upon his Excellency the Governor to suspend Francis S. Thayer, the auditor of the Canal Department, and to appoint a suitable person to perform his duties, if it shall be made to appear to him that the said auditor has violated his duty in respect to the public moneys in his charge and subject to his draft, the particulars of which alleged violations of duty appear in the report of the commission to investigate the affairs of the canals of the State, which has been submitted to this board, and which is herewith transmitted.

"The members of the board who voted in favor of the adoption of said resolution were as follows: The Lieutenant-Governor, Attorney-General, and Secretary of State. The Comptroller voted in the negative. The Treasurer was not present when the vote was taken, by reason of illness.

"WILLIAM DORSHEIMER,
"*Lieutenant-Governor.*
"DANIEL PRATT,
"*Attorney-General.*

"DIEDRICH WILLERS, JR.,
"*Secretary of State.*"

"EXHIBIT F
"EXECUTIVE ORDER FOR THE SUSPENSION OF AUDITOR THAYER

"STATE OF NEW YORK: EXECUTIVE CHAMBER,
"ALBANY, *December, 1875.*

"*Whereas*, The commissioners of the canal fund, by their requisition hereto annexed, have required or recommended the suspension from office of Francis S. Thayer, the auditor of the Canal Department; and, whereas, it has been made to appear to me that the said Francis S. Thayer, as such auditor, has violated his duty in respect to the public moneys in his charge and subject to his draft;

"Now, therefore, in pursuance of the provisions of section 2, of chapter 783 of the laws of 1857, I do hereby suspend the said Francis S. Thayer from his office as auditor of the Canal Department.

"In witness whereof, I hereunto set my name and cause to be affixed the privy seal of the State this 28th day of December, 1875.

{ State of New York. }
{ Excelsior. } "SAMUEL J. TILDEN."
{Executive Privy Seal.}

"By the Governor,
"CHAS. STEBBINS,
"*Private Secretary.*

"Indorsed: Order by Samuel J. Tilden, Governor, suspending Francis S. Thayer, auditor of the Canal Department.

"Filed December 28, 1875, at four and a half o'clock P.M.

"DIEDRICH WILLERS, JR.,
"*Secretary of State.*"

A. E. ORR TO TILDEN

"NEW YORK, *May 19, '76.*

"GOVERNOR TILDEN,—We ended our work on the commission last Tuesday.

"I regret that I could not see you and say farewell, and wish you God-speed in the work with which you are so prominently identified.

"I leave in the faith that fearless honesty will place its heel on fraud and corruption, and that you will be the standard-bearer selected at St. Louis and surely prove victorious in November next.

"The best men of each party are beginning to see the necessity for just such action, and you are daily receiving numerous recruits.

"Don't give way an inch.

"Very respectfully, your friend,
"A. E. ORR."

"MR. TILDEN AND THE DEMOCRATS

[*From the New York "Tribune" (Republican) of May 27, 1876.*]

"Mr. Tilden is by no means the only Democrat at the East whom good citizens might rejoice to see nominated for the Presidency. His name would undoubtedly do honor to the ticket to be made at St. Louis; but it is not essential to the credit of the party, and if some of his own political brethren are bitterly opposed to him, that is, in one sense, a family affair, over which the outside world need not greatly vex itself. As an indication of the tendencies of the Democratic party, however, the causes of the hostility to Tilden becomes a matter of national concern. The first serious manifestation of enmity came from Tammany Hall, and it finds expression in the columns of the *Express*, where it is alleged that Gov. Tilden has made use of his position to organize a personal party. But this is such a strange complaint to come from the Tammany Hall autocracy that there must be something more behind it. The *World*, whose change of proprietorship is generally interpreted as a blow at Mr. Tilden's pretensions, has not a word to say against the Governor; it only insists, with good sense and good temper, that there are other eminent Democrats whose merits and whose chances are entitled to consideration. But on Wednesday a conference of leading Democratic politicians was held at Albany to consider how Mr. Tilden could be most conveniently thrown overboard, and from them it would seem that we ought to obtain some light upon the interesting question which neither the *World*, nor the *Express*, nor Tammany has seen fit to answer. There were present at this conference Chief-Justice Church and Justice Allen, ex-Lieut.-Gov. Beach, ex-Gov. Hoffman, ex-Speaker Littlejohn, and other well-known men, and the judgment of the meeting is understood to have been unanimous that Mr. Tilden, having alienated a large faction of the Democracy, is not the man for St. Louis.

"We mean no reflection upon the integrity of any of these estimable gentlemen, but it is a significant fact that pretty nearly all the most reputable Democrats whose names have been, either rightly or wrongly, connected with the Tweed and Canal Rings, were found on Wednesday in their company. It was probably not the fault of Judge Church and Judge Allen that the Canal Ring and what was left of the old Tammany Ring united in 1874 to run them both against Tilden, first one and then the other, in the canvass for the nomination; but it was certainly their misfortune. That fight of the Rings against Tilden was a matter of notoriety, and the nomination of our present Governor, instead of Judge Church or his cousin, Judge Allen, was generally recognized throughout the

State as a triumph of the better elements of the Democracy over the thieves and corruptionists. It seems to be the same fight that is renewed now. Judge Allen is known as the author of the much-criticised decision of the Court of Appeals which released Tweed from Blackwell's Island. Mr. Beach is remembered as the gentleman who made such a strange exhibition of himself last Summer by publishing a card in which he intemperately denounced a report of the canal investigating commission as "unfounded in every particular," and who then, being subpœnaed by the commission, swallowed his card and convicted himself of official neglect out of his own mouth. The history and affiliations of ex-Gov. Hoffman are well enough known.

"Altogether, it may be said that the Albany conference only brought to the front the men who have always been recognized as Governor Tilden's enemies and rivals, and who, from their peculiar positions, could not be his friends, not because they are not personally good men, but because a reform movement cannot be carried on in New York without hurting their allies and adherents. And if we go outside the State we find the anti-Tilden sentiment confined to the Western inflationists and communists, who hate every man that believes in a dollar, and are perfectly frank in the declaration of their sentiments. Now, as we have said before, the Democratic party is not so poor that it can name no one for the Presidency whose fitness is not so marked as Mr. Tilden's; but if he is to be thrown overboard the country has a right to insist that the reasons for his rejection shall be made quite clear; otherwise it is sure to draw unpleasant conclusions. The Democratic candidate, whoever he may be, must be a man whom repudiators, canal thieves, and the relics of the old Tammany cannot support."

THE FIFTH AVENUE HOTEL CONFERENCE OF 1876

[*From the "Sun," April 7, 1900.*]

"A man with half a memory writes a long letter to the *Evening Post* of this city recalling the circumstances of the once-famous Fifth Avenue Hotel Conference of May, 1876. He thinks the political situation is ripe for another such demonstration on the part of eminent citizens who do not want to vote for McKinley again, yet view with apprehension the probability that Bryan will be the alternative choice. There is as much time now before the two great nominating conventions, he points out, as there was when Carl Schurz and others met in the Fifth Avenue Hotel to save the country. A quarter of a century has considerably idealized his mental picture of that conference and its results. This is his description of it now:

"'It was a gathering of the foremost patriots in the nation, regardless of party affiliations, to discuss the political situation and suggest to the country a programme for the Presidential canvass which was soon to begin. There were philosophers and scholars of the first rank, eminent lawyers, and brilliant editors, and men who had won renown in many a fierce campaign as "practical" politicians and popular leaders. The call which brought them together distinctly disavowed the idea of nominating a candidate or framing a platform, except, possibly, in the barest outlines. The whole purpose of the conference was to end at one stroke some of the false conditions against which the conscience and intelligence of the country were in revolt, but not to pull down anything for which it was not prepared to offer something better as a substitute.'

"This conference to which the writer in the *Evening Post* refers in terms of reverence, amounting almost to awe, met at the Fifth Avenue Hotel on May 16, 1876, in response to a call signed by Mr. Schurz and a few others. There were present about two hundred gentlemen, mostly of the type which afterward came to be known as the Mugwump; that is to say, the type addicted to proclaiming its superior intelligence and conscience in political affairs. As might be expected, the Hon. Carl Schurz, the Flying Dutchman of American politics, was the most conspicuous figure. He made the principal speech, and he was chairman of the committee which prepared and reported a pretentious 'address to the country.' This address to the country constituted the sole fruit of the conference's deliberations.

"Let us supplement the half-memory of the man who wants another such demonstration of the foremost patriots, philosophers, and scholars, under the leadership once more, as we assume from the tone of his letter, of the Hon. Carl Schurz. At the time the conference met there was nothing murky in the political situation. On the Republican side the nomination of Governor Hayes, of Ohio, was clearly indicated. The *Sun* had predicted it long before the patriots and philosophers assembled. Mr. Blaine was an aggressive candidate, and there was some third-term talk about Gen. Grant; but the Conkling-Blaine feud and the Bristow disaffection already rendered practically certain the nomination of a compromise candidate not identified with either faction, and the logic of the situation pointed directly to Governor Hayes. On the other side everything was shaping towards the event which occurred at St. Louis six weeks later, the nomination on the second ballot, by far more than the required two-thirds majority, of Samuel J. Tilden, a statesman and reformer representing with singular closeness the ideal which was declared to be in the minds of Mr. Carl Schurz and his associates.

"That celebrated address which Mr. Schurz drafted, with the assistance of the intelligence and conscience of the country, could scarcely have called more pointedly for Tilden and barred out Hayes as the President desired by the foremost patriots, philosophers, and scholars, had it mentioned their names. We quote from Mr. Carl Schurz's address to the country:

"'We shall support no candidate who, however favorably judged by his nearest friends, is not publicly known to possess those qualities of mind and character which the stern task of genuine reform requires, for the American people cannot now afford to risk the future of the republic in experiments on merely supposed virtue or rumored ability to be trusted on the strength of private recommendations.

"'The man to be intrusted with the Presidency this year must have deserved not only the confidence of honest men, but also the fear and hatred of the thieves.

"'The country must now have a President whose name is already a watchword of reform, whose capacity and courage for the work are matters of record rather than promise.'

"There was much more of the same sort in the address which Mr. Schurz signed and the Fifth Avenue Hotel conference issued. Within a few weeks the Republican party nominated the man whose capacity and courage for the work of reform were matters of promise only, and the Democracy put up the statesman already publicly known to possess those qualities of mind and character which the stern task of genuine reform required.

"What was the sequel? A few weeks later the Hon. Carl Schurz, the author of all the high-sounding professions in the address to the country, was hard at work persuading citizens of the Mugwump type to cast their votes for Hayes and against Tilden; and a few months later, after Mr. Hayes had failed to secure a majority of the electoral vote, but had been counted into the office to which Mr. Tilden was elected, the Hon. Carl Schurz, reformer and leader of the Fifth Avenue Hotel conference, got his pay for partisan activity; it came in the shape of a Cabinet appointment, which he promptly accepted.

"Such is the true story of the May conference of 1876."

JOHN T. MORGAN TO MONTGOMERY BLAIR

"*Confidential.*

"SELMA, ALA., *June 3d, 1876.*

"HON. MONTGOMERY BLAIR.

"DEAR SIR,—I have had two valued favors from you—the last of 25th May. I was chosen as a State elector, and also as a State delegate to St. Louis by our recent convention. It was very large, fully representative, unusually able, and harmonious. The delegation to St. Louis is very able, comprising many of our best men. No instructions were given. I did not even hear much discussion of candidates. The great leading thought is success, and to gain this every man will sacrifice all his preferences for any particular candidate. I think I may state safely (but I do it in personal confidence) that not more than two of our twenty delegates favor now the nomination of any other person but Mr. Tilden. One of these stated to the convention that he was under no pledges to any man. This state of opinion is the result of close scrutiny of the drift of sentiment in the Northern States, and especially in New York. The recent movement of Church and Kelly and others has deceived no one here.

"I am satisfied that Alabama will be very reluctant to take such a lead as would have the appearance of dictating the candidate to the Northern States. The North ought to settle its differences about the minor and purely political question of currency laws and allow us to unite with them in demanding a pure government which will give them a chance for life. If they force us to choose, however, we will certainly be directed solely by the consideration of 'success.' We can't afford to risk anything to gratify a predilection. If you could, Bayard would get the State. I was at Montgomery at the time you refer to as a member of the convention of 1861. I do not remember that Mr. Bayard was there. I feel satisfied he was not there.

"As his friend I would prefer to see him wait a time and mature more thoroughly his great powers in the school of experience. Still, he would now be a most acceptable President to all the people of the Southern States.

"My conviction remains unshaken that Mr. Tilden is the strongest man in N. Y.; that he is an honest Democrat from principle; that he acts squarely on his convictions in everything; that his record is one to inspire confidence in the people; that he will attack fraud and corruption wherever he meets them, without fear or hesitancy; and that his good sense, and the best interests of his own State, will lead him to give to the country with which the great commercial cities are so intimately associated in the means of prosperity, *peace and protection*, while it is working out with honest toil its redemption from poverty and distress. This is all we need. We do not wish the power that springs merely from the weight of numbers in the electoral colleges. We wish no offices, or, rather, we need none, and our wisest men will be glad if we get but few. Let us alone, and we will soon become richer than we have ever been.

"Genl. E. W. Peters, who is Col. Denison's law partner, is in our delegation, and will probably be our chairman. He is a hard-money Democrat, and is much impressed with the necessity of Mr. Tilden's nomination as a matter of success.

"Very truly yours,
"JNO. T. MORGAN."

On the 28th of June the Democratic National Convention at St. Louis nominated Mr. Tilden for President.

The whole vote on the second ballot was 738; necessary to a choice, 492. Tilden had 535; Hendricks, of Indiana, 66; Allen, of Ohio, 54; Parker, of New Jersey, 18; Hancock, of Pennsylvania, 59; Bayard, of Delaware, 11; Thurman, of Ohio, 2. Indiana seconded Pennsylvania's motion to make Mr. Tilden's nomination unanimous, and it was adopted.

In the month of June, 1876, Governor Tilden received a note from a citizen of Minnesota complaining that he could get no evidence of any success achieved by the Governor in his war upon the Canal Ring, and that it was thrown in the face of the people out there that nothing had been accomplished. His letter concludes as follows: "Now, if ever I have seen any disposition of these cases of corruption it has escaped my memory, and to be prepared to answer our assailants on their only one point, with an earnest desire to convert them to Tilden and reform, is solely the object of my writing."

To this letter Tilden wrote the following reply, dated June 15, 1876: "Your letter of June 12th has been handed to me. In reply, I would like to state that it takes time to obtain the evidence and prepare the actions, civil and criminal, in such cases as those against the members of the Canal Ring. The machinery of justice under the State government has not the unity and efficiency that it has under the Federal government, where the district attorneys and marshals are appointed by the Chief Executive instead of being elected in their localities. On the whole, however, these cases have proceeded with more rapidity than could have been expected under the circumstances. You will have become, doubtless, aware before this reaches you that George D. Lord was convicted a few days since at Buffalo. The principal civil suit against Beldon, Denison & Co. is set down for trial on the 12th of July. The trial was put off for a few weeks by the court against the opposition of the Attorney-General. The most important thing, of course, was to break up the system, and that has been done. A secondary object is to deter from the commission of similar offences in future, and that work is going on satisfactorily."

P. H. SMITH TO TILDEN (TELEGRAM)

"SPRINGFIELD, ILL., *June 21, 1876.*

"TO GOV. SAM. J. TILDEN,
"*15 Gramercy.*

"The Chicago *Times* to-day says that you were chairman of platform committee in eighteen hundred and sixty-four which put forth the famous peace resolution pronouncing the war as a failure. Please telegraph the fact. Large majority of this convention for you.

"P. H. SMITH."

MANTON MARBLE TO PERRY H. SMITH (TELEGRAM)

"*June 21, 1876.*

"TO PERRY H. SMITH,
"*Springfield.*

"Your telegram shown me. Governor Tilden was not chairman of platform committee of Chicago convention. James Guthrie was. Tilden opposed resolution containing phrase speaking of war as having thus far failed to restore the Union in committee; got it stricken out; refused to agree to resolution with it in. It was then irregularly restored. Tilden refused to agree to resolutions at all stages, and sent messages by me to McClellan advising him to discard it in letter of acceptance. Tilden made speech in New York delegation against resolution, which was briefly reported by me in *World*, and is copied in *Courier-Journal* telegraphs. I was present in New York delegation and at meetings of committee or in adjoining room."

At the Democratic convention of the State of New York, held at Utica, May, 1876, Governor Tilden was recommended as a candidate for President to the National Democratic Convention, to be held at St. Louis on the 26th of June following. At the meeting of that convention an informal ballot disclosed such a decided partiality for Mr. Tilden over either of the other candidates that he was nominated on the next ballot.

MAJOR-GENERAL HOOKER TO TILDEN

"GARDEN CITY, L. I., *June 29th, '76.*

"To his Excellency, GOV. SAMUEL J. TILDEN.

"MY DEAR GOVERNOR,—I cannot refrain from offering you my sincere congratulations on your nomination to the exalted office of the President of the United States. As a quiet observer of the political events of the nation, I know of no one in my day that has afforded me so much satisfaction, and sincerely hope and believe that the wisdom shown by the selection at St. Louis will be fully ratified by the great mass of our people in November next. We require reform in politics, religion, and morals, and I am convinced that we will receive them generously at your hands. The whole government of the nation has been corrupt—desperately corrupt—and the honor and glory of applying the antidote, I am convinced, will belong to you. If the fact of your nomination does not enhance the material values of the nation I am sure your election will do it. Already I seem to breathe a new atmosphere, as is the case with every well-wisher of the country.

Sincerely yours,
"J. HOOKER."

CLARKSON N. POTTER TO TILDEN

"61 WALL ST., N. Y., *June 29, '76.*

"MY DEAR GOVERNOR,—Your letter was well received yesterday at Union College, and I am glad you sent it.

"I got down last evening just in time to hear of your nomination in the street and take into your house the news. Heaven grant you may be elected. The country needs that, far more than you do or can desire it.

"Faithfully yours,
"CLARKSON N. POTTER."

WILLIAM ALLEN BUTLER TO TILDEN

"NEW YORK, *June 29, 1876.*

"MY DEAR GOVERNOR TILDEN,—I congratulate you most heartily. Whatever may be the fortunes or the fate of the coming struggle, there is nothing but satisfaction to your old friends in your well-earned victory at St. Louis, and you can well understand how specially gratifying it is to

"Yours sincerely,
"WILLIAM ALLEN BUTLER."

ROBERT B. MINTURN TO TILDEN

"NEW BRIGHTON, STATEN ISLAND, *July 3, 1876.*

"MY DEAR GOVERNOR TILDEN,—No one has been more delighted than I by your nomination; and you, knowing how much I have desired it, may have been surprised at not receiving any word of congratulation from me.

"The truth is that, at a time when the mails and the wires have been burdened with messages of felicitation for you, it seemed that you would scarcely care to have any formal expression from those of whose regard and support you were already assured. I may have been wrong in this feeling, and perhaps I should at once have written to tell you how much I was rejoiced at your nomination, and how thoroughly I have admired your noble fight against the worst constituents of our politics—culminating in your victory, at the St. Louis convention, over all the jobbing elements of the party, which were strengthened by a most unprecedented and venomous opposition from your own State.

"My gratification at your nomination has, however (I must confess), been mingled with deep regret at the phrase in the platform which denounces the resumption clause of the act of 1875. I know as well as any one the fraudulent character of that act—I know that the Cincinnati convention refused to endorse it—but, nevertheless, I feel that it was a solemn pledge of the national faith, a pledge which cannot be repudiated without discredit, not to say, disgrace.

"The act of 1875 was a settlement—unsatisfactory and inadequate, no doubt—but still a settlement which, in every point of view, should (as it seems to me) be respected. If present legislation is inadequate to carry it into effect, fresh legislation should be provided. If the time that remains is now too short to make effectual provision for resumption, the period should be extended to admit of proper preparation. But to say (as the platform does) that the resumption clause is itself an obstacle to resumption, and to propose its naked repeal, is (as it seems to me) to talk nonsense, and, what is worse, very dishonorable and disgraceful nonsense.

"Knowing how thoroughly sound you are on this subject, I cannot but believe that you will take some occasion (probably in your letter of acceptance) to relieve yourself and your supporters from the odium of permitting the phrase to pass without explanation. I observe that Mr. Hendricks exults in the expression, as being equivalent to an abandonment of any policy looking towards resumption by the government. But the phrase is capable of receiving a different interpretation, as was shown by one of the Ohio delegates in the convention, who said that it might be taken to express a disapproval of the resumption clause only because it did not contain sufficiently vigorous provisions for a sufficiently early resumption. But if nothing should be said by you, I am satisfied that the interpretation of Mr. Hendricks is the sense which will be affixed to the platform both by friends and foes; and it is a sense which (in my judgment) will do very great harm, and, indeed, is already working mischief.

"I trust that you will not consider it impertinent in me to write thus strongly and with so much frankness. I feel very strongly that the conservative sentiment of this country will not willingly see the settlement of 1875 rudely and thoughtlessly repudiated; and I am confident that not only is this the real feeling of the country, but that it is a noble and honorable sentiment which cannot with impunity be disregarded by those who represent a reform of politics.

"You may be very sure, my dear Mr. Tilden, that if I had not a very genuine confidence in you, and an earnest desire for your success, I should not have ventured to write you thus. Pray take this view of my letter, and believe me,

"Yours most sincerely,
"ROBT. B. MINTURN.

"*His Excellency S. J. Tilden, &c., &c., &c.*"

WHITELAW REID TO BIGELOW

"*Personal.*

"NEW YORK, 23 PARK AVE., *July 9, '76.*

"MY DEAR MR. BIGELOW,—I am sorry that I missed you on Saturday. I had just run over to the Phelps' to assist them in some of their final preparations in sailing again for Europe. You know they took my niece over, returned with her to nurse her, went with me to the West to bury her, and are now just starting back to try to get up their own health again.

"I would like very much to talk over the political situation with you. I am exceedingly sorry that the Hendricks nomination and the platform seem to shut us up to the support of Hayes. At the same time, I feel like congratulating the independent press and honest men of all parties on the great reform they have succeeded in securing in forcing unobjectionable nominations from the Republicans, and compelling the Democrats to take Tilden. It does not seem to me by any means clear that he will not be elected. If he is we ought all to pray night and day that his health may be preserved to protect us against Hendricks.

"Very truly yours,
"WHITELAW REID."

GEORGE TICKNOR CURTIS TO GOVERNOR TILDEN

"NEW YORK, *July 10, '76.*

"MY DEAR SIR,—Gov. Hayes leaves to you a clear field. Since reading his letter I am the more confirmed in the views which I hurriedly expressed on Saturday. You now have a great opportunity to do two things: first, to make the country see that the resumption of specie payments means *measures*, and not *barren promises*; that the attitude of the Republicans in regard to specie payments is like the attitude of the government in regard to its notes—the holder asks for payment, and he gets another paper promise; the country asks to have specie payments restored, and it gets the law wh. says it shall be done in 1879, but takes no step towards a fulfilment of the pledge. Secondly, you now have a grand opportunity to show the inflationists of our own party that they indulge a false alarm about contraction; that the very gist of the problem is to avoid contraction that will hurt anybody by putting the finances of the govt. into a condition to supply a circulating medium that will appreciate in value from the moment of the enactment of the very first measure, and will go on appreciating until it becomes at par with gold in the market and in the purchasing and paying power.

"Let the people see that you are not, as your rival certainly is, a mere puppet in the hands of others. Speak, speak as if *ex-cathedra*; for your position is now one that will cause anything you say, that appears to come from *conscious power to handle the subject*, to sink deep in the public mind. Your opponent not only shows no such conscious power, but he shows that he possesses no more of it than a child; in which respect, indeed, he is a good average representative of his party. Now is your time to strike a blow that will be felt.

"Yours very truly,

GEO. TICKNOR CURTIS."

"*Gov. Tilden.*

C. H. McCORMICK TO TILDEN

"SPRING HOUSE, RICHFIELD SPRINGS, N. Y., *July 11, 1876.*

"MY DEAR SIR,—Your kind expressions of me when at your house yesterday have induced me to make a suggestion to you in *confidence.*

"If uncommitted on the question, and if you could do no better (of course) as Secretary of the Treasury, I venture to submit that in that important [post] I might be able to command confidence to a large extent where I am known.

"With your views as expressed, one word from *you* at St. Louis would have given me the nomination for the 'second place.' I suppose the place above mentioned is of more importance to the public in a 'reform' point of view than the second place. These things, Govr., are only for your consideration, with neither claims nor representations on my part, only asking that if not approved they will not further be thought of.

"When I left St. L., Gen. Preston, of Ky., and other influential friends from other States requested permission to use my name for the V.-P. shd. Govr. H. on any account decline, etc.

In much haste,
"Your frd. & obt. St.,
"C. H. MCCORMICK."

TILDEN TO S. S. COX

"STATE OF NEW YORK, EXECUTIVE CHAMBER,
"ALBANY, *July 22, 1876.*

"DEAR MR. COX,—Your note of the 15th came several days ago, but I have since that time been so exceptionally occupied that I could not give any attention to my correspondence.

"I did, however, immediately direct the messages you desired to be at once sent, and I now will answer your inquiry in respect to the statement of Federal taxation for the year 1870, contained in my last annual message.

"The year taken is that which ends on the 30th of June, 1870, being most nearly identical with that in which and for which the census statements are made.

"The statement is of taxation and not of expenditures. All the statements in the comparative tables are of taxation. In the long run, unfortunately, the expenditures equal the taxes. At any rate, the comparison is a comparison of taxation.

"If you will refer to the first page of the report of the Secretary of the Treasury for December 5, 1870, you will find the receipts for the year ending June 30, 1870, stated as follows:

From customs (in gold)	$194,538,374 44
From internal revenues	185,128,859 07
From sales of public lands	3,350,481 76
From miscellaneous sources	28,237,762 06
Total	$411,255,477 33

"To reduce the gold revenue from the customs to currency requires the addition of the premium on gold. The gentleman to whom I intrusted that computation made an average which fixed the premium at 24 per cent. That is no doubt considerably below the real premium at the times when the revenues were collected.

"The amount of the premium is $46,689,209.86. From that should be deducted premium received on the sales of gold which form the larger part of the 28,000,000 of receipts from miscellaneous sources, and amount to $15,294,137.37, leaving a balance of $31,395,072.49—

	$31,395,072 49
Add	411,255,477 63
	$442,650,550 12
Add to that the amount collected by Postmasters	15,141,623 71
Total	$457,792,173 83

"The estimate of the amount drawn from the people by taxation by the Federal government, contained in the table to which you refer, is made in round numbers $450,000,000.

"There can be no doubt it is below the truth.

"Very respectfully yours."

HENDRICKS TO TILDEN (TELEGRAM)

"*Cleveland, O.*

"REC'D AT ALBANY, *July 15, 1876.*

"TO GOVERNOR TILDEN,
"*Albany, N. Y.*

"I have spent the afternoon here and seen many Democrats. Our gains are large, and we can carry Ohio, but all say it is worth thousands of votes to repeal the resumption clause on some terms. I think you should urge a proper measure of repeal.

"T. A. HENDRICKS."

ABRAM S. HEWITT TO TILDEN

"HOUSE OF REPRESENTATIVES, *July 26th, 1867.*

"MY DEAR GOVERNOR,—We have got over another day, thanks to an election case, without action on the silver bill. We believe now that we shall be able to defeat action, if not vote down the measure. It has been a hard fight, and, if we win, it will be due to considerations of expediency rather than of principles on the part of the Southern members.

"The object of this note is mainly to suggest something in regard to the civil-service plank. A very intelligent newspaper man says that the real issue is not so much in the personnel of the clerks as in the modes and machinery of administration in the several departments of the Govt. In other words, that the abuses are largely due to the defective organization of the department, that the business has outgrown the methods and machinery devised by Hamilton, and that it is the framework of the government machine which needs reformation, reconstruction, and adaptation to the requirements of the public business. In this view, the mere appointment and discharge of a few clerks is of but little consequence, compared with such a reform in the mode of conducting the public business.

"This crude statement seems to contain the germ of a position in politics in regard to civil service, far higher and more practical than the declaration of Hayes.

"The P. S. dept. may be instanced to illustrate the state of affairs. When it was a small affair it was not of such consequence, and before the days of railroads and telegraphs indispensable, perhaps, that it should use its receipts to pay its expenses and pay over to the Treasury any balance that might remain at the end of the fiscal year. Now, however, when the receipts are very great, they should be paid all into the Treasury, and the expenses drawn thence by warrant, as in other departments of the government. This is not the case, but the Postmaster-General, having the control of the money, authorizes and allows expenditures, such as repairs and improvements to buildings, amounting to large sums, without any authority from Congress, such as is necessary in the other departments for such outlays.

"So the bookkeeping of the government is not in accordance with the experience of the times, but is crude, old-fashioned, unsatisfactory, and even contradictory. Now a broad declaration from you that you will endeavor to reform these abuses which are of a gravity far greater than the incompetence or negligence of clerks, and that this reform is the most urgent and will receive careful attention would, I think, strike the public favorably.

"Faithfully y'rs,
"ABRAM S. HEWITT.

"Scott Wicks, of Ill., one of our best members, and who stood by us on the banking and currency committee, has lost his renomination in consequence. It is a severe blow to him and to me, and if we win he must be taken care of. He is a first-class man.

"I do not think you begin to appreciate the bitterness of these Western inflationists."

ABRAM S. HEWITT TO TILDEN

"*Personal and private.*

"SUNDAY, 8 P.M., WASHINGTON, *Aug. 6, '76.*

"MY DEAR GOVERNOR,—I have been very unwell all day, caused by the nervous exhaustion of yesterday's work in the House. And yet I will try to give you some idea of the situation and the results. The banking and currency committee decided to report the repeal of the resumption date on Friday. I persuaded them to wait till Saturday, hoping that your letter would come and change the situation. The letter did come, but the committee were perfectly fixed in their determination to report. I tried to get them to substitute a commission to inquire and report in December on the whole resumption question. They offered to accept this as an amendment, but not as a substitute. To this the hard-money New England men would not agree, and so I decided to offer my substitute, as we could well vote for repeal pure and simple, without measures of preparation. We had a debate of two hours. You will find what I said in the *Record.* After the debate was over they declined to let my substitute be offered. The House was determined to get a vote on it, and so no quorum voted on the motion for the previous question. This brought them to terms, and they allowed the substitute to be offered. It was lost by twelve majority. If the House had been full it would have carried. The vote then recurred on the repeal, and it was carried by 20 majority, all the hard-money men voting against it. There was no hard feeling, and no bitterness remains. The hard-money men have made their record, and the soft-money men have got the repeal, and no longer any excuse for not carrying their States. I think that the matter is in the best possible shape. The party is committed to specie payments by the platform and your admirable letter, and by Hendricks' mushy acquiescence.

"Immediately afterwards we passed a concurrent resolution establishing a commission to consider the silver question and the resumption of specie payments. So that we can say that we have made provision for investigation and the elaboration of a practical scheme for resumption.

"On the whole, I now think that the matter has been managed as well as the difficulties of the situation would admit.

"Your letter gives general satisfaction, especially to the Southern members, who [are] loud in its praise.

"I hope that Congress will adjourn this week, so that we may organize for the campaign. I have in preparation all the necessary documents to show the frauds and corruption of the administration, and if we have means to circulate them I anticipate the best results.

"Faithfully yours,
"ABRAM S. HEWITT."

Considering the friendly and very intimate relations which had subsisted between Mr. Bryant and Mr. Tilden from the latter's early boyhood, it was natural that the Governor should inspire the request contained in the following letter from one of his nephews. The correspondence which ensued, and its results, will be found in Bigelow's *Life of Tilden*, Volume I., page 300. It is proper to repeat here that Mr. Bryant, at the time he wrote his letter declining to be named as one of the Tilden electors, was only a proprietor of half of the *Evening Post* property, and his partner, Mr. Henderson, feared the effect upon the prosperity of the paper which would be likely to result from the appearance of its editor in such conspicuous relations with the Democratic party. Mr. Bryant, however, went so far as to give instructions, which were pretty carefully observed, to permit nothing personally hostile to Mr. Tilden to appear in the columns of the *Post* during the canvass, and voted for him at the election.

Besides the reasons here stated for Mr. Bryant's embarrassing attitude towards Mr. Tilden, there were others communicated to Mr. Tilden a few weeks later by Miss Julia Bryant in the note succeeding Mr. Pelton's.

W. T. PELTON TO JOHN BIGELOW

"*(August, 1876.)*

"MY DEAR MR. BIGELOW,—It seems very desirable that Mr. Bryant should be put on as one of the electors at large, and we must know that he will not decline if nominated. Will you undertake to communicate with him at once? I would suggest that you write him and send a messenger with the letter to Cummington—or perhaps it would be better to write Mr. Godwin, who is there, or was a few days ago. Of course, you can state as strongly as you please how much it is desired *here* that he accept.

"Can't you send Monday morn, train, so as to get reply early.

"Sincerely yrs.,
"W. T. PELTON.

"*Satrdy. evg.*"

JULIA BRYANT TO TILDEN

"ROSLYN, *Sept. 30, '76.*

"DEAR MR. TILDEN,—I am very, very sorry that you and your friends and your enemies will not see the article in regard to the slanders about your income tax which my father wrote at Cummington last Saturday. He bestowed much time upon it, read it to me, and pronounced it himself 'a good article,' and sent it on Monday to Mr. Sperry,[9] with the injunction to publish it entire, whatever might have appeared previously on the subject in the *Evening Post.*

"After our return here this week a letter came from Mr. Sperry begging my father most earnestly *not* to publish the article, as it would certainly be followed by abuse of Mr. Henderson in the *Times*—abuse more virulent than ever before—because in this article the *Times* was attacked, although indirectly, and most *severely censured.* It was *urged* that my father should not persist in publishing what would cause such distress to Mr. Henderson, already so worn by his troubles. On this score my father felt that he must yield, but he did it most unwillingly and quite ungraciously.

"I am anxious, however, that you should know what has passed; and should know, also, that my father, averse as he is to such constant watchfulness, has had much to combat in keeping attacks on you out of the papers, and has insisted that you should not be treated in the *Evening Post* otherwise than with respect. You may think that he has not exerted himself in your behalf, as he might have done for an old and esteemed friend, and one who has done him such good service; but, truly, it has required no small effort on his part to keep the paper as moderate as it is.

"He knows that I am writing this now.

"I am obliged to finish in great haste, as I am just going to town.

Yours truly,
"JULIA BRYANT."

TILDEN TO MISS HUNT

"138 EAGLE ST., ALBANY, *Aug. 8th, 1876.*

"DEAR MISS HUNT,—I lately learned by chance that it is to you that I am indebted for a copy of the new edition of the works of Ed. Livingston on criminal jurisprudence. No information as to the source of the presentation had ever before reached me. I ought, perhaps, to have caused inquiry to be made into that matter, but in the rush of things amid which I have lived, did not. The work which has fallen on me in my present career has been constantly outgrowing my help and my own capacity for attention to the secondary things; and I must confess in myself a tendency to become more and more absorbed, with increasing intensity and increasing persistence, in the parts of the work on which its success depends as on the turning-points of battle—a habit not favorable to secondary things, very unfavorable to the human machine, but surprisingly serviceable to the work which gets the benefit of it.

"I will now say what I would have contrived the opportunity to say earlier, if I had ever known to whom it should have been addressed.

"It is impossible to appreciate more highly than I do the character, abilities, and services to his country and to the world of Ed. Livingston. And then, I have always taken a special interest in the man. Among my early recollections is this of him: He used to come to Lebanon Springs, which is on the edge of the beautiful valley in which I was born and passed my youth. My father's acquaintance with him was the occasion of my seeing him and retaining a recollection of his form and features. His taste for antiquarian researches led him to dig open some mounds in the neighborhood and leaving on the rustic mind some impression of eccentricity. My father had been more intimate with the chancellor, and deprived from him a taste for Merino sheep, and shared in his importations.

"I need not add with how much interest I read Mr. Hunt's biography of Ed. Livingston, which is itself a delicious portrayal of a most attractive character.

"I beg you to accept my thanks for the volumes you were so kind as to send me, and believe me,

"Very truly yours,
"S. J. TILDEN."

MISS HUNT TO TILDEN

"MONTGOMERY PLACE, BARRYTOWN-ON-HUDSON, *Aug. 10th.*

"DEAR GOVERNOR TILDEN,—Your kind note has reached me safely, while mine, sent with the books, never arrived at its destination, as it should have done.

"My aunt, Mrs. Barton, in a spirit of filial piety, had preserved a number of copies for the purpose of presenting them in suitable quarters. But before she could accomplish the object Mrs. Barton herself suddenly died. The duty having consequently devolved on me of distributing the volumes, I felt special satisfaction in offering you a copy of them, who, as the Governor of the native State of Edward Livingston, are so conspicuous for wisdom and devotion to the cause of public reform.

"May I venture to add a few words, and to say that at such a moment as this it is quite impossible not to feel the deepest interest in the work which you tell me has proved so absorbing to yourself. It is, indeed, your high fortune to lead in the reform all over our country, and no one, watching the drift of the national canvass in your favor, can fail to be full of hope and belief in the future.

"Should you ever come in our neighborhood, I beg that you will not pass us by. It would be a great gratification to me to have the pleasure of receiving you at Montgomery Place.

"LOUISE LIVINGSTON HUNT."

TILDEN TO HON. JOHN BRAGG, MOBILE

"138 EAGLE STREET, ALBANY, *Aug. 11th, 1876.*

"MY DEAR SIR,—Mrs. Van Buren has been so kind as to send me your letter to her. I am glad to renew an acquaintance which, although slight, has not wholly passed from my recollection.

"You mention an inquiry of yours in 1872, whether I had entirely abandoned public life. In the sense of official life, I can scarcely be said ever to have any. Tho' I have given almost half my life to public affairs, it has been as a private citizen. In 1846 I went to the Assembly for a special object, to help Mr. Wright in a crisis of his administration, and retired. In 1872 I went again to the same body to obtain the impeachment and removal of corrupt judges who swayed the administration of justice in the metropolis, and again retired. In 1846, and again in 1867, I served in conventions to revise the State Constitution. That is all in that long period.

"I never destined myself to a public career. I did not come into my present trust until I found myself unable in any other way to have it on the side of reforms I had begun three years before, and to which I had surrendered my professional business, attention to my affairs, and my peace and comfort. I had felt gloomily the decay of all my early ideals of my country, and engaged in the effort to restore them in the city and State in which I live, with no idea of any result to myself except of sacrifice. The logic of events has brought me into my present situation. I have been tempted to do so much to satisfy the curiosity of an old acquaintance, and, as I stop, I do not know but I have provoked more than I have satisfied.

"At any rate, it is a real pleasure to refresh what remains of a set of early associations. I think you were something of a pet of Mr. Van Buren, as I was also. He would have been interested in the course of present events; and puzzled about me, for he told me, near the close of his life, when he had observed me for thirty years, that I was the most unambitious man he had ever known.

"I will send you a pamphlet which will give you some idea of the events in this State to which I have alluded.

"With much esteem, I am very truly yours,

"S. J. TILDEN.

"*Hon. John Bragg, Mobile, Ala.*"

SIDNEY WEBSTER TO TILDEN

"NEWPORT, *12 August, 1876.*

"DEAR GOVERNOR,—Since reading your admirable letter of acceptance I have begun two letters to you to say how sincerely I congratulated you, but have destroyed both, chiefly moved thereto by memories of my young days, when I had occasion to know how pestered a candidate for the Presidency is by letters from friends which have no business importance, but which, nevertheless, either consume his precious time by the reading or are turned over to the files. This letter now begun *may* have a better fate!

"I cannot see how an acceptance-letter could have been framed better adapted to the imperative needs of the situation. Repeal of the law of 1875 was on the platform, and you had to deal with it. 'Contraction' is a red rag to our friends in the West and South, and that must be accepted. And along the Atlantic coast are they who fancy their pecuniary salvation depends on *instantly* lifting the greenback to an equality with gold, and these could not be lost sight of. And, finally, you had to keep in mind a *policy* which you could 'work' when you enter the White House next March.

"There was possibly a little peril in departing from the traditional acceptance-letter of fine phrases and loyalty to the platform; but you did wisely to incur that peril, for I do think your letter has practically eliminated the financial issue from the canvass—has prevented an alarming sectional conflict and bad blood between debtors and creditors—and will in the end convince all reasonable people you purpose to 'resume' as rapidly as human power can. And besides this (which may seem a contradiction), I believe you have given a hint to those who are in pecuniary distress and sorrow, and would like inflated business to lift them, as they think, out of their misery, that they had better join hands with the Democracy.

"My idea of the canvass is that the independent voters will soon come to think there is little difference in the purposes of you and Governor Hayes, and the only question is which of you is likely to be most able to carry them out. That, of course, leads to an inquiry into the personal qualities of the two candidates and the temper of the party behind each. On both of those inquiries you *ought* to win, and you will (excepting in a contingency to which I will presently refer) win. If the independent voters appreciated your mental and moral fibre as I do, they would not doubt as to the first; and as to the second, our party is new in power, ambitious to establish a dynasty, and is extremely amenable to reason and fair-dealing.

"I was a little sorry you said anything of a second term. You cannot accomplish much if it is known you won't have a second, and a good way to treat Hayes would be to suggest that he resign at the end of two years (if elected), or never be inaugurated.

"My forecast of the situation is that 'the machine' will squelch the reformer (but of that we can judge better after the Republican *State* nominations); that the financial issue will drop to the rear; and the Republican managers will endeavor to force on us the Southern question and obscure the reform issue. I hope our friends will not dally with the Southern question, but say (defiantly and offensively, if need be) that they will give no moral sympathy or support to those who seek to deprive the negroes of any of their political rights or embarrass the free exercise of them. Rightly or wrongly, they are citizens, and we at the North must look upon them as such. Under the recent decisions of the Supreme Court (which are correct) the Federal govt., certainly the President, can do little; but it does seem to me that your moral influence, if judicially manifested in a letter for publication (as it would be by you), would do good in every respect.

"I have written, as you see—*currente calmo*—and at too great length, for all I wished to express was my appreciation of the wisdom of your acceptance-letter, and my belief in your triumphant victory.

"Faithfully yours,
"SIDNEY WEBSTER."

PARKE GODWIN TO JOHN BIGELOW

"CUMMINGTON, *Aug. 28th, '76.*

"MY DEAR BIGELOW,—I don't know what Mr. Bryant has written, but I presume he has not consented. John and I have both tried to get him to pronounce himself publicly, but he will not, tho' saying that he means to vote for Tilden all the while. I presume he feels himself bound in some way to the E. P. I hope to be in Alb'y on Wednesday or Thursday with Minna!

"Yours very truly,
"PARKE GODWIN."

F. O. PRINCE TO TILDEN

"BOSTON, *Augt. 28, 1876.*

"DEAR MR. TILDEN,—I am much concerned touching the matter about which Messrs. Avery and Collins and myself conferred with you a few days at Albany.

"Although the Fenian sympathizers seem disposed to oppose the nomination of Mr. A.,[10] I think their opposition can be controlled; but a certain candidate, who has hitherto expressed himself willing to waive any claims he may have for the nomination in favor of our man, has now changed his mind and wants it.

"We fear he will cause such discord in the convention as to prevent our offering the nomination to Mr. A. upon the terms upon which he consents to accept it. These are, that it should be made with reasonable unanimity.

"We can carry the convention for our candidate, but not, probably, with such general consent as would be required.

"We have had several interviews with the party causing the trouble, and tried our best to impress upon him the importance of nominating Mr. A. for the sake of our cause *outside* of Massachusetts, but to no effect.

"If we fail in this matter I shall feel that we have lost some of our chances for success.

"Congratulating you upon the auspicious outlook elsewhere,

"I am, very truly, y'rs,
"F. O. PRINCE."

CHARLES F. ADAMS TO BIGELOW

"ADAMS BUILDING, 23 COURT ST., BOSTON, *January 10, 1906.*

"MY DEAR MR. BIGELOW,—I have to acknowledge the receipt of your favor of yesterday, the 9th.

"The extract you make from the letter of F. O. Prince is quite intelligible to me. I remember all the circumstances.

"Mr. Tilden was very anxious, indeed, that my father should be the Democratic candidate for Governor of Massachusetts in 1876. Mr. F. O. Prince was then chairman, I think, of the Democratic committee; at any rate, he was influential. Mr. Tilden, as you very well know, was never at a loss when it came to handling men.

"Mr. Tilden worked through Mr. Prince to accomplish his end. William A. Gaston, afterwards Governor, desired the nomination. It is he who is referred to as a 'certain candidate.' My father was wholly unwilling to accept the nomination unless it came to him unsought, and with 'reasonable unanimity.' The Irish were strongly opposed to him. Their dislike, or rather personal antipathy, to him dated far back—as far, indeed, as 1840, when the questions relating to the burning of the Ursuline Convent at Charlestown were before the General Court of Massachusetts, of which my father was a member.

"Considerable pressure had to be brought to bear upon Mr. Gaston, who finally consented to withdraw, and did, although not with very good grace, nominate my father at the convention. His nomination, of course, gave a certain prestige to the ticket. As a popular candidate in that election my father did not prove a success. A considerable Irish element refused to vote for him.

"It is rather strange to reflect that all these events occurred now thirty-one years ago—nearly the lifetime of a generation; but it is the Irish opposition to which Mr. Prince refers as the 'Fenian sympathizers.' They proved quite irreconcilable. The whole thing is now ancient history.

"Believe me, etc.,
"CHARLES F. ADAMS."

JOHN BIGELOW TO AN INQUIRER

(MR. TILDEN'S WAR RECORD)

"Sept. 1876.

"MY DEAR SIR,—I have an abiding faith that a falsehood never hurts any but those who propagate it. It is also my conviction that no man can pay a much greater homage to another than to deliberately misrepresent him. It is a cowardly confession of weakness and of inferiority. With this sort of homage no public man in this country, so far as I know, has ever been so liberally favored as Mr. Tilden. But two short years ago and there was no American of equal political prominence who could to a greater extent be said to receive the praises of his countrymen, without distinction of party, nor one, perhaps, who had enjoyed fewer of the advantages of adverse criticism. From the moment, however, that he loomed above the horizon as a probable candidate for the Presidency until now, the invention of his political adversaries has been taxed to the utmost to feed whatever appetite remained unsatisfied for calumny and scandal.

"Most of these inventions are so improbable and monstrous that they perish in coming to the birth. As, however, you seem to think the charge of disloyalty during the war has been raised to the dignity of an exception by the recent letter of Gen. Dix, which you enclose, I cheerfully comply with your request to furnish what I trust you and those other Republican friends in Maine, with whom it has been my privilege in times past to co-operate, will regard as a satisfactory answer, not only to the insinuation of Gen. Dix, but to any and every other charge or insinuation that has been or may be made in impeachment of the loyalty or patriotic devotion of Mr. Tilden to the Union, whether before, during, or since the war of the rebellion. To make this perfectly clear I may be obliged to ask your patience, but I will try not to abuse it.

"Let me first dispose of the statement of Gen. Dix that 'Mr. Tilden did not unite in the call for the great Union meeting in New York, after the attack and surrender of Fort Sumter; but he refused to attend it, though urgently solicited to by one of his own political friends.'

"The most charitable construction to be put upon this statement is that the writer had been misinformed; he certainly could have had no personal knowledge upon the subject. It was publicly contradicted when it first appeared in print; it is not true in point of fact; and, if it had been, it would not follow, by any means, that Mr. Tilden did not sympathize in the objects of the meeting.

"Mr. Tilden received a formal written invitation, bearing date the 18th of April, inviting him to act as an officer of the meeting in question. As soon as he found himself at liberty he went to the proper quarter to ascertain what resolutions were to be proposed, and, on being satisfied in regard to them, then and there assented to the use of his name as one of the officers of the meeting. He not only assented to such use of his name, but was himself in actual attendance upon the meeting; and not only did he attend this meeting, but only two days later he attended another meeting of the New York bar, which was called for a similar purpose, and took part in its deliberations.

"Now let me state to you precisely the attitude which Mr. Tilden occupied during the war, and why he manifested so much caution in any action which might possibly influence the course of events at that critical moment.

"It has been my privilege to know Mr. Tilden familiarly, not to say intimately, during his entire public life, embracing a period of nearly or quite forty years. During that time, though we frequently differed about processes, and were often enlisted under opposing political organizations, and though we took widely different views of the fittest way to meet the storm which had been brewing since the repeal of the Missouri Compromise, it never occurred to me for one moment to suppose there was any man in the country less tolerant than he of the doctrine of secession, or prepared to make greater sacrifices to preserve our Union and the republican institutions which had been bequeathed to us.

"At the comparatively youthful age of eighteen years Mr. Tilden had acquired settled opinions upon and shared in the public discussions of the subject of secession. In a speech at a Union meeting, held in Union Square, at which Gen. Dix presided, and Hamilton Fish, William H. Aspinwall, James Brown, Andrew Carrigan, and many other Republicans were vice-presidents, on the 17th of September, 1866, Mr. Tilden, in vindication of President Johnson, incidentally alluded to his early investigation of the subject of secession, and to the conclusion to which he then arrived. He said:

"'The Constitution of the United States is, by its own terms, declared to be perpetual. The government created by it acts within the sphere of its powers directly upon each individual citizen. No State is authorized, in any contingency, to suspend or obstruct that action, or to exempt any citizen from the obligation to obedience. Any pretended act of nullification or secession whereby such effect is anticipated to be produced is absolutely void. The offence of the individual citizen, violating the lawful authority of the United States, is precisely the same as if no such pretended authority ever existed.'

"On the subject of slavery, Mr. Tilden's opinions were no less fixed. Though never what used to be known as an Abolitionist, neither was he ever the advocate or apologist of servile labor. In the controversy which grew out of our territorial acquisitions from Mexico in 1847, he was for doing everything to secure those Territories the benefit of the social and industrial institutions of the North. In that sense he acted in 1848 in opposing the extension of slavery into any of the free Territories by the act of the Federal government; and again, in 1854, when the repeal of the Missouri Compromise was under consideration in Congress, and the flames of sectional controversy broke out afresh, Mr. Tilden was open and decided in his opposition to the repeal, in reference to which he stated in a letter to Wm. Kent in 1860:

"'I used all my influence, at whatever sacrifice of relations, against the repeal ... because I thought a theoretical conformity to even a wise system dearly purchased by breaking the tradition of ancient pacification on such a question and between such parties.'

"Accustomed as I was to converse with Mr. Tilden freely upon all public questions, even when our views were most at variance, having always been in the habit of reading everything which I knew to come from his pen, I feel that I may safely challenge anybody to produce a particle of evidence, either oral or in print, of any sympathy on his part either with secession or with slavery, or any evidence that in the course he felt it his duty to pursue he was not actuated by his best judgment as to what was wise and right for the government and for the welfare of his country. After the breach with the South in 1854, I think I am competent to affirm that he had no partisan relations whatever with slave-holding States. In a letter to the *Evening Post*, written in February, 1863, he speaks of being taunted by Senator Preston King as an object of proscription by the South, and of being asked if he thought his name could pass the Senate of the United States.

"'I answered,' said Mr. Tilden, 'that it was a matter of very little consequence to me whether it could or not; but that it was of great consequence to me that I should do what I thought best for the country.'

"Every act and every expression of his during the war, so far as it has come under my cognizance, was in full accordance with this position, and, what is more, in entire harmony with the whole tenor of his life.

"Better than any person that I knew, he comprehended the irreconcilability of the forces that were arraying themselves against each other in the country. Exaggerating, perhaps, the danger of attempting to rule the country by a sectional party, he deemed it the part of wise statesmanship to postpone as long as possible, in the hope, through the mediatorial offices of time and its inevitable changes, of avoiding a collision.

"No one contested the force of his reasoning on this subject; but they derided his apprehensions of a civil war. So preposterous did they appear to the impassioned multitude in the North, that I remember myself to have been asked by one of his personal friends whether he was quite in his right mind on the subject.

"In 1860, after the failure of the Democratic party at Charleston—though he was then and had been for several years withdrawn from political life—he did not hesitate openly to proclaim his conviction that the dissolution of the Democratic party and the attempt to govern the country by a party like the Republican, having no affiliation in the Southern States, would inevitably result in civil war. He was asked to fill a vacancy in the delegation from New York at the adjourned meeting of the Democratic convention of that year in Baltimore. In that body he made two speeches, in which he portrayed, as an inevitable consequence of a sectional division of the Democratic party, a corresponding division of the States and an armed conflict. These speeches were described by those who heard them as inspired by a solemn sense of patriotic duty and a most vivid perception of impending dangers. After the election of Mr. Lincoln, and when the dangers he had foretold were becoming realities, he took part in several conferences in which Hamilton Fish, the late Charles H. Marshall, the late Daniel Lord, Moses H. Grinnell, the late Wm. B. Astor, Moses Taylor, William B. Duncan, Richard M. Blatchford, A. A. Low, and other gentlemen of more or less prominence participated; and on two of these occasions he made speeches in which he sought to impress upon his hearers a juster sense than was generally entertained of the threatened dangers, and of the fittest means of averting them.

"Earnestly as Mr. Tilden labored to avert the war and to thwart the measures which seemed to him calculated to precipitate it; anxious as he had been to contribute no fresh ingredient of hatred to the seething caldron; when, without any responsibility on his part, the war came, he never for a moment hesitated as to the course he was to pursue. He felt it to be the duty of every citizen to sustain the government in its resistance to territorial dismemberment. To those who thought, as did many then calling themselves Republicans, that on the whole it would be as well to consent to a peaceful separation, Mr. Tilden always answered that peaceful separation was an illusion; that the questions in controversy would be rendered infinitely more difficult by separation, and new ones still more difficult would be created; that, if the antagonized parties could not agree upon peace within the Union, they certainly would not have peace without the Union. They never could agree upon terms of separation, nor could they agree upon the relations to subsist between them after the separation; and, however lamentable might be the consequences, force could be the only arbiter of their differences.

"Though Mr. Tilden was opposed to any illusory concessions to the spirit of disunion; though he was satisfied, after the attack on Fort Sumter, that the differences between the two sections could only be settled by the last argument of kings; and though he was disposed to do everything in his power to make that argument as effective and decisive as possible—his co-operation with the administration of President Lincoln was qualified by a fixed difference of opinion upon several points.

"This opinion was in accord with the view Mr. Tilden had frequently expressed on other occasions, and was also in accord with the opinion which he subsequently gave when his advice was solicited by the then Secretary of War. The week preceding and the week following Mr. Stanton's assuming the duties of Secretary of War, and at his invitation, Mr. Tilden had frequent conferences with him, at the first of which he is reported to me to have said in substance: 'You have no right to expect a great military genius to come to your assistance. The whole human race have been able to furnish such men only once in a century or two; you can only count on the average military talent; you have three times the available population and perhaps nine times the industrial resources of your antagonist; though you occupy the exterior line, you have an immense advantage in the superior capacity of your railways to move men and supplies. What you have to do is to make your advantages available; you must make your combinations so as to concentrate your forces and organize ample reserves to be ready to precipitate them on critical points. In the probable absence of military genius you must rely on overwhelming numbers, wisely concentrated.' Mr. Stanton appeared to adopt these views, but unhappily they did not prevail in the councils of the government.

"A year and a half later, when Mr. Tilden, accompanied by ex-Gov. Morgan, visited Washington for the purpose of securing greater harmony of action between the Federal and State government, Mr. Stanton, in a conversation with Mr. Tilden, referred to this advice, and added: 'I beg you to remember I always agreed with you.' I refer the more freely to the deference which Mr. Stanton testified to Mr. Tilden's judgment in these matters, because it is known not only to the Hon. Peter H. Watson, then Assistant Secretary of War, but to some, at least, of the members of Mr. Lincoln's Cabinet who are now living.

"On the subject of the finances, an element so vital to the successful prosecution of a war, Mr. Tilden's views were at variance with those adopted by the administration; he had more faith in the people, in their readiness to bear the burdens and make the sacrifices which the occasion required, than was manifested by the authorities at Washington. Before their financial policy was fully determined upon he advised that the money for carrying on the war should be chiefly drawn from loans to be supplemented by taxes, and no more Treasury notes not bearing interest issued than were barely necessary to supply the new uses created by the government in its own payments. He was of the opinion that if these measures were promptly adopted, so that the supply should keep pace with the wants of the government, the war might be carried on without any serious embarrassment, without any exorbitant inflation of prices, and without any extreme depreciation of the government bonds. In discussing the financial situation of our own State in his first message to the Legislature in 1875, Gov. Tilden briefly restated the views which he then entertained and expressed upon this subject.

"Though Mr. Tilden foresaw the disastrous consequences of the policy which prevailed at Washington, the wild inflation of prices, the ruinous depreciation of government securities, the extravagant premium on gold, and the certainty that the continuation of that policy would lead, as it has done, to incalculable disaster; and believing, as he did, that it might even endanger the ability of the government to continue the war, he rigorously abstained from any public discussion of them that might tend to create the discredit which he apprehended, and restricted himself to private remonstrances with the more influential friends of the administration.

"While doing all he could to counteract what he deemed the errors of the government, both in the management of the war and of the finances, he was determined neither to be made responsible for nor to be compromised by either. His attitude throughout that pregnant period of our history was, so far as possible for a private citizen holding no official or even active relations with any political party, that of patriotic constitutional opposition to supposed errors of administrative policy, openly co-operating with all the measures of the government of which he approved, and privately discouraging those of which he disapproved.

"At the same time he said, in a speech:

"'That in a time of war we could not deal with our government, although disapproving of its policy, without more reserve than was necessary in debating an administrative question during a period of peace; that the reason was that, if we should paralyze the arm of our own government, we yet could not stay the arm of the public enemy striking at us through it; that it was this peculiarity which had sometimes caused minorities to be suppressed in the presence of public danger, and made such periods perilous to civil liberty.'

"Mr. Tilden was more solicitous than almost any other prominent man in the country to avert the war, because he saw more clearly than most men the grave proportions it was likely to assume; and when it broke out he did not associate himself publicly with the party which he had thought had unwisely precipitated it, because he could not entirely approve of the methods by which they were conducting it. I have yet to see one particle of authentic evidence that, when the war had become inevitable, Mr. Tilden did not do everything that might have been reasonably expected of him to make all the resources of the country available for its vigorous and successful prosecution. Happily my own convictions on this point are confirmed by abundant testimony, some of which it may be a satisfaction to your friends that I recapitulate:

"On the occasion of presenting a stand of colors to the Thirty-seventh Regiment of New York State Volunteers on the 22d of June, 1861, Mr. Tilden was among the speakers, 'and,' says John T. Agnew, who was also present and took part in the ceremony, 'made a stirring appeal to the officers and men of the regiment; a speech not excelled in patriotism by any public speaker during the war of the rebellion.'

"At even an earlier period Mr. Tilden made a journey to Washington, at the request of Brig.-Gen. Ewing, in the especial interest of the Seventy-ninth Regiment of Highlanders.

"The Hon. J. D. Caton, formerly Chief-Justice of the State of Illinois, and the bosom friend of President Lincoln, in a recent letter to the Hon. Mr. Hewitt, which has already been published, says that during the war of the rebellion he had several interviews with Gov. Tilden on the subject of the war, and ever found him ardent and earnest in its support.

"The Hon. Abram S. Hewitt, who, during the war, was in constant intercourse with the War Department, and much depended upon by its chief for his advice at the period, was also in almost daily intercourse with Mr. Tilden. In a recent speech in Congress, which has already become famous, he indignantly repelled the idea that Mr. Tilden ever manifested any sympathy with disunion.

"In October, 1862, Mr. Tilden prepared, in behalf of the Democratic party, a declaration of its adhesion to the Union, and of the war to preserve it. This declaration was made in substance as written, and in so authentic and authoritative a form as to produce a profound popular impression, both in the South as well as in the North. I have examined the manuscript, which has fortunately been preserved, and, with a perfect familiarity with the Governor's handwriting, have no difficulty in verifying its authenticity.

"In 1864, Mr. Tilden, though absorbed by his profession and holding no relations with the public not shared by any private citizen, found himself appointed a delegate to the Democratic National Convention at Chicago. He deemed it his duty to attend. In the delegation he made a speech, the substance of which was briefly reported. The points of it were:

"1. Opposition to any declaration in favor of an armistice.

"2. He insisted that the adjustment of the controversy pending between the North and the South, on any other basis than the restoration of the Union, was manifestly impossible.

"At this convention Mr. Tilden used all his influence to resist, though ineffectually, the adoption of certain expressions in the platform that might have a tendency to discourage the further prosecution of the war; he always refused to acquiesce in them, and subsequently sent a message to Gen. McClellan, the nominee of the convention, urging him to disregard them in his letter of acceptance.

"To these evidences of Mr. Tilden's earnestness in the prosecution of the war, let me add one more, which is perhaps more conclusive than all the rest.

"All the members of Mr. Lincoln's Cabinet were perfectly cognizant of his position during the war, and were in the habit of soliciting his advice; and two of the three who still survive, and with whom Mr. Lincoln had the most intimate and durable relations, are now publicly advocating his election to the Presidency.

"I wish you to realize, as I do, how utterly wanton and shameless is this attempt to associate Mr. Tilden's name with the enemies of his government, and how desperate must be any cause which has to rely upon such methods for success.

"As it seemed to be my duty as a journalist to oppose and often to criticise the course pursued by Mr. Tilden, both before and during the war, I feel it but simple justice to him to bear this testimony to the honorable and patriotic motives with which I never doubted him to be animated.

"JOHN BIGELOW.

"*Highland Falls, Orange County, New York.*"

NELSON J. WATERBURY TO TILDEN

"NO. 152 BROADWAY, NEW YORK, *Sept. 1, 1876.*

"GOV. TILDEN.

"DEAR SIR,—I wish to direct your attention to four acts of Kelly at Saratoga hostile to our success—not for effect upon him, but that they may enter into your mind in respect to action affecting the cause:

"1. He showed disregard of success in placing himself at the head of the electoral ticket.

"2. He tried to defeat the party by his attack upon the Liberal Republicans.

"3. He made a deadly effort to foreclose success by forcing Potter.

"4. He never, during the whole convention, said a word to encourage the Presidential canvass.

"Yours truly,
"NELSON J. WATERBURY."

SAMUEL HAND[11] TO TILDEN

"Confidential.

"SATURDAY EVENING, *Sept. 9th, 1876.*

"MY DEAR GOVERNOR,—I had supposed, after what was said at Saratoga, Tuesday and Wednesday, that our friends tacitly agreed with me that the idea of bringing my name forward for Governor should not be seriously entertained, and therefore I did not think it necessary or becoming to take any further steps about. But I learn, on my return from the North, from Mr. Manning and others, that the project is assuming definite shape and may, unless at once ended, be carried to a nomination.

"I appreciate how high the office is, and of what importance and conspicuousness, and am sensible how much it is beyond anything to which I could at present naturally aspire. I feel gratified that I should have been thought of at all in connection with so great a trust, and am especially proud that you should have deemed me fit successor.

"The more I reflect, however, the more convinced I am that *it will not do.*

"I feel certain that under the present circumstances my nomination would be a mistake, and *know* that it might be fatal.

"Aside from these public considerations, I have private reasons which you would admit sufficient, if I could trouble you with them, to prevent my acceptance of the nomination. I should deeply regret it if these, in fact, interfered with the success of our party, but I am sure such is not the case. I regard them as insuperable, and I have written Mr. Manning a note, of which he can make public use, declining to have my name used at the convention.

"I write this that you may first and at the earliest moment know of my conclusion.

"Yours with the greatest respect,
"SAMUEL HAND."

THE SHERIFF OF NEW YORK CITY TO TILDEN

"SHERIFF'S OFFICE, CITY AND COUNTY OF NEW YORK,
"*September 14, 1876.*

"To his Excellency SAMUEL J. TILDEN,
"*Governor of the State of New York*:

"The recent publications in the newspapers of the capture of William M. Tweed, at Vigo, in Spain, are confirmed by a private telegram received by me.

"There are several indictments for forgery, found by the Grand Jury of this county, against said Tweed, which were untried at the time of his escape on the 4th day of December last.

"He was also at that time in my custody, under an order of arrest, issued in a suit commenced against him by the people of the State of New York, in which a judgment has since been perfected in an amount over $6,000,000, the execution on which has been returned wholly unsatisfied.

"It is said that the government of Spain are willing to surrender said Tweed to the authorities of this county.

"May I ask you to present the subject to the government of the United States, so that prompt and efficient measures may be taken to secure his surrender?

"I remain,
"Your obdt. Servant,
"WM. C. CONNOR,
"*Sheriff.*"

GOVERNOR TILDEN TO HAMILTON FISH

(APPLICATION FOR ARREST OF WM. M. TWEED, A FUGITIVE FROM JUSTICE)

"CITY OF NEW YORK, *Sept. 19th, 1876.*

"SIR,—I transmit herewith for the use of your department a copy of the official application made to me by the Sheriff of the City and County of New York concerning the case of William M. Tweed, a fugitive from the justice of this State, who is understood to be at this time held in custody as such at Vigo by the Spanish government.

"Owing to my being in this city, this document did not come to my knowledge until late yesterday, and, although advised that the Attorney-General of this State has already addressed you to the same effect, I deem it proper now to superadd my earnest request that the government of the United States may employ its efficient and perfectly adequate powers to induce a delivery of this great criminal into the hands of the sheriff at this city.

"Yours respectfully,
"(Sd.) SAMUEL J. TILDEN,
"*Governor of the State of New York.*

"*Hon. Hamilton Fish,*
"*Secretary of State of the United States.*"

L. P. WALKER TO TILDEN

"NEW YORK, *Sept. 19, 1876.*

"MY DEAR SIR,—As a Southern man, whose interest in your election is greater than your own, because it involves the right to live, I beg permission to make a single suggestion, the result of general intercourse here for the last ten days with gentlemen from all sections of the country. The politicians, as a rule, are not overzealous for your success. Could they separate their fate from yours this feeling would be openly manifested. Your self-poise offends their vanity, and they are controlled where they think they should direct. It was the confidence of the people in this phase of your character, as much, even, as the spirit of reform, that secured you the nomination at St. Louis. It certainly greatly influenced my action. Still, I think, if you will allow me to say it, it might be proper for you to recognize and act upon certain suggestions that have been made with reference to the campaign in Indiana. Your election may not depend upon the result in that State in October, but it will be so urged and considered generally, and I am very sure that you have not overlooked this possibility. The suggestion I wish to make is that you would in some proper way manifest such interest in that election as to satisfy your friends in that State and elsewhere that you appreciate the importance of carrying that State in October. My excuse for this letter is the fact, known to you, that I was an original Tilden man, and, I will add, I have seen no reason to regret it.

"I shall leave to-day for Alabama, carrying with me the conviction that your election is almost an assured fact. God grant it. With high respect, yours very truly,

"L. P. WALKER."

ACTING SECRETARY OF STATE TO GOVERNOR TILDEN

"DEPARTMENT OF STATE, WASHINGTON,
21st September, 1876.

"To his Excellency SAMUEL J. TILDEN,
Governor of the State of New York, Albany.

"SIR,—I have to acknowledge the receipt of your letter from New York of the 19th inst., accompanied by a copy of one addressed to you by the Sheriff of the City and County of New York, concerning the case of William M. Tweed, a fugitive from the justice of that State. In reply, I have to assure you that it may not be doubted that if the person adverted to should come into custody of authorities of this government he will be received for the purpose of being transferred to the proper authorities of New York, agreeably to your Excellency's request.

"I am, Your Excellency's Obedient Servant,
"(Sd.) W. HUNTER,
"*Acting Secretary.*"

W. C. BRYANT TO JOHN BIGELOW

"CUMMINGTON, MASSACHUSETTS, *September 21st, 1876.*

"DEAR BIGELOW,—The attacks on the personal character of Mr. Tilden are shameful. There was no need of asking me to see that a fair and just treatment of his statement in refutation of the story about the income tax should be accorded to him in the *Evening Post.* I wrote to Mr. Sperry yesterday on the subject, telling him that I thought that the paper should express as great indignation at the slander, as soon as its refutation should be made public, as if the Republican candidate had been the subject of it. I only wish that the opportunity for such an expression had been given a little earlier.

"Yours very truly,
"W. C. BRYANT."

CHARLES O'CONOR TO TILDEN

"NEW YORK, *Sept. 22d, 1876.*

"To his Excellency SAMUEL J. TILDEN,
"*Governor of the State of New York.*

"SIR,—It is probable that William M. Tweed, a noted delinquent, who went abroad many months since, will be tendered to the custody of the Sheriff of the City and County of New York within a few days.

"At the time of his departure the same sheriff held him in formal custody under an order of arrest in a civil action requiring bail in $3,000,000. Since his departure judgment has been recovered against him in that action at the suit of the State to an amount exceeding $6,000,000.

"For his negligence in permitting the escape there was, in fact, no ordinary civil remedy against the sheriff except a very trivial and inadequate one on his official bond. The proper steps for securing this measure of redress have been pursued with all proper diligence; and, until this time, there did not seem to be any utility in prosecuting any other line of action. But as Tweed may be again in custody at an early period, it has now become important to consider what course should be adopted for the purpose of rendering that custody safe and secure. As already stated, the remedies allowed by law against the delinquent custodian who allows his prisoner to escape are totally inadequate. Consequently, should Tweed be again in legal custody, there will be no effective security for his detention to meet the awards of civil and criminal justice, except what may be afforded by the personal and official fidelity and vigilance of the custodian.

"Your predecessor, Governor John A. Dix, made a public and official remonstrance against the palpable favoritism displayed towards this person in his then existing custody as a prisoner in the Penitentiary. During the same year the Sheriff of the City and County of New York, by gross negligence, suffered the escape of Genet, a convict of the same general class as Tweed.

"With these circumstances to excite vigilance, the present sheriff nevertheless allowed Tweed to enjoy a sort of free custody, precisely similar to that which had been accorded to Genet; and Tweed, availing himself of the facility, left the State.

"Would it be proper, on Tweed's return, to place him in charge of the same officer? I think you will answer this question in the negative.

"The Constitution, arts. 10, secs. 1 and 5, together with the act of 1848, Edmonds Statutes, vol. 3, p. 330, affords to you as Chief Executive the means of meeting the exigency. You can, on brief notice to him, remove the present sheriff and appoint a perfectly reliable custodian to receive the prisoner.

"Perhaps all the office I ought to assume in this matter properly ends here. But, when one acts at all in an important affair, he ought to do all that his best judgment dictates towards accomplishing the object in view.

"The history of Tweed's prosecutions, imprisonments, judicial releases, and ultimate deliverance from custody is well known to you and the public. To it I refer for a justification of my further remarks.

"The person whom you may appoint to fill the place made vacant by a removal of the present sheriff can hold only until the end of the present year. A new sheriff, elected by the people, with full notice of their needs in November next, will enter on his duties on the 1st of January, 1877. For the short term of about three months created by the removal, I take leave to recommend the appointment of General Francis C. Barlow. His persistent hostility to official swindlers, and his zealous activity in prosecuting Tweed to conviction, are well known to you. Tweed would not escape from his hands. I have consulted no one on this subject, nor have I any knowledge that General Barlow would accept the office. Should he do so, you will have well performed your duty; and, in any event, your tender of the appointment will effectually refute all assertions that you owe Tweed favor, or fear his disclosures.

"Yours, &c.,
"CH. O'CONOR."

WM. M. TWEED PLACED AT THE DISPOSAL OF THE NEW YORK AUTHORITIES

"DEPARTMENT OF STATE, WASHINGTON, *Oct. 10, 1876.*

"To his Excellency SAMUEL J. TILDEN,
"*Governor of the State of New York.*

"SIR,—Referring to the letter which your Excellency addressed to me from the city of New York on the 19th Septr. last, with reference to the case of William M. Tweed, at that time understood to be held in custody by the Spanish government, and to the acknowledgment of that letter by the Acting Secretary of State on the 21st ultimo, I have the honor to state that in the month of July last there were received in this department duly authenticated copies of two indictments, found in the Court of General Sessions for the city and county of New York, against William M. Tweed and others for forgery and other offences.

"In the month of June last a person believed to be Tweed, but passing under the name of John Secor, had clandestinely landed on the island of Cuba, and the authorities of that island, with the sanctions of the Spanish government at Madrid, purposed to deliver him to the United States, but he escaped from the island on or about the 27th day of July, and sailed for a port in Spain.

"The Captain-General of Cuba despatched a steamer in pursuit, which failed to intercept his flight, and on his arrival at Vigo he was immediately arrested and placed in confinement.

"Instead of returning him to Cuba, the Spanish government decided to deliver him directly to the United States, and placed him on board the U. S. steamer *Franklin*, which left the port of Vigo on or about the 28th day of September with Tweed, *alias* Secor, on board, under orders to sail for the port of New York, where she may be expected to arrive some time from the 20th to the last of this month. After the news of the arrest in Spain became known, the sheriff of the city and county of New York also addressed me a letter, stating that he had process against Tweed, requiring the custody of his person in the county of New York, from which he escaped in December last, and requesting such action on the part of the government as will secure his return to answer the behest of the process in his hands, and offering to bear all the necessary expenses of conveying him to New York.

"The uncertainty at that time attending a surrender by the Spanish government prevented any definite reply to the sheriff, or any more positive answer on the subject than that which was addressed to you on the 21st September.

"But now, as the person referred to has been actually delivered by the Spanish government to the government of the United States, and as no doubt seems to exist that this person, calling himself Secor, is William M. Tweed, the President, in pursuance of the intention with which he decided to receive him, deems it proper to place him at the disposal of the authority of the State of New York, and instructs me for that purpose to inform your Excellency, as Governor of the State, that on the arrival of the *Franklin* orders will be given to the naval officers for the delivery of Tweed into the custody of the sheriff of the city and county of New York, such being the disposition theretofore requested by you in your letter.

"Inasmuch as such orders must necessarily pass through the proper channels of the Navy Department and should be explicit, and in New York awaiting the arrival of the steamer, to be executed immediately upon such arrival, I venture to request the earliest possible expression of any particulars or details which you may desire carried out to insure the proper transfer of the custody of this person into the hands of the authorities of New York, so that the instructions may be in the proper hands by the 20th of this month; and I venture to suggest that it may greatly tend to facilitate the matter if no public information be given as to the details of the matter.

"I have the honor to be,
"Your Excellency's obedient Servant,
"HAMILTON FISH."

HORATIO SEYMOUR TO GOV. TILDEN

"UTICA, *October 25, 1876.*

"MY DEAR SIR,—I have reason to know that your opponents in and out of the party count upon the large towns to defeat you. They rely upon distress among Democrats, hard times, and the use of money. The word 'reform' is not popular with working-men. To them it means less money spent and less work. Most of these men are Catholics. You will see that the Republicans have dropped the school question. I think it important that some quiet, judicious person should visit the large towns and see the leading Irishmen and call their minds back to the hostility of Hayes and the Republicans to their nationality and religion. There is danger of a loss of vote among the class.

"I am still out of health, and I write with difficulty. I gain slowly, but I do not expect to enjoy hereafter full health and vigor.

I am truly yours, &c.,
"HORATIO SEYMOUR."

C. B. SMITH TO TILDEN

"RICHMOND, IND., *Oct. 27th, 1876.*

"MY DEAR OLD CLASSMATE,—Permit me to thank you for your letter on the 'rebel claims.' It is worthy of you, and that is saying, in the estimation of all your old friends, *all* that can be said in its praise. It is indeed noble and strong, while it crushes with the force of fate. It spikes the last gun of the administration. It is indeed a triumph and a victory.

"We are all proud of you, and look forward with joyful and confident anticipations of soon seeing you the Chief Magistrate of this great nation. Your mission is a great and noble one, but you are equal to every possible condition and emergency. I firmly believe this era has raised you up to bring the nation back to its old historic thought respecting honesty and economy, and make it fit for honest men to live in.

"Pardon my familiarity and earnestness, for the feelings of boyhood are sure to control me when writing to or of a classmate.

"Yours truly,
"C. B. SMITH."

R. D. RICE TO S. J. TILDEN

"*Confidential.*

"PORTLAND, *Oct. 27, '76.*

"HON. S. J. TILDEN.

"DEAR SIR,—As I was just ready to leave N. York last evening, some facts came to my knowledge of which it may be well for our friends to be appraised (in case they are not already) as to the *then* last line of policy of our opponents. You are aware that Z. Chandler and Tyner were both in the city and at the wheel. Your State is substantially abandoned by them; the fight is, of course, to be kept up there *nominally*, at least. The *real* fight is to be made in the Carolinas, Louisiana, Florida, etc., in the South, and some of the doubtful States in the North and N. West, including *Indiana.* To carry these States by the *commercial element* in each has been *fully resolved*, and the *means put in requisition* for that purpose to an extent, especially in Ind., exceeding the amounts used in the last election is, I think, beyond a doubt. Larger hopes are entertained from the greenback element. They *must* contest this battle to the last, however desperate it appear. Excuse this hasty note. Our people here are in ecstasies over your letter, and in the best of spirits.

Yours Truly,
"R. D. RICE."

L. W. WALKER TO GOVERNOR TILDEN

(APPROVING GOVERNOR'S LETTER ON REBEL CLAIMS)

"HUNTSVILLE, ALA., *Oct. 27th, 1876.*

"MY DEAR SIR,—I have read with sincere pleasure and approval your letter of the 24th inst. to the chairman of the national Democratic committee. It states only the literal truth as to the South. I think I know as well as any one the sentiments of the people of this State, and I am sure there is not a man, woman, or child in it who entertains the idea that the government could, would, or should pay for the loss of slaves, or for the loss of any other property during the war, belonging to persons who were engaged in, or sympathized with, what has been judicially designated the rebellion.

"The South absolutely surrendered at Appomattox the whole sectional past, and now looks alone, in perfect good faith, to a common American future.

"In this campaign of unparalleled profligacy waged by the Republicans, no greater calumny has been uttered against the people of the South, and against the possibilities of your administration, should you be elected President, than this charge, first made noticeable, not by the character, but by the ability and official position, of Mr. Blaine, the unanswered license of whose statements, after the passions incident to the election shall have subsided, must shock the conscience of the whole nation, and consign him to immortal infamy.

"With sincere regards, your very truly,
"L. W. WALKER."

C. K. FOOTE TO S. J. TILDEN

"MOBILE, *Nov. 2, 1876.*

"To his Excellency SAMUEL J. TILDEN,
"*Governor of the State of New York.*

"SIR,—Your letter of 24th ult., in reply to the Hon. Abram S. Hewitt, relative to the 14th amendment and 'rebel debts,' is no doubt a good campaign card, and well played at this particular time in check of the clamor and misrepresentations, and its use and effect in the pending Presidential election.

"I beg to assure you of an abiding confidence in your election to the Chief Executive office of our government, and to promote this great 'reform' the intelligence, the property, and the integrity of the South is solid and zealous in this great work, believing and trusting in your known and tried integrity to the principles of justice and right to all.

"In the matter of the 'cotton tax,' from June, 1865, to September, 1868, after peace was restored and promised, it was not an element of the 'war,' nor was it 'an incident to military operations for maintaining its existence.' The compiled record of H. H. Smith, Esqr., clerk of the committee on war claims of the 43d Congress, may be official facts, and are no doubt the truth, so far as the guilty persons are concerned that have rendered infamous and odious the offices they have prostituted to embezzlements, thefts, and wickedness. The facts connected with that 'cotton tax' have not come to the surface. Those that have made haste to buy and sell, and to bribe and lobby their way through a most foul administration, are not the standard or measure for honest claimants that have patiently waited, with the evidence of the money paid into the United States Treasury, against the day of 'reform' and the return to honesty, and a just discrimination on the merits and facts of the case; nor should it be ruthlessly set aside without a fair investigation and examination by discreet, honest men.

"Your 'veto' and your integrity will be accepted together, trusting in the latter all the time, and the use of the former on all suitable occasions, and for the good of the nation.

"With sentiments of highest esteem and admiration, I am,

"Respectfully yours,
"C. K FOOTE."

THE ELECTION OF 1876

On the 7th of November, 1876, the people of the State of New York, and the people of the United States, expressed their preferences among the several Presidential candidates to succeed President Grant, as follows, according to the Albany *Evening Journal Almanac*:

For Tilden in New York State	522,043
For Hayes	489,225
Tilden's majority	32,818

It is to be remarked that Tilden's vote was larger than any of the State or local candidates', and was vastly larger than had ever been cast for any other man.

The vote for Grant in 1872 in New York State was	440,745
Tilden's vote larger than Grant's vote in 1872, when the latter carried the State by 53,466	81,298
Tilden's vote in 1876 larger than Greeley's vote in 1872	134,764
Grant's vote in 1868 was	419,883
Tilden's vote in 1876 larger than Grant's vote in 1868	102,160
Seymour's vote in 1868 was	429,883
Tilden's vote in 1876 larger than Seymour's in 1868	92,160

The total vote for Tilden in the United States in 1876 was	4,300,316
For Hayes	4,036,015
Tilden's majority	264,301

Grant's vote in 1872 was	3,596,742
Tilden's vote larger than Grant's vote, in 1872, when the latter's majority was 761,844	703,574
Greeley's vote in 1872 was	2,834,888
Tilden's vote in 1876 larger than Greeley's in 1872	1,465,418
Grant's vote in 1872 was	3,013,188
Tilden's vote in 1876 larger than Grant's	1,287,128
Seymour's vote in 1868 was	2,703,600
Tilden's vote in 1876 larger than Seymour's in 1868	1,596,716

JUST WHAT CHANDLER DID, AND HOW THE PLAN WAS LAID TO DEFEAT THE POPULAR CHOICE FOR PRESIDENT

[*From the New York "Times" of June 15, 1887.*]

"The New York *Sun*, after three days of hard labor, has finally produced a curious reply to the *Times's* comments upon Mr. William E. Chandler's connection with the election of 1876. The best answer to its series of misrepresentations will be found in the following statement of what did actually occur at the Fifth Avenue Hotel on the morning of Nov. 8 of that year.

"As stated on Saturday last in the *Times*, a gentleman entered the Fifth Avenue Hotel at the Twenty-third Street door about 6.30 o'clock in the morning, possibly a little before that hour. He went at once to the rooms of the national committee and found them occupied only by a number of servants in the hotel, who were engaged in cleaning and setting the rooms to rights. He was informed that everybody had gone home or to bed a couple of hours before. He left the room and started for the clerk's desk to ascertain the number of Mr. Zachariah Chandler's room. While opening the first door in the direction of the reading-room, on his way to the office of the hotel, he came in collision with a small man, wearing an immense pair of goggles, his hat drawn down over his ears, a great-coat with a heavy military coat, and carrying a grip-sack and a newspaper in his hand. The newspaper was the New York *Tribune*. The gentleman did not recognize the stranger, but the stranger recognized the gentleman immediately. The stranger cried out: 'Why, Mr. Blank, is that you?' The gentleman knew the voice, and said: 'Is that you, Mr. Chandler?' He answered: 'Yes, I have just arrived from New Hampshire by train. D—n the men who brought this disaster upon the Republican party.' The gentleman replied: 'The Republican party has sustained no disaster. If you will only keep your heads up here, there is no question of the election of President Hayes. He has been fairly and honestly elected.'

"Chandler replied: 'Look at this paper.' The answer was that the paper had not the news, and the gentleman began to give Mr. Chandler an idea of the situation, when Chandler interrupted him, saying: 'I have just got the key to my room; come up-stairs.' Upon entering the room, Mr. Chandler placed his grip-sack in the corner, took off his overcoat, sat down in a chair—the gentleman taking the only other one in the room—and Chandler said:

'Now go ahead.' The visitor went over the ground carefully, State by State, from Maine to Oregon, counting the electoral vote in each State, and showing the vote as it was finally counted for Hayes and Tilden. After he had finished, William E. Chandler said: 'Well, what do you think should be done?' The gentleman replied:

"'Telegraph immediately to leading Republicans, men in authority, in South Carolina, Florida, Louisiana, California, Oregon, and Nevada.' Mr. Chandler made no direct reply to this proposition, but said:

"'We must go and see Zach.'

"The gentleman said:

"'Do you know the number of his room?' William E. Chandler replied:

"'Yes, I know where it is.' To which the gentleman answered:

"'If you don't know exactly, I'd better go to the office and get the number; I was going there when I met you.' Chandler said: 'No, I know where it is,' and led the way around to the Twenty-fourth Street side of the hotel. After proceeding a short distance down the corridor he looked up at the number over a door and said: 'This is Chandler's room.' Then he began to knock and kick at the door. The noise at once awakened the inmate, and there proceeded from the room a series of shrill screams and shrieks, followed by an affrightened female voice crying out: 'What do you want? Go away; I'm a lone woman.' Chandler immediately darted down the corridor. The gentleman said: "See here, if you don't know the number of the room we'd better go immediately down to the office and get it; we don't want anything more of this kind." Chandler insisted that he would be right the next time, however, and walking still further down the corridor he selected a room about four doors below the first one he had attacked. The response to his knock was immediate and not uncertain. There was no scream in this case, but the inmate shouted in angry tones: 'Get out; I'm a lady. Why do you disturb me at this hour. Go right away, or I will call the servants.' Chandler then remarked: 'I guess I'll have to go down to the office.' Whereupon he darted down-stairs, ascertained the number of Zachariah Chandler's room, which was between those of the two ladies whom he had thus unceremoniously aroused, and he began kicking and knocking at the door, of the right room in this case, and did so for a little time without effect. The gentleman then joined with him in thumping and kicking the door, remarking: 'We'll wake up the whole house and will have the police down on us if we don't look out,' when in a moment came the well-recognized voice from the inside, 'Who's there?' to which William E. Chandler replied: 'It's me, Chandler; open the door, quick.' The door was shortly opened, and

Mr. Zachariah Chandler was discovered standing in his nightdress. Mr. William E. Chandler then said, closing the door: "Here is a gentleman who has more news than you have, and he has some suggestions to make.' To which Zach Chandler replied: 'Yes, I know him. What is it?' With this he seated himself on the edge of his bed. William E. Chandler then said: 'The gentleman will tell you the story himself. He understands the case better than I do.'

"The gentleman then went over the details of the election, and added the recommendations he had made to William E. Chandler.

"The chairman of the national committee laid down and said: 'Very well, go ahead and do what you think necessary.' The two visitors left the room and went to the telegraph office in the hotel. It was just five minutes before seven by the hotel clock when they arrived there. The telegraph office was not open, and they were informed that it would not be open until 8, possibly later. The two men stood by the receiver's shelf at the little telegraph inclosure, Chandler with his back to the door opening towards Twenty-third Street entrance. The other gentleman faced Chandler, leaning on the shelf, with his back to the door leading into the great hall of the hotel. The only other persons in the room were a few servants and a clerk in the newsstand. The gentleman said: 'I'll have to take these messages to the main office of the Western Union.' Chandler called a servant and directed him to have a carriage brought to the Twenty-third Street entrance. Then Chandler said: 'Well, what do you want to do?' The gentleman replied: 'We'll first telegraph to Gov. Chamberlain, of South Carolina.' The gentleman dictated the despatch, which appeared in the *Sun*, and which was as follows:

> "'*To D. H. Chamberlain, Columbia, S. C.*:
>
> "'Hayes is elected if we have carried South Carolina, Florida, and Louisiana. Can you hold your State? Answer immediately.'

"Mr. Chandler took the despatch in shorthand, as dictated. The gentleman then proposed to send a similar despatch to S. B. Conover, of Florida. Mr. William E. Chandler immediately objected, saying that Conover was as much of a Democrat as he was a Republican, and would probably show the despatch to the Democrats as early as he would to any Republican in town. At any rate, the Democrats would get it first. The gentleman remarked:

"'Have you any other proposition to make, or have you any one in your mind whom it would be safer or better to address?' Mr. William E. Chandler scratched his ear with his pencil, and after a moment's consideration said he had not. The gentleman then said it was imperative that some one should be woke up down there, and if Mr. Chandler could think of no one else it was essential to telegraph to Conover. Mr. Chandler hesitated for an instant, and said: 'Well, I suppose we must; something has to be done.' The gentleman accordingly dictated to Chandler the Conover despatch. Here it is:

> "'*To S. B. Conover, Tallahassee, Fla.*:
>
> "'The Presidential election depends on the vote of Florida, and the Democrats will try and wrest it from us. Watch it and hasten returns. Answer immediately.'

"The gentleman then suggested S. B. Packard as the proper person to address in Louisiana, and the Packard despatch was dictated to, and taken down by, William E. Chandler in shorthand:

> "'*To S. B. Packard, New Orleans, La.*:
>
> "'The Presidential election depends on the vote of Louisiana. The Democrats will try to wrest it from you. Watch it and hasten returns. Answer immediately.'

"The gentleman then asked: 'To whom shall we send in Oregon?' Mr. Chandler said: 'John H. Mitchell.' The Oregon despatch was then dictated:

> "'*To John H. Mitchell, Portland, Oregon*:
>
> "'Without Oregon Hayes defeated. Don't be defrauded. Hasten returns. Answer.'

"The gentleman suggested that George C. Gorham, of San Francisco, was the proper man to receive a telegram. Chandler at once assented. Then the gentleman suggested that probably he might be able to do something with Nevada and Oregon, and a despatch something as follows was prepared:

> "'*To George C. Gorham, San Francisco, Cal.*:
>
> "'The Presidential election depends on our having both Nevada and Oregon, which are reported for Hayes. Telegraph both those States immediately. Watch them and hurry results. Answer immediately.
>
> "'W. E. CHANDLER,
> "'*Fifth Avenue Hotel.*'

"Chandler says, in his testimony before the Potter committee, that he found the Gorham despatch among some papers. This happened in this way: After the despatch had been written some verbal changes in it were suggested. Mr. Chandler found some trouble in making them on the telegraph blank, and the gentleman who dictated the despatch remarked: 'You'd better write that despatch over again; you'll save time.' Chandler did so, and the original despatch got into his pocket with the rest of his papers.

"William E. Chandler signed with his own name the despatches to Oregon and to Gorham, of San Francisco. To the despatches sent to Conover, Packard, and Chamberlain the narrator's recollection is he signed the name of Zachariah Chandler. William E. Chandler at once took telegraph blanks and wrote from his stenographic notes the five despatches above printed, the gentleman standing by him taking every despatch as he finished it and carefully reading it. When the last despatch was transcribed, Chandler handed it over to the gentleman and said: 'Are they all right?' He was informed that they were. Chandler immediately started to open the door from the reading-room to the Twenty-third Street entrance that the gentleman might make a hasty exit, but Chandler made a bungling job of it; finally the two reached the outer door. The gentleman jumped into the carriage there waiting and told the driver to get to the main office of the Western Union with all possible speed. Probably the quickest time ever made by a carriage from the Fifth Avenue Hotel to the Western Union was made that morning. Arriving at the Western Union office the gentleman went to the receiver's desk and handed in the despatches. The receiver, who knew the gentleman very well, said: 'Good-morning.' The gentleman said: 'Get these despatches off as quickly as possible, and charge the Republican National Committee.' The receiver replied: 'The National Committee has no account here, and we can't do it. Why not charge them to the New York *Times* account?' The gentleman replied, 'All right,' and the receiver immediately handed them back to him to be countersigned. This was promptly done, the gentleman returned to his carriage and was driven back to the Fifth Avenue Hotel. There was still nobody stirring connected with the National Committee.

"And now a few extracts, which the *Sun* failed to discover in the Potter committee's report, are pertinent. First, in regard to the telegram to George C. Gorham, in San Francisco, Mr. Chandler testified:

"'I found among those papers this copy of a telegram which I sent from the Fifth Avenue Hotel. I think before daylight on the morning of Nov. 8. It bears date of the 7th of November, but it was really written and sent on the morning of the 8th.'

"Immediately after this comes the following sentence, bear in mind, from William E. Chandler's testimony before the Potter committee:

"'The remaining copies are in shorthand, and I will read them.'

"If these messages were not dictated to Mr. William E. Chandler, why should he have written them in shorthand? When time was so precious, is it to be believed that William E. Chandler wrote his own messages first in shorthand and then transcribed them? Further down on the same page (526) of the testimony occurs the following:

"'This paper [handing to the chairman a paper from which he had read] is worn from carrying it in the pocket.'

"The chairman: 'Who made these stenographic marks?'

"The witness: 'Those are my own. I learned to write shorthand many years ago.'

"It is perfectly clear from this (Chandler's own testimony) that these messages were dictated to Chandler by another person. They were so dictated exactly as described in the foregoing narrative. The New York *Times* has never to this day been reimbursed by the National Committee or William E. Chandler, nor has William E. Chandler or any national committee ever offered to pay the *Times* for the telegraph tolls or for any of the expenses incurred on that morning.

"Mr. Chandler's efforts in behalf of the grand old Republican party on the morning of Nov. 8, 1876, may therefore be briefly summarized as follows:

"First.—He frightened two lone women nearly out of their wits.

"Second.—He finally discovered the number of Zachariah Chandler's room.

"Third.—He acted as an amanuensis for a gentleman who dictated five despatches. (Work well done.)

"Fourth.—He asked a servant to bring a carriage around to the Twenty-third Street entrance of the Fifth Avenue Hotel. (Result satisfactory.)

"Fifth.—He attempted to open a door to enable the gentleman bearing the despatches the more readily to reach the street. (Made a mess of it.)

"Mr. Zachariah Chandler, chairman of the National Committee, asked the gentleman above alluded to, on the evening of Nov. 8, if it would not be well to send William E. Chandler to Florida. The gentleman thought it would. Mr. William E. Chandler left for Florida on the following day at 6 P.M. Mr. William E. Chandler, therefore, did not initiate the idea of going to Florida. The truth is that Zachariah Chandler wished to send to Florida a gentleman who had been formerly a private secretary to William H. Seward, but the person was not at hand and could not be reached in time. William E. Chandler for this important mission was a second choice.

"The whole scheme of sending what were afterwards called 'visiting statesmen' to the doubtful States originated in the brain of Zachariah Chandler, not William E. Chandler.

"If the New York *Sun* and Mr. William E. Chandler can find any comfort in the foregoing plain narration of facts they are entirely welcome to it."

Notwithstanding Mr. Tilden's popular majority, the public needs not now be told that he was counted out by the instrumentality of an extemporized tribunal, not only unknown to the Constitution, but in distinct disregard and violation of the provisions of that instrument for counting the electoral votes for Presidents and Vice-Presidents. A detailed account of the processes by which this great national crime was initiated will be found in the first chapter of the second volume of Bigelow's *Life of Tilden*. To that record, however, some important testimony has since been disclosed which appears to have escaped the biographer's notice.

At a meeting held at Chickering Hall on the evening of November 12, 1891, to sympathize with Governor Nichols's war on the Louisiana lottery system, the late Abram S. Hewitt was one of the speakers. In the course of his remarks in denunciation of the lottery gambling in Louisiana, Mr. Hewitt said:

"I can't find words strong enough to express my feelings regarding this brazen fraud.

"This scheme of plunder develops a weak spot in the government of the United States, which I would not mention were it not for the importance of the issue. We all know that a single State frequently determines the result of a Presidential election. *The State of Louisiana has determined the result of a Presidential election. The vote of that State was offered to me for money*, and I declined to buy it. *But the vote of that State was sold for money!*"

A day or two after this anti-lottery meeting the New York *Sun* recites this passage of Mr. Hewitt's speech, and accompanies it with the following pertinent and instructive comment:

"We do not remember that this highly important testimony has ever before been elicited from Mr. Hewitt in any public declaration. He says that he has personal knowledge that the vote of Louisiana was sold to Mr. Hayes' managers for money; that the same vote was offered for money to him as Mr. Tilden's representative, and that he declined to buy it—very properly, as all patriotic citizens and all honest men will agree.

"Some time in the summer of 1878, when the great crime was less than two years old and the beneficiaries of that crime were still in the full enjoyment of its fruits, there occurred a spirited, we may even say a bitterly personal, controversy between the Hon. Henry Watterson and Mr. Hewitt as to the extent of the latter's responsibility for the failure of the Democratic party to obtain its rights by the seating of Mr. Tilden in the office to which he had been elected. Col. Watterson acrimoniously, and, as we are glad to believe, unjustly, charged Mr. Hewitt not only with a mismanagement of Democratic interests at the time of the electoral count, but also with suppressing the fact of Mr. Tilden's personal disapproval of the electoral commission bill at a critical time in the deliberations of Mr. Tilden's friends at Washington.

"The merits of the Watterson-Hewitt controversy are not now of living interest. Time doubtless has softened the sentiments of each of the two statesmen with reference to the other's part in the events of 1876 and 1877. We refer to the incident merely to say that even under the strongest provocation to disclose all that he knew about the theft of the Presidency, Mr. Hewitt withheld the statement which he made so distinctly and emphatically at an anti-lottery meeting in Chickering Hall fifteen years after the crime.

"There was also, as it may be remembered, a searching investigation into all of the circumstances surrounding the theft of the vote of Louisiana, conducted by the special committee of the Forty-fifth Congress, known as the Potter committee. The object was not to remedy the irremediable, but to bring out the whole truth, to fix the responsibility where it belonged, and to make a repetition of the crime forever impossible. Those Democrats who possessed special knowledge bearing upon the crime came forward and testified. The report and testimony of the Potter investigation fill about twenty-five hundred printed pages, but on no page is there any piece of evidence more important than that which Mr. Hewitt volunteered on Thursday night before a mass-meeting called for an enterprise of moral and social, rather than political, reform.

"We speak of the Potter investigation merely to say that the Hon. Abram S. Hewitt was not among the witnesses before that committee. He did not appear to testify to the sensational facts which he gave so freely to the anti-lottery meeting in Chickering Hall. In all the twenty-five hundred pages he appears only once, and then indirectly. Major Burke testified that when he went to Mr. Hewitt as the ostensible manager of Mr. Tilden's case in the House, and asked him whether Louisiana was to be abandoned by the Democratic managers, Mr. Hewitt replied, among other things, that 'the Democratic party could not afford to take the responsibility of plunging this country into anarchy and strife, upsetting values and disturbing trade.'

"But Mr. Hewitt's silence on previous occasions, when his testimony would have been so valuable, does not render it less interesting, now that its importance is mainly historical."

In *Harper's Magazine* for the month of March, 1907, will be found an article from the accomplished pen of Frederick Trevor Hill, entitled "The Hayes-Tilden Contest—A Political Arbitration," in which occurs the following statement of an incident of the nefarious transaction under consideration, which no one has ventured to contest, and which leaves no longer a doubt that Mr. Tilden must have been declared President instead of Mr. Hayes, despite all the other devices by which he is believed to have been counted out, but for the forgery of signatures to the returns from Louisiana which escaped the attention of the perhaps too-eminent counsel in charge of Mr. Tilden's case, a forgery for the concealment of which Senator Ferry seems to be indirectly responsible:

"The proceedings opened as usual with the reception of the conflicting certificates from the Senate chamber—five documents in all—and while these important papers were being perfunctorily examined and initialed by the presiding justice, the journalists in the gallery watched the scene, the lawyers whispered together and prepared for the coming contests; the general public waited, bored and inattentive, and some of the Republican managers sat quaking with fear.

"Judge Clifford finally laid aside his pen, and it was ordered that the various exhibits which he had been marking be printed and copies furnished for the convenience of the counsel and commissioners. Had a single objection to this routine been interposed; had prudence, habit, or even curiosity impelled any of the Democratic counsel to scrutinize the original documents, or had enterprise prompted any journalist to examine and compare them, a sensational exposure would have been inevitable, for one of the Republican certificates was clumsily, even obviously, forged.[12]

"Had this been discovered, it is not improbable that one or more of the Republican commissioners, who were suspected of wavering in their party allegiance, would have voted for a thorough investigation, and an entirely different result might have been effected. Neither suspicion nor inspiration, however, put the Democratic champions on their guard, and the opportunity passed unheeded, never to return."

FRANCIS C. BARLOW[13] TO JOHN BIGELOW

"NEW YORK, *Nov. 6, 1876.*

"MY DEAR SIR,—I believe I have never thanked you for the legislative documents, which I beg now to do.

"I did not overlook the last clause of your letter, in which you express a hope that you may see me on the stump for Tilden. I have been on the stump for Hayes, doing what I can, and I have the strongest confidence that we are going to elect him, and that because I believe there is too much good sense in the American people to turn over this govt. and its credit to those who 10 or 12 years ago were trying to destroy it. I think this will carry us through.

"Neither Mr. Tilden nor any one else can stem the rebel influence if he is elected.

"I have always said that I thought that Tilden, if elected by the Republican party, would make an admirable President, but with the rebels and copperheads and the Democratic party, with all its villainies behind him, he will ruin us.

"On Wednesday you will be as sorry that you did not advocate Hayes, as I shall be (win or lose) glad that I opposed Tilden.

Yours truly,
"FRANCIS C. BARLOW."

In the last paragraph of this letter the general got both his boots on the wrong legs. When John Sherman, as the Warwick of the Hayes dynasty, was sending all of the staff officers of the Republican party into the South to see not if, but that, Hayes was elected, General Barlow was one of the number, and the only one, I regret to say, of that formidable crowd who had the manliness to admit on their return that the ballot had been tampered with, and that Hayes was not honestly entitled to the electoral vote. The general, however, unfortunately both for himself and the country, was too strong a party man to publicly assail the corrupt scheme devised by the conspirators to place in the Presidential chair one who was not the choice of the nation.

I do not think that he was as glad that he had opposed Tilden as I was and am that I did not advocate the election of Mr. Hayes.

FRANCIS KERNAN TO TILDEN

"UTICA, *Nov. 8, '76.*

"MY DEAR SIR,—Assuming, as I do, that you are elected, I greatly rejoice. I congratulate you, and I congratulate the country. I have never felt so much solicitude as to any political matter as in reference to the result of this election. The welfare of the people and their govt. demanded a change. The entire people will be blessed by the restoration of economy and honesty in the administration of the Federal govt. Under you I am confident we will have the greatly needed reforms.

"We did not do as well in this county as I expected and believed we would. But our young men, especially, worked hard and deserved success. But the Republicans made a very great effort to and did hold their people pretty well; and a good deal of money, wherever it came from, was used in the county, and they, with this, got most of the purchasable vote. I hope you are well. Take care of your health.

"Yours Truly,
"FRANCIS KERNAN."

GEO. W. QUACKENBOS TO TILDEN

"TEN O'CLOCK, A.M., 58 WALL STREET,
"NEW YORK, *Nov. 10, 1876.*

"DEAR SIR,—A meeting of Republican chiefs was held at Washington night before last, at which it was decided to send some one by express train or special train to Florida.

"Report is that the person sent to go was Zac. Chandler himself.[14] Whoever he was, he was expected to reach Palatka about daybreak this morning. The steamboat, with returns from the outlying counties, was expected at Palatka at 3 o'clock this morning, and the messenger was to receive these returns at once.

Yours truly,
"GEORGE W. QUACKENBOS."

AUGUST BELMONT TO TILDEN

"SUNDAY MORNING, *Nov. 11, '76.*

"MY DEAR GOVERNOR,—The *Herald* and *Post* have the following despatch from Conover on their bulletin:

"'The agony is over. Florida has gone Democratic.' Gold has at once declined from 109¾, ⅞ to 109¼, and is now 109⅜.

"God grant that Conover's telegram may be confirmed.

"No other solution but your election can end the agony of the country and prevent the most disastrous consequences.

"Yours most truly,
"AUGUST BELMONT."

EDWARDS PIERREPONT TO TILDEN

"103 FIFTH AVENUE, *Nov. 11, 1876.*

"THE HONORABLE SAML. J. TILDEN.

"DR. SIR,—I did the best I could to elect our candidate. You beat us overwhelmingly, and you have showed a level head since. We cannot elect the U. S. Senator; you ought to take that place. It gives you just enough of time before the spring of 1879[15] to make useful acquaintance, but not enough to create personal irritations and jealousies.

"*No man* can be two years Governor of New York without destroying many ambitious hopes and making many bitter enemies.

"Tho' these suggestions come from a political opponent, they are not the less genuine.

"Yours truly,
"EDWARDS PIERREPONT."

WM. A. WALLACE TO TILDEN

"CLEWFIELD, PA., *Nov. 14, 1876.*

"MY DEAR SIR,—Your firmness and courage now is the only hope for the perpetuity of our institutions. The country is with you, and will sustain you in any event and at all hazards.

Very truly yours,
"WILLIAM A. WALLACE."

BENJAMIN RUSH TO TILDEN

(SUGGESTS GOVERNOR GIVE A PUBLIC DECLARATION OF HIS VIEWS ON THE SITUATION)

"1728 CHESTNUT STREET, PHILA., *18th Nov., 1876.*

"DEAR SIR,—May I venture, with great respect, to offer a suggestion which, in this extraordinary crisis, might, it seems to me, if you approve, have a good effect with the other side.

"Would not a public expression of your well-considered views *now*, in the present state of things, tend to exercise a good influence? Your friends all remember how much good was done, on a different occasion, by that admirable letter to Mr. Hewitt, shortly before the election, about rebel claims, etc.

"Might not the calm, patriotic, and therefore assuaging utterances of your pen *now* tend to an early settlement upon the basis of right and justice by bringing to bear, with accumulated force, upon the bad men so conspicuous in the disputed States, the just indignation and censure of honest and influential men of their own party, who could not fail to be influenced by such an expression from you, causing those men, at least, to *pause* in their mad career?

"Might it not, at least, have the effect of *gaining time*, and smoothing the way for the dispassionate and final and possibly controlling judgment of the better elements of the Republican party?

"Pray pardon the freedom of the suggestion. It is doubtless not new to you or the friends about you, but this may at least serve to show how the suggestion strikes another mind at a distance.

"Suffer me to avail myself of the occasion to congratulate the American people and yourself upon the unmistakable majority of the Electoral College and immense popular majority in your favor.

"I have the honor to be, with the highest respect.

"Your friend & obt. serv't,
"BENJAMIN RUSH."

GID. J. PILLOW TO TILDEN

"*Confidential.*

"MEMPHIS, TENN., *Nov. 18th, 1876.*

"His Excellency SAMUEL J. TILDEN, etc.

"Enough has developed itself since my former letter to confirm the correctness of the views there expressed. I see indications of a weakness in the *backbone* of the Republican leaders, and if they stood without a controlling power over them they would yield. But the President has his *own purposes to accomplish*, and he will not let them yield.

"On and after the 5th of March next, if there be no President or Vice-President elected and inaugurated, there is no provision *in the Constitution* for the *further existence* of any *government.* The Constitution, which is the chart of the government, will have *expired*, leaving nothing but the *physical skeleton* of the constitutional government. Grant knows this and sees it, and will shape *everything* to *bring about that end.* He will, by his measures, *defeat you and Hayes* both by shaping the means to the end.

"The constitutional government, thus ended, with no power or provision anywhere for its *reorganization*, Grant finds himself in possession of a physical government, without the restraints of a Constitution—with the army, navy, and treasury at his command; he will be the *absolute ruler* of a government of *force*, in which his *will* will be the law. If Congress should prove *refractory* he will know how to deal with that body. There are three notable historical parallel cases for his guidance.

"His professions of a purpose to have a *fair count*, using his *army* and *navy* to bring it about, is one of the means by which he will delude the people and *conceal* his *real purpose.* His purpose will not be lost sight of, and he will hold to the *Republican party* and its *confidence* until his *usurpation* is *assured.*

"You are the only man who can save the government—*preserve* the Constitution and the liberties of the people. To accomplish these ends, you *must act.* In the end, *three-fourths* of the American people will *sustain you.* The time will soon pass when *action* will *accomplish anything* or will be *possible. Time by action* may *possibly avert* the great *national calamity*, but without *action* the case is hopeless.

"I do not expect you to answer my letters. I cannot write more fully. I can only make *suggestions*. Let your private secretary say my letters are received. If deemed necessary I would visit you.

"Your friend,
"GID. J. PILLOW."

GEO. W. MORGAN TO TILDEN

"MOUNT VERNON, OHIO, *Nov. 18th, 1876.*

"MY DEAR MR. PRESIDENT,—For so I still believe you to be. Your course during the late canvass inspired me with great confidence in your judgment, and nothing but the momentous issue now upon us could induce me to make suggestions for your consideration.

"A party that drifts in a crisis like the present is certain to wreck upon the breakers. And whatever policy is to be adopted should be carefully considered, promptly be determined, and be decisive. The inauguration of two Presidents means a war which in its destructiveness would dwarf the rebellion. Not to count the electoral vote and declare an election would be to create a dictatorship which would soon result in armed conflict. This is one side of the picture.

"If you are counted out by fraud, as is probable, would acquiescence cause a repetition of the wrong four years hence; or would it electrify the country and cause an outburst of indignation against the wrong-doers?

"Again, is it certain that an armed conflict would not disintegrate the Union? If they found the battle going against them would not the pretended Republicans of the North offer to recognize the independence of a Southern confederacy?

"If two Presidents are inaugurated then comes the problem of money and munitions. New York and other ports would be put in blockade, and revenue be thus cut off.

"Men who do not dream of going into the conflict themselves may glibly advise a recourse to arms.

"If your policy be one in the interest of peace, then a patriotic address to your countrymen would give you a noble immortality, preserve constitutional government, and restore the Democracy to power at the next election. Should such be your determination, meetings should be simultaneously held throughout the Republic, declare your election, but waive the administration of the government, and denounce the usurpers who seek to overthrow the Constitution.

"In conclusion, I have but to say, if the facts show that you are elected, for one I will stand by you, let the result be what it may.

"With great respect for your ability and entire confidence in your patriotism, I have the honor to subscribe myself,

"Your very obedient servant,
"GEORGE W. MORGAN."

J. THOMAS SPRIGGS TO TILDEN

(SUBSTANCE OF A CONVERSATION WITH SENATOR CONKLING)

"UTICA, SUNDAY, *Nov. 19, 1876.*

"PRESIDENT TILDEN.

"MY DEAR SIR,—I have had an hour's talk to-day with Senator Conkling, and I am happy to inform you he is sound as a bullet all through. He says of course he is desirous his party should succeed, but if it is expected he will consent to succeed by fraud they are mistaken. He is sound in all the questions that will arise, and means to act with his friends.

"He is devoting himself to the law, and means to act with our friends in the Senate.

"He asked me what position our people meant to assume, and whether they meant to act upon the *good-boy principle* of submission, or whether we mean to have it understood that Tilden has been elected and by the Eternal he shall be inaugurated? Thinks the latter course advisable; the submission policy he don't much believe in.

"You may rely entirely upon his *hearty co-operation.* I hope to see you soon, but I fear shall not be able to come down before the 1st of December.

"I don't know whether the Senator will unbosom himself to Kearner, but I know he is all right, and I am correspondingly hopeful and happy as ever.

"Yours truly,
"J. T. SPRIGGS."

AUGUST BELMONT TO TILDEN

"*Private.*

"*Thursday (Nov. 23, 1876).*

"MY DEAR GOVERNOR,—I had a long talk with Curtis, and have made it all right. He *volunteered* the information that he wrote the *Sun's* article yesterday, but without entering into the discussion of the merits of his argument I told him that all our friends viewed the question differently.

"*He will keep quiet*, I know, and I hope Barlow has been equally successful with Dana. No pains ought to be spared to get him all right so as to end, as far as he can, the mischief of yesterday's article.

"Curtis is anxious for your success, but he is a *vain* man, who likes to be made something of. I think some little notice of him by you or your friends in the way of asking his legal advice or other co-operation would secure him completely to your interests and silence his constitutional croaking.

Yours sincerely,
"AUGUST BELMONT."

The editorial of the *Sun* here referred to, after giving in detail the provisions of the Constitution for the counting of the electoral votes for President and Vice-President, proceeds to give the advice which so disturbed Messrs. Belmont and Barlow:

"We[16] now proceed to state what, in our opinion, the Constitution means by counting the votes. It is to be noted that the Constitution commits the choice of a President and Vice-President, in the first instance, to a body of electors who are to be chosen in each State as its legislators may direct. These electors are to meet, to vote, and to make and sign and seal up a certificate of their votes. These instruments, denominated in the Constitution 'the certificates,' are to be transmitted to the President of the Senate 'sealed.' They are, in our opinion, not merely *prima facie*, but they are conclusive, evidence that the Electoral Colleges of the States from which they come gave the votes which they purport to certify.

"We can conceive of no reason why the Constitution required the electors to make and sign and certify lists of the votes which they gave, excepting that it was required in order to give legal verity to the contents of the certificates. For the same reason we hold that to 'count the votes' so certified does not import or imply a power to inquire into the legality, sufficiency, or regularity of the appointment of the electors whose appointment is duly certified by the State authorities whose duty it is to give to the two Houses of Congress legal information of that appointment. It will never do, in our judgment, to draw analogies for the government of this matter from the practice of legislative bodies in judging of the rights of their members to seats. That practice rests upon an express constitutional provision; and it is from that express power to determine the legality of an election that their whole authority to go behind the certificate of a sitting member is derived.

"But these Electoral Colleges are peculiar bodies, whose appointment is committed wholly to the States, whose certificates, when their official character has been duly vouched by their States, become by force of the Constitution the sole and exclusive legal evidence that the votes of those States have been cast for such and such persons as President and Vice-President. It cannot be, therefore, that any authority can reside anywhere to try any question, or to find any fact, that is to warrant the two Houses in rejecting the votes of any Electoral College of whose authority to give those votes the State, through its constituted authorities, has legally informed Congress. All such questions and all such facts belong to the proper authorities of each State to try and determine before the persons supposed to be chosen electors are assembled to give their votes. Any attempt by the two Houses, or either of them, to go behind the certificates and to determine the right of the electors to give the votes which they have certified, when the State has determined that right by its competent authorities, will lead to conclusions in which the people of this country will not acquiesce.

"Thus, if it shall be found on an inspection of the certificates of the Electoral Colleges, when they are opened in the presence of the two Houses, that Mr. Hayes has received 185 votes, or more, that result must be accepted by the people as the legal result, whatever may have been the frauds committed in Louisiana or any other State in taking or returning or counting the popular vote. It is perfectly proper for Congress to ascertain the fact of such frauds in an authoritative and conclusive manner for the information of the people, but the certainty that there are such frauds cannot affect the legally certified election. Mr. Hayes must be inaugurated and acknowledged as President, even if the legal result is so tainted with fraud that honest men revolt at the very thought they must submit to. There is no alternative but civil war; and that forms an unnecessary and inadequate remedy, and is not to be thought of. If Hayes shall be declared President, with grave reason to believe that he has not been honestly and fairly entitled to have the electoral votes of certain States, he and his party must bear the consequences. Those consequences, if his opponents are wise, will be, not that his title to the office is to be resisted, but that the people are to be appealed to to use their constitutional and peaceful methods of redressing all wrongs and punishing all outrages—namely, by the ballot-box. No such appeal can be made if the country is to be plunged into anarchy by denying Hayes' title to the office. Our government must be preserved and perpetuated; and that it may be, grievous as the wrong will be that takes from Tilden States in which he has certainly carried a majority of the popular vote, we must submit to that wrong, in the entire certainty that the party responsible for it will in due time be rewarded with political annihilation.

"We shall therefore deprecate and oppose any action by the House of Representatives looking to any dispute of the regular electoral certificates from any of the States. The responsibility for what is done in the three controverted States is with the Republicans, and there let it rest. All that the House of Representatives can properly do in the premises is to ascertain and determine the precise nature, methods, and extent of the frauds, and then leave the question to the judgment of the country, and to the legal and constitutional remedy afforded by the next elections."

SAML. WARD TO TILDEN

(WANTS GOVERNOR TO ASSIST EVARTS IN UNVEILING STATUE OF DANIEL WEBSTER)

"Private.

"BREVOORT HOUSE, *24th Nov., 1876.*

"DEAR MR. PRESIDENT-ELECT,—A cat may look at a king, and an old fossil like myself may offer a suggestion to a much wiser man.

"I humbly suggest that you assist at Evarts' oration to-morrow, upon the unveiling of the Webster statue in Central Park.

"If he meditates mischief your presence will check him, and if he intends preaching from the Constitution it will encourage him. If he carries out the doctrine of State-rights as against Conkling's speech of last winter, he covertly justifies nullification and secession.

"Yours faithfully,
"SAML. WARD.

"*His Excellency Governor Tilden, President-elect.*"

WM. P. CRAIGHILL TO G. W. MORGAN

"BALTO., MD., *Nov. 24, 1876.*

"DEAR GENERAL,—Now is a time, it seems to me, when every true lover of our country will desire to do all he can to allay excitement and to reach an honest and fair conclusion upon the question about which all are thinking—Who ought to be the next President? I believe a great majority of the American people, North and South, desire peace and quiet, as well as an honest decision on that question; but there are, unfortunately, some in both sections, and perhaps in Congress, who have nothing to lose and may gain something by turmoil, strife, and excitement.

"When the pot boils much froth and scum rise to the surface, which otherwise might never be known to exist.

"It appears to me the *crisis* will be upon us when the two Houses of Congress meet to count or see counted the electoral votes. Disputes must arise about many questions, by reason of the complications now surrounding the situation. Who shall decide between them? The great want is a tribunal to whom may be referred at once, *without debate* or excitement, all disputed points. This tribunal should not only be honest and impartial and able, but the Congress and the people should *believe* so. Could not such a tribunal be organized *before the dispute begins*? It might be extraconstitutional, but its decrees could be made binding in this particular case by consent of all concerned.

"Let Congress request Mr. Tilden to select the chief judge in his State or in New Jersey or Virginia, and let Mr. Hayes take the chief judge of Ohio or Pennsylvania or Illinois or Massachusetts; let these two be joined by the Chief Justice of the U. S. as a third member.

"The last named has never been a violent partisan, and is specially acceptable to the bar in Richmond, Virginia, and elsewhere in the South. Let this tribunal decide all disputed points in accordance with the Constitution and precedents, as far as applicable, by common law and common-sense. Let their judgment be final and conclusive. By such a course justice would be done and all parties satisfied.

"Very truly yours,
"WM. P. CRAIGHILL.

"*Gen'l Geo. W. Morgan,*
"*Mount Vernon, Ohio.*"

G. W. MORGAN TO TILDEN

"MOUNT VERNON, OHIO, *Nov. 27, 1876.*

"MY DEAR MR. PRESIDENT,—Colonel Wm. P. Craighill, the writer of the inclosed, is an officer of the Engineer Corps, and is one of the finest and ablest men in our military service. He does not dream that you would see his letter, but I deem it proper to submit it for your consideration.

"I remain, Mr. President, with great respect,

"Your very obedient servant,
"G. W. MORGAN.

"*His Excellency Samuel J. Tilden.*"

CERTIFICATE OF THE ELECTORAL VOTE OF THE STATE OF NEW YORK IN 1876

"STATE OF NEW YORK, *ss.*:

"We, the Secretary of State, Comptroller, Treasurer, and Attorney-General of the said State having formed a Board of State Canvassers, and having canvassed and estimated the whole number of votes given for *Electors of President and Vice-President*, at the general election held in the said State, on the seventh day of November, in the year 1876, according to the certified statements received by the Secretary of State in the manner directed by law, do hereby determine, declare, and certify, that

Horatio Seymour,	Atherton Hall,
De Witt C. West,	Henry D. Graves,
Parke Godwin,	William J. Averell,
Thomas H. Rodman,	Daniel B. Judson,
Edward Rowe,	Edmund A. Ward,
Thomas D. Jones,	Ansel Foster,
Oswald Ottendorfer,	James McQuade,
Thomas Mackellar,	Bartholomew Lynch,
Anthony Dugro,	Calvin L. Hathaway,
Augustus Schell,	George W. Knowles,
Frederick Smyth,	William C. Dryer,
Joseph J. O'Donohue,	Frederick O. Cable,
Samuel F. Barger,	John McDougall,
Jordan L. Mott,	Jerome Lee,

James H. Holdane,	Charles B. Benedict,
William Voorhis,	Cyrus Clarke,
Addison P. Jones,	Porter Sheldon,
Eli Perry,	

were, by the greatest number of votes given at the said election, respectively elected *Electors of President and Vice-President* of the United States.

"Given under our hands, at the office of the Secretary of State, of said State, in the city of Albany, the twenty-fifth day of November, in the year of our Lord one thousand eight hundred and seventy-six.

"JOHN BIGELOW, *Secr'y of State.*
"L. ROBINSON, *Comptroller.*
"CHARLES N. ROSS, *Treasurer.*
"CHARLES S. FAIRCHILD, *Attorney-General.*

"State of New York, }
"Office of the Secretary of State.} *ss.*:

"I CERTIFY the foregoing to be a true copy of an original certificate of the Board of State Canvassers, on file in this office, and of the whole thereof.

[SEAL]

"Given under my hand and seal of office, at the city of Albany, the twenty-fifth day of November, in the year of our Lord one thousand eight hundred and seventy-six.

EDGAR K. APGAR,
"*Deputy Secretary of State.*"

FRANK CROCKER TO TILDEN

WASHINGTON, D. C., *Jan. 15, '77.*

"HON. S. J. TILDEN.

"SIR,—I have in my possession a telegram sent to Z. Chandler, chrm. Repn. com., by O. C. Babcock, dated Chicago, Dec. 4/76.

"I consider it not only very valuable, but the *key* to the editorials and political arguments on the 'electoral count' which has filled the columns of the *National Republican*, the administration organ, for the past month.

"Respectfully Yours,
"FRANK CROCKER,
"617 6th St., N. W."

O. C. BABCOCK TO Z. CHANDLER (TELEGRAM)

"Chicago, *Dec. 4th, 1876.*

"HON. Z. CHANDLER,
"*Chairmn. Repn. Com., Washington.*

"The Illinois electors here have agreed they will vote an open ballot. If any elector refuses so to vote, or refuses to throw a ballot for Hayes and Wheeler as he votes, they will immediately declare a vacancy in the district thus represented by such judge and elect another in his place; they claim that such action is not only perfectly justifiable, but that it cannot be reviewed by any tribunal, as the action of the electors is final. If this meets with your approbation I suggest you to telegraph this programme to every Republican State.

"O. C. BABCOCK."

The subscriber of the last preceding letter during the Civil War was on the staff of General Grant, and when the latter became President acted as his private secretary. He was indicted in 1876 by the Grand Jury of St. Louis for frauds upon the revenue and for the "safe-burglary conspiracy" referred to in the following testimony of one of the witnesses in the trial, Col. H. C. Whitley, who was one of the parties charged, but desired, before doing so, to place on the record a conditional pardon granted him.

> "'Harrington took a letter from his pocket and asked me if the signature was that of A. B. Cornell, and I said it was not. He said that some of Pinkerton's detectives were here, and I should send some of my men to work in with the memorialists and find out what they were doing. I sent men out. Harrington gave me some names on a paper whom he wished to be worked in with. I don't remember the names. I told Harrington that I would send men over, naming Mr. Nettleship. I went to New York on the same night (15th) and sent Mr. Nettleship over, giving him the names, and telling him that they were the parties to be worked. I don't remember that I gave Nettleship any instructions to report to Harrington at this particular time. I was again in this city on the 29th of March, having previously sent over a man named Oberworth with Nettleship. I found on my arrival that Oberworth had

been arrested for peddling cigars without a license, and I told Harrington that he (Oberworth) was one of my men, and he was released. Mr. Harrington complained that the men were good for nothing, and he wanted men who would push matters along and work to some purpose. Harrington said something must be done; that he had a plan which would throw dirt and ridicule on the memorialists. He said they thought that Evan's books were in his office, and they were trying to get them, and he thought that to have his office robbed was the best plan; he said he did not care if his safe was knocked or blown to hell, as the damned safe belonged to him. I said I did not wish the men to get into trouble, and Harrington replied that there was no danger, as he was district attorney, and they should not be hurt. I came from New York on the 29th, and returned the same night. I came again on the 8th of April, and saw Gen. Babcock at his office. I asked how matters were about the investigation, and he said all right, that Harrington kept him posted up.

"'I was again in Washington on the 27th, arriving in the afternoon, four days after the safe was blown up. I went up to Harrington's house, and he told me about what had transpired during the blowing of the safe. He said that everything would have worked all right except for the interference of Major Richard, the superintendent of police, who would not co-operate with him. After that I called upon Gen. Babcock at his office in the White House. He spoke about the safe burglary, saying that it was very badly managed; that he thought I was smarter than to allow things to go on as they did. The next time I saw Babcock was in New York, in the May following. I went up to the Fifth Avenue Hotel in that city. After talking to him a while I said that I expected that there would be some more trouble about the case. Babcock said: "No; stand by your guns; I'll protect your rear." I spoke to him about Bluford Wilson, then the Solicitor of the Treasury, investigating my office in New York for the purpose of ascertaining whether any of the secret-service men were connected with the safe burglary, and then told him I would do it, that is, stand by my guns if he protected the rear.

"'Soon afterward I had an interview with Harrington at the Metropolitan Hotel, New York. I complained to him that the whole matter of the safe burglary seemed to be falling upon the secret service, and that we would likely get into trouble about it. Harrington said: "No; I am the real district attorney at Washington, and I will protect all of you." I told him that Somerville wanted some money, and Harrington gave me $500 for him. I paid it all to Somerville as part of his fee. Harrington did not say what particular service Somerville rendered. During the same month I had an interview with Babcock here. I called to see him at his house. Harrington then lived a few doors from him on the same row. I told Babcock I wanted to see Harrington, and Babcock sent after him. Harrington came in by the alley gate to Babcock's yard. I told Harrington that Somerville wanted more money, but do not remember that Babcock heard me speak to Harrington, or that he knew the money was to go to Somerville. All I remember is that Harrington brought me the money, and that I gave it to Somerville, who said he wanted to use it to get Benton, the burglar who was arrested on the night of the burglary, out.'

"In speaking of other interviews with Babcock, Whitley testified as follows:

"'In the autumn of 1875 I called at Babcock's cottage at Long Branch and had a talk with him. I told him that Albert Cunz and Delome, two former secret-service men, had been thrown out of employment in consequence of the safe burglary and their connection with it. Babcock said he would try and get them in the New York Custom-House. I told him that I would like for myself a commission to go somewhere, and Babcock said he would see the Secretary of the Treasury, and have me sent to Europe with some bonds. I told him I did not want to go to Europe, but wanted to go to Colorado. Babcock said: "If any trouble comes up you can 'slide off,'" or words to that effect. I told him I had had trouble enough in connection with the case, and did not want any more.

"'I had a conversation with Harrington after we were indicted in the fall of 1874 in the Metropolitan Hotel. I told him I did not like the idea of being indicted in the matter. He told me it would be all right, that he would pay counsel for me. He directed me to write and employ Gen. S. S. Henkin, of Washington, as my attorney, which I did. That case resulted in a hung jury. This spring, previous to going before Proctor Knott's committee, I called at the White House to see Gen. Babcock, and requested him to do all he could to have Mr. Rice, who was with me, appointed postmaster at Pueblo, Colorado. He said he would assist all he could. As I was leaving the room, I remarked to him: "Things look like we will have more trouble." He answered: "Yes, things do look squally; but it will all blow over again.""""[17]

Babcock was acquitted, with the aid of a deposition by General Grant, and only a few weeks before this trial was promoted to a colonelcy.

Only four months before the indictment and trial of Babcock, Secretary Belknap, a member of President Grant's Cabinet, was impeached and put on trial before the Senate at Washington. During the trial the late George F. Hoar, one of the Republican Senators from Massachusetts, addressed the Senate, and closed his discourse with the following fearful arraignment of the administration during the Presidency of Grant, and gave a transparent exposure of the reasons why the satellites of the President were determined to shrink from no crime necessary to prevent the inauguration at Washington of a President who had become famous by the havoc he had already made of the Tweed Ring plunderers in New York and the Canal Ring plunderers at Albany, and whose advent to Washington would put to flight the horde of miscreants who then infested both ends of the capitol:

> "My own public life has been a very brief and insignificant one, extending little beyond the duration of a single term of Senatorial office, but in that brief period I have seen five judges of a high court of the United States driven from office by threats of impeachment for corruption or maladministration. I have heard the taunt from friendliest lips, that when the United States presented herself in the East to take part with the civilized world in generous competition in the arts of life, the only product of her institutions in which she surpassed all others beyond question was her corruption. I have seen in the State in the Union foremost in power and wealth four judges of her courts impeached for corruption, and the political administration of her chief city become a disgrace and a by-word throughout the world. I have seen the chairman

of the Committee on Military Affairs in the House, now a distinguished member of this court, rise in his place and demand the expulsion of four of his associates for making sale of their official privilege of selecting the youths to be educated at our great military school. When the greatest railroad of the world, binding together the continent and uniting the two great seas which wash our shores, was finished, I have seen our national triumph and exaltation turned to bitterness and shame by the unanimous reports of three committees of Congress, two of the House, and one here, that every step of that mighty enterprise had been taken in fraud. I have heard in highest places the shameless doctrine avowed by men grown old in public office that the true way by which power should be gained in the republic is to bribe the people with the offices created for their service, and the true end for which it should be used when gained is the promotion of selfish ambition and the gratification of personal revenge. I have heard that suspicion haunts the footsteps of the trusted companions of the President. These things have passed into history. The Hallam, or the Tacitus, or the Sismondi, or the Macaulay who writes the annals of our time will record them with his inexorable pen; and now, when a high Cabinet officer, the constitutional adviser of the Executive, flees from office before charges of corruption, shall the historian add that the Senate treated the demand of the people for its judgment of condemnation as a farce, and laid down its high functions before the sophistries and jeers of the criminal lawyer? Shall he speculate about the petty political calculations as to the effect of one party or the other which induced his judges to connive at the escape of the great public criminal; or, on the other hand, shall he close the chapter by narrating how these things were detected, reformed, and punished by constitutional processes which the wisdom of our fathers devised for us, and the virtue and purity of the people found their vindication in the justice of the Senate?"

CHARLES MASON TO TILDEN

"'ALTO,' NEAR EDGE HILL,
"KING GEORGE, VA., *Dec. 5, '76.*

"DEAR SIR,—Although I am confident if any one in the U. S. has the ability to cope with the rogues who are bent on cheating the people out of the hard-earned victory they have achieved, in the Presidential contest, it is yourself; yet, at the risk of being thought highly presumptuous, I venture on a few suggestions I have not observed thrown out by any one.

"That the Constitution does not provide for the extraordinary condition of things in which we are placed by the Congress, nor that any of its annotators furnish an apt construction, is certain; and for the same reason, I suppose, as that given by Bishop Warburton, why no allusion was made in the Pentateuch to a future state. The patriots of the Revolution, like the Patriarchs after the creation, no doubt thought the proposition so self-evident and the provisions so ample for pious and honest men that they did not dream of the world's being peopled by such a race of sinners and corruptionists.

"If precedent is to be weighed in counting the votes, let the spirit of the first example be wholly and rigidly observed. There is doubt, in the first election of Gl. Washington, the president of the Senate did perform that ministerial duty. But the order of the Senate, prepared by a committee, and signed by John Langdon, the prest. 'elected for that purpose,' expressly says 'the underwritten, appointed president of the Senate for the sole purpose of receiving, opening, and counting the votes of electors, did, in the presence of the Senate and House of Representatives,' etc., leaving it to be inferred (and no other conclusion will hold water) that in doing this his functions ceased. Subsequently, as you know, there were some variations from this practice, but all going to the mere ministerial agency of that officer.

"The bald attempt of McDonald, present chief clerk of the Senate, to cite a different practice, in the case of Harrison, when James W. Watson was president of the Senate, by construing his action in his (McDonald's) own language, as to imply judicial authority, does great violence to the truth of history and the greatest injustice to that astute and cautious statesman, who struggled all his life against the exercise of doubtful powers and was never known to practise one. This little incident on the part of McDonald is only a part of the well-laid scheme to revolutionize the government by seizure in the count of either of the returning boards in the subjugated States, should be conscience-stricken and obey the mandates of the Decalogue, rather than the tyrant's order, and cast the electoral vote for you, to whom all justly belong.

"Going through the pageant of a public inauguration is by no means called for, as you are well aware; and I would suggest that instead of allowing Sunday to intervene, that Grant's term expires at 12 o'c. at night on the 3d of March, when his power as Commander-in-Chief will cease, and when Sherman will not dare use the army for their hellish purposes. I make this suggestion for the reason that there is a tradition in the family of Mr. Jefferson, to whom I am nearly allied by marriage, handed down by himself, that being informed commissions were to be made out by Mr. Adams for judges and other officers after midnight, he (Jefferson) entered the office of Secretary of State precisely at 12 o'c. on the 3d of Mar. and demanded it of the Secretary, John Marshall, I think, who, after some remonstrance, yielded and delivered the keys to Mr. Jefferson. Allusion is made to those midnight appointments in his correspondence, but no mention is made of those particular circumstances. I had them from Col. L. G. Randolph, his grandson, confidential friend, executor and sole custodian of his papers until sold to Congress.

"Some persons apprehend that if the election devolves upon the House (which I cannot conceive possible on any reasonable grounds) we shall lose the Vice-President, whose choice will have to be decided by the Senate; but this cannot be, as the contingency will not arise for such a resort. For the Constitution expressly provides that 'the person having the greatest number of electors shall be President, if such number be the whole number of electors *appointed*.' Now, how can they be appointed unless lawfully done, and who is to judge of such legality? Certainly the House, or it may be both Houses. So if the electoral vote of a State be rejected by either, because of fraud, it is a nullity—no vote at all—and therefore not *appointed*, and cannot be estimated in the count, leaving you with 84, an undisputed majority of the electors actually *appointed*. For, mark! The Constitution does not require a majority of the whole Electoral College, but of those *appointed*.

"If there should be any discussion about the authority of the 'great seal of a State,' you are aware that it has been nowhere so fully ventilated as in the famous New Jersey contest for Congressional seats, when, if my memory serves me, the Govr's. certificate was only respected when there was no suspicion of fraud.

"I am, with great respect & haste,

"Your humble servt.,
"CHARLES MASON."

CHARLES A. DANA TO TILDEN

"Dec. 15, 1876.

"DEAR SIR,—Here is a note from my regular Washington correspondent, which I send to you for your information.

Yours sincerely,
"C. A. DANA."

A. M. GIBSON TO DANA

"WASHINGTON, D. C., *Dec. 13, 1876.*

"MY DEAR SIR,—There is undoubtedly danger of defection among Southern Democrats. The friends of Hayes are certainly bidding high in that direction, and I *know* that their propositions are being entertained—listened to, considered. The combination between Jay Gould, C. P. Huntington, and Tom Scott, spoke of ten days since in my despatches, is now openly admitted here. Central Pacific gets all west of Ft. Worth and one-half of T. P. east of Fort Worth. The subsidy for T. P. is part of programme, as well as counting in of Hayes. Packard and Chamberlain are to be abandoned, and a new departure in Republican party policy is to date from Hayes' inauguration. I know what I am talking about. Can't you give Tilden a hint? His managers here don't get below the surface of things.

"Very truly,
"A. M. GIBSON."

GENERAL WINFIELD SCOTT HANCOCK TO GENERAL SHERMAN

"CARONDELET P. O.,
"ST. LOUIS CO., MO., *December 28th, 1876.*

"MY DEAR GENERAL,—Your favor of the 4th inst. reached me in New York on the 5th, the day before I left for the West. I intended to reply to it before leaving, but cares incident to departure interfered. Then, again, since my arrival here, I have been so occupied with personal affairs of a business nature that I have deferred writing from day to day until this moment, and now I find myself in debt to you for another letter in acknowledgment of your favor of the 17th, received a few days since.

"I have concluded to leave here on the 29th (to-morrow), p.m., so that I may be expected in New York on the 31st inst. It has been cold and dreary since my arrival here. I have worked 'like a Turk' (I presume that means hard work) in the country, in making fences, cutting down trees, repairing buildings, etc., etc., and am at least able to say that St. Louis is the coldest place in the winter, as it is the hottest in summer, of any that I have encountered in a temperate zone. I have known St. Louis in December to have genial weather throughout the month; this December has been frigid, and the river has been frozen more solid than I have even known it.

"When I heard the rumor that I was ordered to the Pacific coast I thought it probably true, considering the past discussion on that subject. The *possibilities* seemed to me to point that way. Had it been true I should, of course, have presented no complaint, nor made resistance of any kind. I would have gone quietly if not prepared to go promptly. I certainly would have been relieved from the responsibilities and anxieties concerning Presidential matters which may fall to those near the throne or in authority within the next four months, as well as from other incidents or matters which I could not control, and the action concerning which I might not approve. I was not exactly prepared to go to the Pacific, however, and I therefore felt relieved when I received your note informing me that there was no truth in the rumors.

"Then, I did not wish to appear to be escaping from responsibilities and possible dangers which may cluster around military commanders in the East, especially in the critical period fast approaching. 'All's well that ends well.' The whole matter of the Presidency seems to me to be simple and to admit of a peaceful solution. The machinery for such a contingency as threatens to present itself has been all carefully prepared. It only requires lubrication, owing to disuse. The army should have nothing to do with the selection or inauguration of Presidents. The people elect the President. The Congress declares in a joint session who he is; we of the army have only to obey his mandates, and are protected in so doing only so far as they may be lawful. Our commissions express that! I like Jefferson's way of inauguration. It suits our system. He rode alone on horseback to the capitol (I fear it was the 'old capitol'), tied his horse to a rail-fence, entered, and was duly sworn; then rode to the Executive Mansion, and took possession. He inaugurated himself simply by taking the oath of office. There is no other legal inauguration in our system. The people or politicians may institute parades in honor of the event, and public officials may add to the pageant by assembling troops and banners; but all that only comes properly after the inauguration, not before, and it is not a part of it. Our system does not provide that one President should inaugurate another. There might be danger in that, and it was studiously left out of the Charter. But you are placed in an exceptionally important position in connection with coming events. The capitol is in my jurisdiction also, but I am a subordinate, and not on the spot, and if I were, so also would be my superior in authority, for there is the station of the General-in-Chief.

"On the principle that a regularly elected President's term of office expires with the 3rd of March (of which I have not the slightest doubt), and which the laws bearing on the subject uniformly recognize, and in consideration of the possibility that the lawfully elected President may not appear until the 5th of March, a great deal of responsibility may necessarily fall upon you. You hold over! You will have power and prestige to support you. The Secretary of War is the mouthpiece of a President; you are not. If neither candidate has a constitutional majority of the Electoral College, or the Senate and House, on the occasion of the count, do not unite in declaring some person legally elected by the people, there is a lawful machinery already provided to meet that contingency and decide the question peacefully. It has not been recently used, no occasion presenting itself, but our forefathers provided it.

"It has been exercised, and has been recognized and submitted to as lawful, on every hand. That machinery would probably elect Mr. Tilden President and Mr. Wheeler Vice-President. That would be right enough, for the law provides that in a failure to elect duly by the people, the House shall immediately elect the President, and the Senate the Vice-President. Some tribunal must decide whether the people have duly elected a President. I presume, of course, that it is in the joint affirmative action of the Senate and House, or why are they present to witness the count if not to see that it is fair and just? If a failure to agree arises between the two bodies there can be no lawful affirmative decision that the people have elected a President, and the House must then proceed to act, not the Senate. The Senate elects Vice-Presidents, not Presidents. Doubtless, in case of a failure by the House to elect a President by the 4th of March the President of the Senate (if there be one) would be the legitimate person to exercise Presidential authority for the time being, or until the appearance of a lawful President, or for the time laid down in the Constitution. Such course would be peaceful, and, I have a firm belief, lawful.

"I have no doubt Governor Hayes would make an excellent President. I have met him, know of him. For a brief period he served under my command, but as the matter stands I can't see any likelihood of his being duly declared elected by the people unless the Senate and House come to be in accord as to the fact; and the House would, of course, not *otherwise* elect him. What the people want is a peaceful determination of this matter, as fair a determination as possible, and a lawful one. No other administration could stand the test. The country, if not plunged into revolution, would become poorer day by day, business would languish, and our bonds would come home to find a depreciated market.

"I was not in favor of the military action in South Carolina recently, and if Genl. Ruger had telegraphed to me or asked for advice, I would have advised him not under any circumstances to allow himself or his troops to determine who were the lawful members of a State Legislature. I could not have given him better advice than to refer him to the special message of the President in the case of Louisiana some time before.

"But in South Carolina he had had the question settled by a decision of the Supreme Court of the State—the highest tribunal which had acted on the question—so that his line of duty seemed even to be clearer than the action in the Louisiana case. If the Federal court had interfered and overruled the decision of the State court there might have been a doubt certainly, but the Federal court only interfered to complicate, not to decide or overrule.

"Anyhow, it is no business of the army to enter upon such questions, and even if it might be so in any other event, if the civil authority is supreme, as the Constitution declares it to be, the South Carolina case was one in which the army had a plain duty.

"Had General Ruger asked me for advice, and if I had given it, I should, of course, have notified you of my action immediately, so that it could have been promptly overruled if it should have been deemed advisable by you or other superior in authority. General Ruger did not ask for my advice, and I inferred from that and other facts that he did not desire it, or that, being in direct communication with my military superiors at the seat of government, who were nearer to him in time and distance than I was, he deemed it unnecessary. As Genl. Ruger had the ultimate responsibility of action, and had really the greater danger to confront in the final action in the matter, I did not venture to embarrass him by suggestions. He was a department commander and the lawful head of the military administration within the limits of the department; but, besides, I knew that he had been called to Washington for consultation before taking command, and was probably aware of the views of the administration as to civil affairs in his command. I knew that he was in direct communication with my superiors in authority in reference to the delicate subjects presented for his consideration, or had ideas of his own which he believed to be sufficiently in accord with the views of our common superiors to enable him to act intelligently according to his judgment and without suggestions from those not on the spot, and not as fully acquainted with the facts as himself. He desired, too, to be free to act, as he had the eventual greater responsibility, and so the matter was governed as between him and myself.

"As I have been writing thus freely to you, I may still further unbosom myself by stating that I have not thought it lawful or wise to use Federal troops in such matters as have transpired east of the Mississippi within the last few months, save so far as they may be brought into action under the article of the Constitution which contemplated meeting armed resistance or invasion of a State more powerful than the State authorities can subdue by the ordinary processes, and then only when requested by the Legislature, or, if it could not be convened in season, by the Governor; and when the President of the United States intervenes in that manner it is a state of *war*, not peace.

"The army is laboring under disadvantages, and has been used unlawfully at times, in the judgment of the people (in mine, certainly), and we have lost a great deal of the kindly feeling which the community at large once felt for us. 'It is time to stop and unload.'

"Officers in command of troops often find it difficult to act wisely and safely when superiors in authority have different views of the law from theirs, and when legislation has sanctioned action seemingly in conflict with the fundamental law, and thus generally defer to the known judgment of their superiors. Yet the superior officers of the army are so regarded in such great crises, and are held to such responsibility, especially those at or near the head of it, that it is necessary on such momentous occasions to dare to determine for themselves what is lawful and what is not lawful under our system if the military authorities should be invoked, as might possibly be the case, in such exceptional times when there existed such divergent views as to the correct result. The army will suffer from its past action if it has acted wrongfully. Our regular army has little hold upon the affections of the people of to-day, and the superior officers should certainly, as far as lies in their power, legally and with righteous intent, act to defend the right—to us—the *law* and the institutions we represent. It is a well-meaning Constitution, and it would be well if it should have an opportunity to be recognized as a bulwark in support of the people and *the law.* of the people and *the law.*

"I am, Truly Yours,

(Signed) "WINFD. S. HANCOCK.

"*To General W. T. Sherman,*
"*Com'd'g Army of the U. S., Washington, D. C.*"

HON. GEORGE HOADLEY TO THE "EVENING POST," JULY, 1901

(MRS. SPRAGUE AND THE ELECTORAL COMMISSION OF 1876)

"To the Editor of the 'Evening Post.'

"SIR,—My attention has been called to an article which appeared in the *Evening Post* of Saturday, June 30, giving an account of the various Democratic national conventions, in the course of which there is, I think, a cruel and untrue attack upon the memory of a lady who had hard luck enough in this world, without being followed into her grave, the late Mrs. Katherine Chase (Sprague). The statement is directly made that a bolt from the decision of the electoral tribunal which counted in Hayes in 1877 had been organized by Mr. Conkling, but that he was deterred from executing it by Mrs. Sprague's interference, based on revenge for Mr. Tilden's opposition to her father's nomination by the Democratic convention in 1868.

"I do not believe there is one word of truth in this story, so far as it relates to Mrs. Sprague. It is perfectly true that Mr. Conkling organized such a bolt, and that he secured the adhesion of Senators enough to have reversed the decision of the electoral tribunal in the matter of the Louisiana electoral vote, and would in this way have made Mr. Tilden President had circumstances not happened to break up the scheme, in consequence of which he went to Baltimore, and was not in the Senate and did not vote on the subject that day.

"I was in Washington at the time, and possessed the confidence of the Democratic leaders, and argued, as you know, the Florida and Oregon cases. My information was, in one sense, second hand. I possessed Mr. Conkling's confidence with regard to the general subject. I knew perfectly what his views were. He did not hesitate to express them fully, even going so far as to state them at length in conversation with myself and my wife and Senator John W. Stevenson, of Kentucky, on the street in front of the Arlington, a few days before the decision of the electoral tribunal. He put the case as it stood in his mind in the most vivid terms. He was a master of vituperative language, as you know, and he did not spare anybody; but more especially he put the matter as a question of law, and with more ability than I have ever heard it done by any one else, but I have not time within the confines of a letter to repeat what he said. Whether Mrs. Sprague was in Washington at this time I do not know.

"The only person on the Democratic side who communicated with Mr. Conkling was Senator William H. Barnum, of Connecticut, chairman of the Democratic National Executive Committee. Mr. Barnum talked to others, as he deemed it discreet, but we all thought it unwise that any one on our side should approach any one on the opposite side of politics, except Senator Barnum. During the afternoon of the day before the final vote was given in the Senate on the Louisiana case, Senator Stevenson, whose daughter was the wife of one of my partners, and who was until he died my very dear and honored friend, communicated to me, as having come to him from Senator Barnum, all the details of what I may call, for brevity's sake, 'this plot' to arrest the high-handed dealings of the Republicans, and I went to bed that night in full confidence that Mr. Tilden would be placed on a legal basis for inauguration to the Presidency in the morning. Eight (or nine) Senators had agreed with each other to cast their votes in the Senate so as to reverse the judgment of the electoral tribunal in the Louisiana case.

"When I came down to breakfast in the morning, William R. Pelton, Gov. Tilden's nephew, told me that 'the fat is all in the fire'; that at two o'clock in the morning *one of the Senators*, whose name, for reasons personal to myself and to him, I do not feel at liberty to use, had come to Senator Conkling and told him that he did not dare to go any further with the enterprise; that his political and perhaps his personal future would be ruined if he did not vote for Hayes. Conkling thereupon made up his mind that the game was lost, and took the earliest train to Baltimore, where he would, as Pelton said, spend the day, and where he did, as I afterwards learned, spend the day. Although I possessed Mr. Conkling's confidence and regard (I have a letter from him somewhere, couched in more earnest terms of gratitude than I ever received from any other human being), I never spoke with him on this subject. My information was derived entirely from Senator Stevenson and William T. Pelton, with the latter of whom I was, as I have already explained I was with the former, on terms of confidence.

"During this period I never heard Mrs. Sprague's name mentioned. I do not know whether she was in Washington or not. I was her father's friend, as you probably know, and I was her friend, and in the matter of the divorce from Gov. Sprague I was (with Winchester Britton, of Brooklyn) her counsel, and procured her divorce. I have had many consultations with both Pelton and his uncle upon various political and personal matters, but never heard this matter alluded to by either of them, or by Mrs. Sprague, and I do not believe that the story has any foundation in truth whatever. She knew perfectly well, for many years before she died, that I was a friend of Gov. Tilden's; that my wife and I both had enjoyed his personal hospitality, and knowing, as she did, my feelings towards her father, and having been her legal agent and representative, as I was, in association with the late Richard T. Merrick, in an attempt, which never came to daylight, to kill Judge Warden's grotesque biography of S. P. Chase, this is the first time I ever heard any interference of hers in the matter of the electoral tribunal even referred to. Mrs. Sprague has left children and friends who mourn over her sad fate and grieve at her death, and, among others,

"GEO. HOADLEY.

> "[Judge Hoadley's means of information are certainly unsurpassed. We accept his statement as conclusive on the point at issue.—ED. *Evening Post.*]"

It was currently rumored in the clubs, and even found expression in the public prints, that Mrs. Sprague, a daughter of Chief-Justice Chase, was influential in preventing Mr. Conkling from taking a stand in the Senate against the findings and decision of the electoral tribunal in favor of Mr. Hayes. As the report savored of scandal, it was, of course, rapidly circulated and heedlessly credited, though out of respect to all parties interested, the stories slumbered for many years until the means by which Mr. Hayes was inaugurated as President could be more dispassionately discussed than on the eve of the distribution of the patronage of a new administration. Fourteen years after Hayes' inauguration the scandal was revived for partisan purposes in part, and in part, presumably, in the interest of historic justice. A phase of the discussion at that time in the New York *Evening Post* provoked the foregoing letter from Hon. George Hoadley, ex-Governor of Ohio, which probably gives the most authentic information the country can ever expect to have of the mysterious and vacillating conduct of Mr. Conkling. My attention was called to it by the Hon. Smith Ely, formerly Mayor of New York, to whom I sent the following acknowledgment:

JOHN BIGELOW TO HON. SMITH ELY

"HIGHLAND-FALLS-ON-HUDSON, *June 19, 1904.*

"MY DEAR MR. ELY,—I am extremely obliged to you for the clipping you sent me from the *Evening Post.* Though familiar with rumors of that nature, it is the first statement with any semblance of authenticity I have met with of the reasons why Conkling did not keep faith with our friends. I am not sure that Conkling himself did not weaken at the pinch as much as the recalcitrant Senator. Had he stood up on that occasion, as he should have done, he would have established for himself a reputation for virtues which no biographer can now claim for him.

"I do not remember the name of the Senator alluded to, because I never knew the fact. Was it Kernan?

"Yours truly.

"P. S.—Cannot you give us a candidate for the Presidency without making prostitutes of the judiciary?[18] When we made judges elective we went as far in that direction as was safe, and farther than was prudent. It was a perversion of the representative system when we submitted the choice of experts, like judges and district attorneys, to the popular vote. If we encourage judges to aspire to the Presidency the suitors for justice will have to take their check-books to court, and their cases will be argued, as they are said to be, before Turkish cadis.

"Yours Truly,
"JOHN BIGELOW."

About the middle of January, 1877, and before the Electoral Commission had given its decision, I received a telegram from Washington that a friend of the Honorable S. S. Cox, then a representative in Congress from New York city, wished to confer with me in reference to the Presidential contest pending in Washington. Cox's friend proved to be Mr. Corbin, a brother-in-law of President Grant. I replied to my correspondent that he might arrange for an interview with me anywhere in New York city except in Mr. Corbin's house, Corbin at that time having a residence in New York city.

It was arranged that we should meet at the Westminster Hotel, about noon, on the 27th of January. I had known something of Corbin through my relations with Colonel Benton many years before, and had become slightly acquainted with him. What I did know of him disinclined me to give him my confidence. I had no idea of the motive which led him to invite this interview. He had intimated to Mr. Cox that he would talk with me, but with no other of Mr. Tilden's friends. The grounds for his taking me into his confidence exclusively was equally unintelligible, beyond the fact that we had been political friends of long standing as common friends of Senator Thomas Benton, of Missouri.

He opened the interview by giving at considerable length what he regarded as evidence of Senator Sherman's expectation that his brother the general would have been nominated at Cincinnati in 1876 instead of President Hayes, and of the intrigues already making for the general's nomination of 1880. At length he proceeded to speak for and in the name of his brother-in-law, the President. He said Grant wished to retire with grace and honorably from his office, and had no special interest in the success of either of the candidates whose fate was depending upon the action of the Electoral Commission. He said that for himself he preferred Tilden forty times to Hayes, and that all the ladies of Grant's family were champions of Tilden. He wound up by saying that if he could be useful in letting the President's views be known to Governor Tilden, when they might serve a useful purpose, he would be glad to do so, and that that was the special purpose of his inviting this interview.

I said to him that in a contingency not difficult to imagine there might be two persons claiming a title to the White House on the 4th of March, one by the choice of the Senate, another by the choice of the House of Representatives, and that it would interest Governor Tilden very much to know whether General Grant would think it his duty to solve that problem with the sword, or leave it to the solution of time and events. Corbin replied that he would tell me what must not go beyond me and Governor Tilden. Some time ago, he said, Grant sent a number of boxes to his house at Elizabeth for safe-keeping, and in stating his intention to do so, he observed that as the inauguration would occur on Sunday at 12 M. he proposed to vacate the White House Saturday night; whoever, therefore, said Corbin, gets into it first will have a very substantial advantage. The President might perhaps stay in until the following day if sufficient reason were shown for so doing. But, said I, suppose our candidate gets the White House and the other gets the Capitol, what then? Corbin paused a little, and then said: "The keeper of the Capitol is under the control of the Commissioner of Public Buildings. The Commissioner of Public Buildings is an engineer officer, under the orders of Chief-Engineer Humphreys. The present Commissioner of Public Buildings is Babcock; like St. Paul, he is generally believed to have an eye 'to the recompense of reward.' Then, those Irish doorkeepers may be worth looking to." Such was the substance of an interview which occupied about two hours.

What may have prompted Corbin to take the trouble to come all the way from Washington to give me this hint, beyond a desire to give himself importance in the eyes of Mr. Tilden, and how far President Grant countenanced his mission, if he knew anything about it, are questions which I never troubled myself to solve. There is no doubt that President Grant thought Tilden had been elected, and found no satisfaction in the prospect of having Hayes for his successor; but if he had wished to convey to Mr. Tilden any intimation that he would find the White House vacant and ready for his occupation on the night of the 3d of March, I find it difficult to believe that he would have selected Corbin for his emissary. However that may be, neither Mr. Tilden nor myself thought his communication worthy of serious consideration.

On the second day of March the House of Representatives, by a vote of 137 to 88, adopted the preamble and resolutions which follow, declaring that Samuel J. Tilden had been duly elected President, and Thomas A. Hendricks duly elected Vice-President of the United States. If these 137 votes in favor of Tilden and Hendricks represented the requisite constitutional number of States in the Union, it is not easy to see what more was necessary to make the one President and the other Vice-President two days later than simply to take the oaths of office prescribed by the Constitution.

RESOLUTIONS ADOPTED BY THE HOUSE OF REPRESENTATIVES DECLARING TILDEN THE PRESIDENT ELECTED

The following is the text of the declaration of the House of Representatives that Samuel J. Tilden has been duly elected President of the United States, and Thos. A. Hendricks Vice-President of the United States:

> "WHEREAS, It is not disputed that the electoral votes of the following-named States, to wit., Alabama, Arkansas, Connecticut, Delaware, Georgia, Indiana, Kentucky, Maryland, Mississippi, Missouri, New Jersey, New York, North Carolina, Tennessee, Texas, Virginia, and West Virginia, amounting in all to 184, were in conformity to the Constitution and laws of the United States cast for Samuel J. Tilden, of the State of New York, for President, and for Thos. A. Hendricks, of the State of Indiana, for Vice-President of the United States, by legally qualified electors appointed by said States, and severally in the manner directed by the Legislatures of said States, lists of which said votes were duly signed, certified, and transmitted sealed by said electors respectively to the seat of government, directed to the president of the Senate and by him opened in the presence of the Senate and House of Representatives, as required by the Constitution of the United States; and
>
> "WHEREAS, The evidence taken and reported to this House in pursuance of the orders thereof, shows conclusively that on the 7th day of November, in the year of our Lord 1876, the following-named persons, to wit., Wilkinson Call, J. E. Yonge, R. B. Hilton, and Robt. Bullock, each of whom was in all respects legally eligible and qualified to be appointed elector for President and Vice-President of the United States, were duly appointed electors by the State of Florida, in the manner directed by the Legislature of said State; and, whereas, the said Wilkinson Call, J. E. Yonge, R. B. Hilton, and Robert Bullock, after having been so appointed electors for President and Vice-President of the United States by said State of Florida, in the manner directed by the Legislature

thereof, did, on the 6th day of December, in the year of our Lord 1876, meet in the city of Tallahassee, in the said State of Florida, that being the time and place fixed by the Constitution and laws of the United States, and of the State of Florida, at which the electors appointed by said State should meet; and having so met, as the electors duly appointed by the State of Florida as aforesaid, did then and there, in pursuance of the Constitution and laws of the United States, cast by ballot four votes for Samuel J. Tilden, of the State of New York, for President of the United States, and in like manner cast four votes for said Thomas A. Hendricks, of the State of Indiana, for Vice-President of the United States, naming in separate and distinct ballots the person voted for by them for President and the person voted for by them for Vice-President, and then and there made distinct lists of the persons voted for by them for President and Vice-President of the United States, and of the number of votes cast for each, which lists were by said electors signed, certified, and transmitted by them sealed to the seat of government, directed to the president of the Senate, and by him opened in the presence of the Senate and House of Representatives, as required by the Constitution of the United States; and

"WHEREAS, The evidence taken and reported to this House, in pursuance of the order thereof, conclusively shows that on the 7th day of November, in the year of our Lord 1876, the following-named persons, to wit., John McEnery, R. C. Wickliffe, L. St. Martin, E. P. Poche, A. De Blanc, W. Seay, R. G. Cobb, K. A. Cross, each of whom was in all respects legally eligible and qualified to be appointed electors for President and Vice-President of the United States, were duly appointed electors by the State of Louisiana, in the manner provided by the Legislature of said State; and

"WHEREAS, The said John McEnery, R. C. Wickliffe, L. St. Martin, E. P. Poche, A. De Blanc, W. A. Seay, R. G. Cobb, K. A. Cross, after having been so appointed electors for President and Vice-President of the United States for the State of Louisiana, in the manner directed by the Legislature thereof, did, on the 6th day of December, in the year of our Lord 1876, meet in the city of New Orleans, in the said State of Louisiana, it being the time and place fixed by the Constitution and laws of the United States, and of the said State of Louisiana, at which the electors appointed by the said State should meet, and having so met, did, then and there, as the electors duly appointed for the State of Louisiana, as aforesaid, in pursuance of the laws and Constitution of the United States, cast by ballot eight votes for Samuel J. Tilden, of New York, for President of the United States, and in like manner cast eight votes for Thomas A. Hendricks, of the State of Indiana, for Vice-President of the United States, naming in separate and distinct ballots the persons voted for by them for President, and the person voted for by them for Vice-President of the United States, and then and there made distinct lists of the persons voted for by them for President and Vice-President of the United States, and the number of votes cast for each, which lists were by said electors signed, certified, and transmitted by said electors sealed to the seat of government, directed to the president of the Senate, and by him opened in the presence of the Senate and House of Representatives, as required by the Constitution of the United States; and

"WHEREAS, The evidence taken and reported to the House in pursuance of the orders thereof, shows conclusively that certain persons who pretended to have been appointed electors by the State of Florida, and who pretended as such to cast four votes for Rutherford B. Hayes, of Ohio, for President of the United States, and four votes for William A. Wheeler, of New York, for Vice-President of the United States, to wit., F. C. Humphreys, C. H. Pearce, W. H. Holden, and T. W. Long, who were not appointed by the State of Florida, but were falsely and fraudulently declared elected, when in truth they had each and every one of them been defeated by a clear majority, as was well known by the then Governor of Florida and the other canvassing officers of that State, who falsely and fraudulently made such declaration; and

"WHEREAS, The evidence taken and reported to this House in pursuance of the orders, further shows conclusively that certain persons, namely, William Pitt Kellogg, J. H. Burch, Peter Joseph, Lionel A. Sheldon, Morris Marks, A. B. Levisee, O. H. Brewster, and Oscar Joffrion, were falsely, fraudulently, and corruptly declared to have been appointed electors by the State of Louisiana, and did falsely, fraudulently, and corruptly pretend to cast eight votes for Rutherford B. Hayes for President, and eight votes for William A. Wheeler for Vice-President of the United States, when in truth and in fact they had never been appointed electors by the said State of Louisiana, but had been defeated by a majority of several thousands of the legally qualified voters of said State, at a fair, peaceful, and legally conducted election, held in pursuance of the law of said State, all of which was well known to the Board of Returning Officers, who made the false, fraudulent, and corrupt declaration of their pretended appointment as electors, and who, under the Constitution and laws of the said State of Louisiana, had no jurisdiction or authority to make any such declaration or statement; and

"WHEREAS, The pretended votes were given by F. C. Humphreys, Charles H. Pearce, William H. Holden, T. W. Long, William Pitt Kellogg, J. H. Burch, Peter Joseph, Lionel A. Sheldon, Morris Marks, Aaron B. Levisee, O. H. Brewster, and Oscar Joffrion, electors, now, therefore, in view of the foregoing facts, the truth of which is attested by an overwhelming array of sworn testimony, as well as by the intelligence of the American people,

"*Resolved*, By the House of Representatives of the United States of America, that it is the duty of the House to declare, and this House does hereby solemnly declare, that Samuel J. Tilden, of the State of New York, received 196 electoral votes for the office of President of the United States, all of which votes were cast and lists thereof signed, certified, and transmitted to the seat of government, directed to the president of the Senate, in conformity with the Constitution and laws of the United States, by electors legally eligible and qualified as such electors, each of whom had been duly appointed and elected, in the manner directed by the Legislature of the State in and for which he cast his vote as aforesaid; and that said Samuel J. Tilden, having thus received the votes of a majority of the electors appointed as aforesaid, he was thereby duly elected President of the United States of America for the term of four years, commencing on the 4th day of March, A.D. 1877.

"And this House further declares that Thomas A. Hendricks, having received the same number of the electoral votes for the office of Vice-President of the United States that were cast for Samuel J. Tilden for President, as aforesaid, the said votes having been cast for him by the same persons who voted for the said Tilden for President, as aforesaid, and at the same time and in the same manner, it is the opinion of this House that said Thomas A. Hendricks, of the State of Indiana, was duly elected Vice-President of the United States for a term of four years, commencing on the 4th day of March, A.D. 1877."

H. A. POPE TO TILDEN

"COLUMBUS, MISS., *Jany. 8, '77.*

"HON. SAML. J. TILDEN.

"SIR,—Although a citizen in private life, I, nevertheless, feel, I trust, as profound interest as any one in the welfare of our common country. In its life it has had crises, but none more alarming since '60 than that which grows out of the Presidential election between you and Gen. Hayes.

"Of your election I do not entertain a doubt; and it were simply to render our beautiful system of self-government on the part of the people a burlesque and reproach to allow a set of gambling politicians to set at defiance the expressed will of the sovereign people.

"Of course we of the South are powerless in the premises, and were it otherwise I am not prepared altogether to suggest the proper course. At this critical juncture peace is more than ever a social and political necessity. But, then, how can we ever expect to preserve constitutional liberty if such a precedent—so violative and destructive of the distinctive and peculiar feature of our more peculiar system of govt., submission to the legally expressed will of the majority—is tolerated.

"To you, sir, I look for counsel, and I trust you will be endowed with more than your recognized distinguished sagacity.

"I have been very much surprised, and not a little amused, at the contradictory opinions which even the learned in the law and governmental science have given both as to the law and practice in the case of the counting of the electoral votes, and as to the ultimate tribunal known to the Constitution as the final arbiter in the premises. Cushing, the learned parliamentarian, and no mean statesman, has gone so far as to intimate Gen. Grant could, under certain circumstances which may exist, hold over after the 4th of March next and continuously—till, indeed, the succession transpires; and so teaches Senator Bogy in a speech in St. Louis.

"A fearful and most dangerous suggestion, verily! And amazing that it should ever have found lodgment and utterance from so distinguished a source. But it has not the semblance of law or the slightest approach to truth in it.

"Cushing reasons from analogy, and says because officers in many of the States hold over till their successors are installed he therefore sees no reason why Gen. Grant should not do so.

"The ready answer to this opinion, however, is very plain and fatal to the force implied in it. In the case of the State officer, he acts in the instance mentioned by express authority of law. But in the case of the President, he is elected for a term of four years, no more or less, and there being no enabling act authorizing him to protract the term a moment beyond the limitation mentioned, should he do so he would be a usurper and deserve death as such at the hands of any citizen. In the cases you at once see there is no analogy whatever, and hence Cushing is certainly mistaken. As to the force and aspect of the 22d rule or any other rule or rules, about which a volume has been written, in solving adverse views, a word or two disposes of them. They are these modes of procedure—centures of the private action of both Houses of Congress, adopted for their convenience and the harmonious despatch of business. But they are dead letters if they contravene the Constitution of the U. S. or attempt to execute any of its requirements.

"Laws are required for the purpose, and not rules. Laws to which all the departments of legislation are necessarily, by law, parties—Congress and the Executive.

"As rules, moreover, they bind only the particular Congress adopting them; and do not lap over, save by acquiescence, express or implied. Hence, as I've said, the 22d rule is dead till revived as suggested, and has therefore no application to the case between you and Hayes.

"But to the general issue. In the event it should be formed from any cause, real or supposed, and *purely in the opinion and discretion of Congress*, neither you nor Mr. Hayes has the requisite number of 185 electoral votes required to confer the office, then to my apprehension the 12th amendment becomes the law of the case—*exclusively and supremely so.*

"You are familiar with it.

"It refers the whole question to Congress, and if, upon a review of the facts in the case, if it should decide there has been no election and the two Houses *can't agree that there has been*, whether the disagreement is real or feigned, then *the House* must *choose the President* and the Senate the Vice-President.

"If you will carefully consider the amendment, with the history of the question of electing the President in the Madison papers, you will, I think, agree with me that Congress is empowered with power similar to the omnipotence of Parliament in the premises considered.

"When I remember the House is Democratic I rejoice greatly at the fact, and esteem it most fortunate for the whole country, for your election is certain.

"Although, sir, a very stranger to you, I am, nevertheless, a lover of my whole country—desire peace and the prevalence of law and order, and the perpetuation of constitutional liberty. And with the hope, possibly, of exciting in your mind a new and perhaps valuable train of thought upon the subject, I have ventured to write.

"If you find anything worthy of your consideration I shall be gratified to know.

"With the greatest respect and prayers for the prolongation of your life, I am,

"Your obt. Servt.,
"H. A. POPE."

W. C. P. BRECKENRIDGE TO G. W. MORGAN

"LEXINGTON, KY., *Jan. 13th, 1877.*

"MY DEAR GENERAL,—I am requested to invite you to meet a few gentlemen of Kentucky, Ohio, Indiana, and possibly Tennessee, at the Galt House on the evening of the 17th instant, the evening before our State convention. It is proposed to have such conference for the purpose of agreement. May I trouble you to let me know if you can be present? I will be here until the night of the 16th, and then at the Galt House.

"Yours truly,
"WM. C. P. BRECKENRIDGE.

"*General George W. Morgan.*"

GEO. W. MORGAN TO TILDEN

(ABOUT INSIDE HISTORY OF LATE CONVENTION)

"MOUNT VERNON, OHIO, *Jan. 15, 1877.*

"MY DEAR MR. PRESIDENT,—A word as to the inside history of our late convention. Knowing the temper of our people, as a precaution against extreme action I wrote to Governor Allen, and to Hancock, of Texas, asking for letters which I could use in committee on resolutions by way of modifying of the wild advice which was certain to be given. Allen answered: 'In the present condition of things, threats of force and war would, in my judgment, very greatly prejudice our cause.'

"Hancock answered by a long letter, conservative in its tone. In conclusion he said: 'It is inconsistent with the genius of our institutions that any official position should be attained by force of arms. A result so accomplished would be a sad commentary on our statesmanship, and nothing but a correction by the people through peaceful modes would prevent our becoming Mexicanized, and the loss of republican government.'

"I read these letters to the committee. To the letter of Allen no comment was made, but Mr. Hancock's was objected to by Mr. Hurd on the ground that Hancock had been a Union man in Texas during the war. It was desired that either Mr. Cook or myself should be chairman of the committee. He declined on the ground of ill-health, and I foresaw that the tone of the resolutions was likely to be extreme.

"A sub-committee, composed of White, Heisley, Ewing, Vance, and myself, was appointed to report resolutions for the action of the full committee. The first and fifth resolutions were mine. The third was drawn by Alex. Long or Hurd. Heisley moved to strike out of that resolution all after 'will be resisted by the people.' The vote stood:

"Ayes—Heisley and Morgan.

"Noes—Ewing, Vance, and White.

"Ewing then moved to strike out all after the words 'last extremity.' The vote stood:

"Ayes—Ewing, Heisley, and Morgan.

"Noes—White and Vance.

"When the sub-committee reported to the committee, Hurd moved to amend by adding after the words 'last extremity' the words, 'even to an appeal to arms.' In the mean time Ward had been called away to preside over the convention, and some one else withdrew. The vote was nine for the amendment, eight against it. The resolution as to the national convention would have been carried by the same vote, but after a declaration in favor of an appeal to arms it was allowed to go by default. All of the speeches but my own were written and in type before the convention met. The convention struck up the 'Marseillaise,' and I took step to the music.

"I still have strong hopes of your inauguration, and if you are not our country will be in peril.

"With great respect,

Truly yours,
"GEORGE W. MORGAN."

GEORGE W. MORGAN TO HON. W. C. P. BRECKENRIDGE

"MOUNT VERNON, OHIO, *Jan. 16th, 1877.*

"DEAR SIR,—From some cause yours of the 13th instant has only this morning been received. My engagements are such as to prevent me from being with you to-morrow. All movements, political or otherwise, must have a recognized leader. Mr. Tilden is ours. I have reason to believe that the action of our convention went beyond his wishes. Mr. Pelton wrote to me just before our convention, and not long since I had a note from Mr. Hewitt. The tone of both indicate a policy less pronounced than that taken by Ohio.

"The last clause of our third resolution was adopted by one majority, and would have been rejected had not two of the committee been absent when the vote was taken. I regret that I cannot have a full exchange of views with the gentlemen to be present. My judgment is that we should defer to the views of Messrs. Tilden and Hendricks.

"Truly y'rs,
"GEORGE W. MORGAN.

"*Hon. W. C. P. Breckenridge.*"

CHARLES F. ADAMS TO TILDEN

"31 PEMBERTON SQUARE, BOSTON, *16th Jan., 1877.*

"MY DEAR MR. TILDEN,—You must excuse me for failing to call on you at 11 o'cl. Monday, as you requested. The snow-storm worked a very sudden change in my plans, and I hurriedly took the morning train for Boston instead of the afternoon, as I intended.

"For the object I had in view, however, my failure to see you again is of little consequence. Mr. Godwin is fully possessed of my views, and, if they are worth anything, can present them to you.

"The point can be stated in a few words. I am impressed with the idea that the true lead to get us out of our present complication should come from the two Presidential candidates, and not from irresponsible gatherings or a Congressional town-meeting. If the candidates could agree on a practical way out of the trouble, and unite in jointly recommending it to Congress and the country, its adoption would seem inevitable. To bring this about the candidates must be put in communication with each other, the way for which is rendered perfectly simple and obvious through the friendly relations still existing between those who joined in the 5th Avenue conference of last spring.

"My own view is that nothing will satisfactorily settle this question but an appeal to the ballot. The simple, fundamental, direct, democratic appeal to the one great tribunal. If the two candidates would unite in asking to have the people decide between them the path would be plain. But I will not dilate on this, as, if you want my views in detail, Mr. Godwin can give them to you.

"Begging you again to excuse my failure to call upon you, I remain, etc.,

"Very respectfully, &c.,
"CHARLES F. ADAMS, JR."

LOUISE LIVINGSTON HUNT TO TILDEN

"*(Jan. 21, '77.)*

"DEAR GOVERNOR TILDEN,—I have just received a letter from my brother in New Orleans, a portion of which I copy, because I feel sure it will interest you as an evidence of the genuine feeling at present in Louisiana.

"He says: 'Our people are in an *admirable temper*, and will do their whole duty. You will find Nichols all that you pronounce him, and I agree with you in thinking he has outshone even Hampton. The latter made a bad mistake in writing to the Pretender Hayes. Has not Mr. Tilden proved himself? Has he not led the South with consummate success until she has for the first time a fair prospect? He has, God bless him for it, shown the whole country a new future, and aroused in it the ancient spirit of truth and courage and zeal for liberty. Nowhere has he been stronger than in his perception of the capacity and will of the people, in his faith in their public virtue and attachment to free government, which ever did and ever must depend upon an honest count of the ballots lawfully cast. The change you observe in public opinion announcing his expected appearance in the Presidency will continue to grow until he is borne where he merits to be—into his great office.'

"How I wish, instead of being only a woman at such a time as this, that I were a Senator or member, endowed with the bold spirit and overruling genius of your own great ancestor! There would be quick work with the present Congress at Washington!

"Forgive me if my letter makes the one-hundredth-and-one of the day; it requires no answer. One word more before I stop. On reflection, I am certain my Uncle Randall alluded to the fact that I was the favorite niece of Mrs. Edward Livingston, my grandaunt, who died not many years since, at a very advanced age. I was very stupid not to think of this solution to the problem at once.

"Very truly yours,
"LOUISE LIVINGSTON HUNT."

THE ELECTORAL COMMISSION AND MR. TILDEN

The following statement, in the handwriting of George W. Smith, Mr. Tilden's private secretary, was from Mr. Tilden's dictation:

"Mr. Tilden's views of the policy which the Democratic party in Congress ought to pursue in respect to the counting of the electoral votes cast for President and Vice-President in 1876 were perfectly defined and freely expressed to all who consulted him long before the meeting of Congress in December of that year. It was to stand firmly and inflexibly on the unbroken series of precedents formed by the twenty-two Presidential counts from 1793 to 1872.

"While the committees of investigation in respect to Louisiana, Florida, and South Carolina, appointed by the House of Representatives, were engaged in their duties, Mr. Tilden caused a collection of all those precedents to be made and printed. At his request the Hon. John Bigelow prepared an analytical and expository introduction which was prefixed to this volume, and they were printed together by the Messrs. Appleton in the latter part of December, 1876. Mr. Marble assisted in preparing an appendix to the introduction, containing citations of authorities on the various points. This introduction was also issued separately and used in large numbers by the Democratic National Committee. It presents a clear, strong, and well-fortified statement of the position which Mr. Tilden thought the Democratic party ought to assume.

"On the 22d December two committees of the House of Representatives were appointed: the first on the powers and privileges of the House of Representatives in respect to counting electoral votes; the second to confer with a committee of the Senate on the same subject. The *Congressional Record* of that date contains the following entry:

"'*Committee to ascertain and report what are the privileges, powers, and duties of the House of Representatives in counting the votes for President and Vice-President of the United States*: Mr. Knott, of Kentucky; Mr. Sparks, of Illinois; Mr. ——, of Virginia; Mr. ——, of Pennsylvania; Mr. Burchard, of Illinois; Mr. Seelye, of Massachusetts; and Mr. Monroe, of Ohio.

"'*Committee to meet with the Senate committee as to the counting of the electoral votes for President and Vice-President*: Mr. Payne, of Ohio; Mr. Hunton, of Virginia; Mr. Hewitt, of New York; Mr. Springer, of Illinois; Mr. McCrary, of Iowa; Mr. Hoar, of Massachusetts; and Mr. Willard, of Michigan.'

"During the Christmas holidays, and for some days after the 1st of January, leading members of the House of Representatives were in New York and had interviews with Mr. Tilden. He was frank, open, and earnest in his conversations with them, and with many others, in advocating the making of an issue first in the House of Representatives and then in the Senate. He was for asserting, by formal resolution, the exclusive right of the two Houses acting concurrently to count the electoral vote and determine what should be counted as electoral votes, and for denying, also by formal resolution, the pretension then set up by the Republicans, that the president of the Senate had any lawful or constitutional right to assume that function. He was for urging that issue in debate in both Houses and before the country. He thought that if the attempt should be really made to usurp for the president of the Senate a power to make the count and thus practically control the Presidential election, the scheme would break down in process of execution, and that, in any event, it was in the interest of popular elective government not to yield to the menace of usurpation, all which actual usurpation could take for itself if completely successful.

"On the request of some member of the House of Representatives, Mr. Tilden himself drew two resolutions for the purpose of making this issue. The Democratic members of the Committee on Privileges, &c., found themselves best able to agree on the simplest form of asserting their principles and deemed that most expedient. Resolutions of that character were prepared by them, transmitted to Mr. Tilden for his advice, and returned with his approval. These resolutions were reported by the Hon. Proctor Knott, chairman of the committee. They will be found in the Congressional Record of Jan. 12, 1877. They are as follows:

"This policy seemed to have been generally agreed upon by the Democratic members of the House of Representatives, and it had been recommended persistently by Mr. Tilden for weeks to all who consulted him upon the subject.

"On the afternoon of Friday the 12th of January, Senator Barnum, passing through New York on his way home for the purpose of getting his family to take them to Washington on the following Tuesday, called on Mr. Tilden and expressed his conviction that a majority of the Senators would concur in denying the right of the president of the Senate to make the count. He had not heard a word of the proposed electoral contrivance. It was afterwards ascertained that the Democratic Senator from New York had been left in equal ignorance.

"On the evening of Saturday, 13th of January, Mr. Marble called on Mr. Tilden, found him in receipt of the McCrary House bill with the amendments proposed by Mr. Hewitt, and a letter from Mr. Hewitt informing him that his counsel would be asked the next day about this bill. Mr. Tilden and Mr. Marble sat late into the night analyzing it. Mr. Tilden invited Mr. Marble to come the next day when Mr. Hewitt should be there to consider this bill, which was supposed to be the axis upon which the deliberations of the House were revolving.

"Mr. Marble was therefore present on the following day, which was the 14th of January, when Mr. Tilden received from Mr. Hewitt his first information that the other measures had been abandoned, and that the subject upon which he wished to confer was the Electoral bill.

"Before he read the new bill Mr. Tilden was told that the Democratic members of the Senate committee were already absolutely committed to this bill, and would concur with the Republican members of the committee in reporting it to the Senate whether the House committee should concur or not.

"'Is it not rather late, then, to consult me?' said Mr. Tilden.

"'They do not consult you,' replied Mr. Hewitt. 'They are public men and have their own duties and responsibilities. I consult you.'

"The examination and analysis of the bill then proceeded. Mr. Tilden said, in the progress of the conference, 'I can't advise you to agree to the bill. I will advise you as to its details.'

"In respect to the provision by which six judges were to be described in the bill and one of them to be eliminated by lot, Mr. Tilden said, emphatically, 'I may lose the Presidency, but I will not raffle for it.'

"Mr. Tilden further said, if an arbitration were to be adopted, the tribunal ought to be fixed in the bill itself and not left to chance or intrigue.

"He said, also, that if an arbitration were to be adopted, the duty of the arbitrators to investigate and decide the case on its *merits* should be made mandatory and not left as a question of construction.

"With both the vital points, the choice of men to compose the tribunal and a function to be performed by the tribunal, left at loose ends, he treated the whole thing as a sort of gamble.

"In the course of the discussion Mr. Tilden said: 'If you go into a conference with your adversary and can't break off because you feel you must agree to something you cannot negotiate—you are not fit to negotiate. You will be beaten upon every detail.'

"Replying to the apprehensions of a collision of force with the executive, Mr. Tilden thought them exaggerated, but said: 'Why surrender now? You can always surrender. Why surrender before the battle, for fear you may have to surrender after the battle is over?'

"Mr. Tilden was pressed to say that if the bill could be modified so as to fix the five judges by a position provision, he would give it his approval, and it was urged that a modification could not succeed unless it was stated that that would make the bill acceptable. He firmly declined.

"Mr. Hewitt stated that the committees of the two Houses were to meet that evening at the house of Senator Bayard, and that he was expected to telegraph them the result of his interview.

"It was perfectly evident that what was sought was not Mr. Tilden's advice, but Mr. Tilden's adhesion. His refusal to give it caused the meeting for that evening to fall through.

"Mr. Tilden condemned the proposed action as precipitate. It was a month before the time for the count, and he saw no reason why there should not be an opportunity afforded for consideration and consultation by the representatives of the people. He treated it as a panic in which they were liable to act in haste and repent at leisure. He did not ask any time for himself or time to decide what he would do in respect to the proposed means. He never for a moment evinced the slightest hesitation or doubt about that; he was clear and inflexible, but he advised more deliberation upon the part of those who were to act in Washington. He believed in publicity and discussion and a wider consultation. He had an inherent and incurable distrust of the scheme, and has frequently said since that so great a stake as the government of forty millions of people with immense civil expenditures and a hundred thousand office-holders to be disposed of by a small body sitting in the Capitol would become the sport of intrigue or fraud.

"Mr. Tilden also disapproved of the secrecy with which the proceedings were shrouded. He thought it unwise to compromise the rights of the members of the two Houses without consulting them, by taking a hasty step which left no different policy practicable than the one thus imposed. Two days later, in a telegram to Mr. Hewitt, he expressed himself again and decidedly on this subject.

"In the whole of this conference Mr. Tilden was never asked to advise what the two committees should do jointly or what the Senate committee should do. He was expressly and repeatedly told that the Senate committee, including the Democratic members, Messrs. Bayard, Thurman, and Ransom, had already determined upon their course whatever his advice or wishes might be. The difficulty on the part of the House committee, in carrying out an independent policy, was pressed upon him as a reason for advising their acquiescence. No argument or persuasion could extract from him a word of personal sanction to the scheme. If, however, it was to be adopted, if it was a foregone conclusion, he manifested a desire that the provisions of the bill should be made to operate as much good and as little mischief as possible, both in their legal effect and in the manner of their execution. He was willing to advise and help in respect to specific provisions, but took care, in doing so, not incidentally to adopt the bill.

"The next day, Jan. 15th, Mr. Hewitt telegraphed from Washington to Mr. Edward Cooper:

"'WASHINGTON, *Jany. 15, 187-.*

"'To E. C.

"'The Senate committee will probably reject five- and report six-judge plan immediately. Our Senators feel committed to concur. House committee will not concur, and for present will probably not report.'

"The answer was as follows:

"'N. Y. *Jany. 15, 187-.*

"'To A. S. H.

"'Procrastinate to give few days for information and consultation. The six-judge proposition inadmissible.

"'E. C.'

"On the following day Mr. Hewitt telegraphed again:

"'WASHINGTON, *Jany. 16, 187-.*

"'To E. C.

"'After protracted negotiations Senator receded from six-judge. Declined five-judge and offered four senior associate justices who are to choose the fifth judge excluding chief justice. Our Senate friends earnestly favor acceptance, because they don't believe it possible to pass over Field. The Democrats on the House committee believe this is the last chance of agreement. We cannot postpone beyond eleven to-morrow, and if we decline Senate committee will report their original plan to which our friends are committed. Telegraph your advice.'

"To this telegram the following answer was sent:

"'N. Y., *Jany. 17, 2 a.m.*

"'Be firm and cool. Four-judge plan will not do. Perhaps worse than six. Complaints likely to arise of haste and want of consultation with members, and embarrassment in exercise of their judgment after plan is disclosed by premature committal of their representatives. There should be more opportunity for deliberation and consultation. Secrecy dangerous; probably mistake in itself, and if it results in disaster would involve great blame and infinite mischief.'

"In the evening of Tuesday, the 16th of January, Mr. Marble went to see Mr. Tilden and found him in his library. Several other gentlemen were present. The foregoing telegrams were read. The situation was freely canvassed. In their presence, Mr. Tilden dictated another and longer telegram, which was sent to the committee-room for transmission to Washington. As it was translated into cypher at the committee rooms and had to be retranslated at Washington, it was not delivered until after the committees had taken definitive action. It was not addressed to Mr. Hewitt and therefore was not seen by him. The only value of this telegram now is as a record made at the time in the presence of half a dozen well-known gentlemen, of Mr. Tilden's views, similar to those he had habitually expressed and somewhat fuller than in the other telegrams.

"Mr. Marble having seen all these telegrams at the time, and being familiar with them, requested copies for the present occasion. In assenting to that request, Mr. Tilden desired Mr. Marble, in any use he might make of them, to say explicitly that Mr. Tilden has never doubted Mr. Hewitt's perfect good faith in the transaction to which the telegrams relate, and believes him to have been actuated by the most patriotic motives.

"'Jany. 17, 1877 Midnight.

"'No need of hot haste, but much danger in it. Some days' interval should be taken; the risk of publicity harmless. No information here nor any opportunity to get information which could justify abstinence from condemning such an abandonment of the Constitution and practice of the government, and of the rights of the two Houses and of the people. Nothing but great and certain public danger not to be escaped in any other way could excuse such a measure. We are overpressed by exaggerated fears and forget that the other side will have greater troubles than we unless relieved by some agreement. They have no way out but by usurpation; are bullying us with what they dare not do or will break down in attempting. So long as we stand on the Constitution and settled practice we know where we are. Consequences of new expedient not enough considered. Only way of getting accessions in the Senate is by House standing firm—and judicious friends believe in that case we will go safely through. Opportunity to consult such friends should be given before even tacit acquiescence, if that is contemplated. Though details may be properly discussed, final committal by House committee should be firmly withheld.'"

THE HAYES FRAUD AND THE LOUISIANA LOTTERY

(*From the "Sun," Friday, November 20, 1891.*)

"We print elsewhere an interesting review of the events which have brought the Louisiana Lottery question to its present familiar phase.

"According to this statement, which is verifiable so far as it deals with the open facts of history, one of the most powerful influences in enabling Mr. R. B. Hayes to carry out the infamous political bargain which was the result of the Wormley conference, was that of the Louisiana Lottery.

"The representatives of Mr. Hayes secured the completion of the electoral count at Washington in 1877 by pledging the fraudulent administration, in advance, to do certain things desired by certain Southern Democrats. One of these things was to accomplish the overthrow of Packard in Louisiana, although Packard had received for Governor in that State a vote larger than Hayes' for President.

"When Mr. Hayes was seated in the office to which he had not been elected, he proceeded to redeem the promises made in his behalf by Stanley Matthews and Charles Foster. But he was able to fulfil his part of the bargain mainly through the intervention of the Lottery Company, which furnished at New Orleans a sufficient number of Republican legislators elect, willing to join with the Democrats in organizing the Legislature that destroyed Packard and seated Nicholls.

"Thus the bargain was carried out upon Mr. Hayes' side by the assistance of the concern once powerfully described by the Hon. Benjamin Harrison as the Great Beast. And to that service on the part of the Great Beast, according to our correspondent's recital of the facts, the Louisiana Lottery owes in return its present position of advantage in the State.

"Is there any doubt as to the pledge to overthrow Packard, which the Great Beast helped Hayes to redeem? Mr. William H. Roberts of New Orleans, among others, has testified that when the electoral count was pending, he received this assurance from a distinguished Republican statesman and a close personal friend of Mr. Hayes:

"'You need not be uneasy. I see that you are all restless and nervous; I see that Blackburn and those men are controlling the Southern men. I assure you that it will be all right; and when I assure you that you are to have your

State government, you ought to know me well enough to know that I am telling you the truth.'"

The distinguished Republican statesman and personal friend of Hayes was the Hon. Charles Foster, of Fostoria, Secretary of the Treasury under the administration of the Great Beast's enemy, the Hon. Benjamin Harrison.

Is there any doubt as to the understanding of the pledge by the Southern Democrats who were active in arranging the bargain, afterwards carried out by Hayes with the aid of the Louisiana Lottery? "If we should lose the national government we may be able to save Louisiana," said the Hon. Lucius Q. C. Lamar to Mr. Roberts of New Orleans early in the progress of the negotiations. And later, when certain Democrats in the House were proposing to stand out to the last against the consummation of the fraud, Judge Lamar sent to one of their number, the Hon. John Ellis of Louisiana, this letter of vindication and appeal:

> "I have just learned from an unquestionable authority, which I will give, if you wish it, that Foster said to a gentleman, my informant, that the speech he made to-day, which so significantly but indirectly hints at Hayes' Southern policy, that he made it after consultation with Mr. Matthews, Mr. Hayes' brother-in-law, and Mr. Matthews told him and urged him to say squarely that Hayes would have nothing to do or to say to Packard.
>
> "Now, Ellis, this is the first thing I have ever heard as coming from Hayes, directly or indirectly, that is worth acting upon by any Southern man. We do not want offices, but we do want to get our States and our people free from the carpet-bag government. Ought you not, if an available opportunity offers you to serve your State and people, to spring forward at once and see if you can't free your State? I think you should at once see Mr. Stanley Matthews and ask him if Governor Hayes will give you some assurance that he will not nominate Packard in his domination of your people."

This Judge Lamar is the gentleman who afterwards served as a member of Mr. Cleveland's cabinet, and who received from Mr. Cleveland an appointment to the bench of the Supreme Court of the United States.

BIGELOW TO JUDGE STEPHEN J. FIELD

(AN ADDRESS OF THE MINORITY OF THE ELECTORAL COMMISSION)

"21 GRAMERCY PARK, *January 31, 1894.*

"HON. STEPHEN J. FIELD.

"MY DEAR JUDGE,—The son of Judge Josiah Gardner Abbott, of Mass., handed me a few days since in Boston a copy of the proposed address of the minority of the electoral commission of 1877 protesting against the decisions of the majority of that commission. At the close of this address, or somewhere on it, was the following endorsement:

"'This address was drawn up at the request of some of the minority members of the electoral commission, to whom it was submitted and approved by them. But some doubted the wisdom of publishing the address at the time, and so it was not signed.

"'(Signed) J. G. ABBOTT.'

"I would like much to know if the Democratic minority concurred in this protest, and the reasons which decided them or any of them against its publication. I am expecting to be delivered one of these days of something about that electoral commission, and, of course, I would like to speak of this address, if at all, by the book. I would like, also, to know if you can tell me why Judge Abbott refused to allow of the publication in his lifetime; if there was any other reason than that it was never signed.

"I hope you will think these questions will involve matters of sufficient gravity to warrant me in troubling you for an answer which no one else that I know can give.

"Yours very truly,
"JOHN BIGELOW."

STEPHEN J. FIELD TO BIGELOW

"SUPREME COURT OF THE UNITED STATES,
"WASHINGTON, D. C., *February 2, 1894.*

"HON. JOHN BIGELOW.

"DEAR SIR,—Your letter of the 31st of January was received yesterday. You state that the son of the late Judge Josiah Gordon Abbott, of Massachusetts, had handed to you a few days before, in Boston, a copy of 'The proposed address of the minority of the electoral commission of 1877, protesting against the decision of the majority of that commission,' and add that at the close of the address, or somewhere in it, was the following endorsement: 'This address was drawn up at the request of some of the minority members of the electoral commission, to whom it was submitted and approved by them; but some doubted the wisdom of publishing the address at the time, and so it was not signed. (Signed) J. G. ABBOTT.'

"You express a wish to know if the Democratic minority concurred in this protest, and the reasons which decided them, or any of them, against its publication. In answer to your inquiry, I would state that I remember very well the preparation of the address undertaken by Mr. Abbott, the draft of which was submitted to me and approved, and I supposed then that it would receive the signatures of all the members of the Democratic minority and be published. Soon afterwards Mr. Abbott informed me that some of the members of the minority had expressed a doubt of the wisdom of publishing the address at that time. It was not, therefore, signed. I know of no other reason. None was given that I can recall except the existence of the doubt mentioned.

"Perhaps Mr. Bayard could give you more definite information upon this point. I know that it was a disappointment to me that the address, either as prepared, or as it might be amended by suggestions of members of the Democratic minority, was not published.

"I think that when the members of the commission separated it was Mr. Abbott's intention to prepare some document with reference to the action of the commission for publication, with the consent of other members of the minority, but that intention was subsequently abandoned by him for reasons which I cannot state.

"You also state that you would like to know if I could tell you why Judge Abbott refused to allow of the publication in his lifetime. I know of none except the fact that the document was never signed. Some years afterwards, when Mr. Abbott was at Washington, he expressed to me a regret that the document which he had prepared had not been signed and published.[19]

"I am very respectfully yours,
"STEPHEN J. FIELD."

The following letter, received in reply to one addressed to its writer by Mr. George W. Smith, one of the executors and trustees of Mr. Tilden's estate, gives the substance of a very important statement bearing upon the election for President in Louisiana in '76, the authorship of which statement, however, is suppressed in compliance with the request and for the reasons assigned by the one who heard it. As the gentleman, whose name is here left blank, has long been dead, it is permissible to say that he was quite the most prominent Republican politician in Louisiana at the time the statement purports to have been made.

A. M. WILCOX TO G. W. SMITH

"BRIGHTON, ENGLAND, *April 19th, '94.*

"DEAR MR. SMITH,—Your letter of April 4th came this morning, having been forwarded from home.

"The letter you speak of is not in existence, having been destroyed when I broke up my home ten years ago. It was not from Kellogg, but from ——. That part referring to the election read about as follows:

"'You ask as to the election. Tilden carried the State by 9 to 14,000 (I am not positive as to the figures, either may be wrong), but this will be overcome in some way; how has not as yet been decided, but you can be certain the State will be returned for Hayes.'

"I cannot be mistaken as to the substance of his letter, as it made a deep impression on me at the time. Had it not been personal and *confidential*, I should have given it publicity at the time.

"In case Mr. Bigelow should make any use of it—the information—kindly see that he avoids using ——'s name for the reasons above given.

"I sincerely regret I cannot produce the letter itself or make a more satisfactory reply to your inquiry.

"Mrs. Wilcox formerly resided in Louisiana, and —— was a frequent guest at her father's house, which explains the frankness of his answer to her letter asking for information in the matter.

"With my best wishes to you.

"Very truly,
"A. M. WILCOX."

WILLIAM BIGLER TO TILDEN

"CLEARFIELD, PA., *Jan. 24th, 1877.*

"MY DEAR SIR,—After a careful examination of all the plans of adjusting the Presidential embroglio at Washington, I came to the conclusion that the plan reported by the committee is the best—most certain to promote the peace and dignity of the country, and to secure your inauguration as President. In the first place it involves an abandonment of the plea for the right of the president of the Senate, and in the next it recognizes the right of the commission to go behind the certificates on an allegation of fraud. Besides, I have special confidence in one of the judges who will be selected as a Republican. He will be just and impartial in his action, with slight inclination to our side.

"The difficulty in the way of the power of the House consists in the obstacles that can be interposed against reaching the point at which that power can be safely and properly exercised. The order laid down in the Constitution must be followed. First, the certificates shall be opened. Second, the vote shall then be counted. Third, if there has been a failure to elect by the States then the House shall immediately proceed to elect a President. The counting will go on smoothly until Florida is reached, and then objection will be made and the Senate will retire. It will decide to count the vote for Mr. Hayes, and the House will reject the vote or count it for you, and then when will they come together again? Perhaps at the end of a week the House may give up Florida to go on with the count and then will come Louisiana, and this the House cannot yield without losing everything. Some say at this point the House should proceed to elect a President, but the vote has not been counted as the Constitution requires, and the assumption that there has been no election in the face of the fact that there are but two candidates, and that it is not possible to so divide the vote as to have a tie, cannot be overlooked. The plan of conceding everything but Oregon, which comes last, has been favored by some. My own impression is that you will become President by the rejection of the vote of Louisiana. That will be done by the commission, and may be done by a vote of the Senate. I think the vote in the Senate, taken at any time, would be very close on the rejection of the vote of Louisiana.

"The danger now is that the plan of the committees will be defeated by persistent debate. I have no fear of Grant. At present he would sign the bill.

"I should have remained at Washington but for an imperious demand for me in a business matter at this place.

"With much esteem I remain,

"Your friend,
"WM. BIGLER.

"Florida is becoming so clear for you that the whole matter may yet be settled by that State."

TILDEN TO GOVERNOR WADE HAMPTON

"NEW YORK, *Feb. 3, 1877.*

"DEAR GOV. HAMPTON,—I have just emerged from ten days of exceptional intensity of pressure in occupations, which at best were not light. During this time your letter of the 22d Jany. arrived. It does not seem to me more than two or three days since I first saw it, but my count of time may have been imperfect.

"Certain I am that I take my first interval to acknowledge it and to reply.

"One only of the newspaper publications which you mentioned had come under my observation; and that I had cursorily looked at rather than read.

"It is enough to say that none of these criticisms has made the least impression on my mind unfavorable to your perfect good faith in your political actions or relations, or to my confidence in your friendly disposition toward me. You were quite right in thinking, as you say, that an explanation was unnecessary, though for great caution you have chosen to write to me on the subject. I have not only faith in you, but great admiration for your personal bearing under difficult and trying circumstances. I have no element of suspicion in my nature, and have looked on the recent contest in no selfish aspect, not even in that refined form which thinks of the honor of being associated with the right in so great a cause. And I appreciate the wrongs to which the people of your State have been subjected.

"I beg, my dear sir, that you will excuse my great haste and believe me,

Very truly your friend,
"S. J. TILDEN."

THOMAS COTTMAN TO S. J. TILDEN

"343 FIFTH AVENUE, NEW YORK, *Feby. 22d, 1877.*

"GOVR. SAML. J. TILDEN.

"MY DEAR SIR,—Your card of this morning confirms my opinion that the defeat of the Democratic party is due measurably to the manipulation of inexperienced or overconfident directors. I hope you will insist on Chandler's exhibit, now they have made all possible mischief out of your account. There has been too much willingness on the part of the Democrats to compromise, and Senator Kernan to say the least of it has acted unwisely. Patrick Kennedy's[20] testimony fully substantiates my views in regard to Louisiana—Wells has been unskilfully handled. But there is no use in crying over spilt milk.

"The 'occasional correspondent' in the *Herald* of this morning overstates the case in reference to dissatisfaction in the party. But of its existence no one can doubt. Not so much South as here and in the West, and from a totally different cause from that assigned in the *Herald.* I had opportunities [of] observing it, and exerted my utmost power to assuage or avert it. There is no necessity now for adverting to the cause, but I will simply remark that the old Hunkers considered themselves ignored to give prominence to Barnburners and new men, personal favorites—and that feeling at one time came near losing you this city and Brooklyn. I have never doubted the feasibility of obtaining a *fair and honest return* of the vote in Louisiana, if the proper means were resorted to which in no wise included pecuniary consideration. It was a political question and political consideration was desired as testified by P. I. Kennedy, who is a very different man from Dr. Hugh Kennedy, whose name Wells offered as the fifth man on the Returning Board, and had laid on the table for future action. Whenever I mentioned the subject to those in *authority here,* I was met with the information that Genl. Taylor was *here* looking to Louisiana. Genl. Taylor is à very estimable gentleman, but most cordially hated by both Wells and Kennedy. When I reflect on the management '*here,*' I can only say you were slaughtered in the house of your friends: not from design, for I believe they were honest and true, zealous and uncompromising, but conceited from the want of experience in politics; not the want of capacity, but an overweening confidence in themselves and the justice of their case. In the name of Louisiana, I unhesitatingly repudiate the assertion of the *Herald's* occasional correspondent of an indifference towards your election.

She cast her vote for you, and it would have been so returned if your lieutenants here had not overestimated their powers.

"Very truly your obt. servt.,
"THOS. COTTMAN."

N. W. HAZEN TO S. J. TILDEN

"ANDOVER, *Feb. 28, 1877.*

"HON. SAMUEL J. TILDEN.

"DEAR SIR,—I hope it is not too late to make some use of the views stated in the paper enclosed, which seem to me so obvious that I have constantly hoped to see them presented from some one of many sources.

"Very respectfully,
"Your obt. servt.,
"N. W. HAZEN."

Whenever it appeared to Congress that no person had a majority of the electoral votes, the whole subject of the election of President, by force of the Twelfth Amendment, passed into the exclusive jurisdiction of the House, and no proposals for joint proceedings, or for any action by the Senate in relation to it were in order.

That no person had a majority appeared from the double returns from some of the States from the opening of the returns, and is admitted by the passage of the electoral law.

The choice being given to the House by the Constitution, it belonged to the House solely to make any investigations which it should find necessary to the proper performance of this trust.

When the Constitution gives the choice to the House, it confers by necessary implication whatever authority is requisite to the full exercise of the power, including, of course, exclusive control over the whole subject.

It may be remarked, by way of illustration, that the first duty is to determine who are the three persons from whom a choice is to be made: acting with the Senate, a fourth person might be rejected from this number, whom, if he were before it, a majority of the House might choose to elect.

The record of the proceedings of the commission will show them to be without warrant or authority in the Constitution, which contains ample provision upon the same subject.

The commission usurps a power conferred upon the House when the House itself was established, which is one of its highest functions, and whose exercise it cannot surrender without dishonor.

1. Upon the motion to be made in the House to accept the report of the commission it should not be entertained, because in violation of the constitutional rights of the House, and not in order therefore.

2. If it has been accepted, the whole proceedings should be declared for this reason null and void.

3. The House should proceed to the choice of President according to the Twelfth Amendment, that it may not fail in the performance of one of the highest duties it owes to the Constitution, and in the exercise of its greatest powers; that some person may be duly chosen, so that its candidate may have the legal title before the law and before the people.

JOHN A. McCLERNAND TO TILDEN

"SPRINGFIELD, ILL., *March 2nd, 1877.*

"DEAR SIR,—It is done, and the Presidential office, fairly awarded you by the voice of the people and the electoral colleges, passes to another. I sympathize with you in this your deprivation of right and official dignity. I sympathize also with the country in its consequent humiliation. A stain is cast upon its escutcheon and Republican institutions.

"The result might have been different but for a mistake, honest, doubtless, though it was. If the chairman of our national committee had not wavered and hesitated at a decisive moment, and thereby awakened doubts as to your purpose, the spirit and courage of the Democracy, then showing a bold front, would have precluded the possibility of the electoral commission and its decision, and have settled everything satisfactorily without a blow. I say this in the belief that the capital and business of the country would not have seconded the Republican leaders in an appeal to arms to uphold fraud and usurpation. Right armed with confidence is seldom vanquished.

"But regrets are now idle. Our part is to repair the past in the future. Your leadership in the late canvass regenerated and renewed the Democratic party, and brought it back to the mansion of its fathers. It revived its ancient energy and devotion. It is now capable of great achievements. This is saying much for both you and it, yet not more than the truth. You are now the acknowledged leader of the *reform Democracy*, and your leadership must be continued for the contest of 1880. This is the sentiment and demand of the *Old Guard* who never desert or surrender.

"Your ob't ser't,
"JOHN A. MCCLERNAND."

ROBERT M. McLANE TO TILDEN

"BALTIMORE, *3rd March, '77.*

"MY DEAR GOVERNOR,—Certainly it is not an agreeable greeting I have to offer, but I cannot let the communication of the foul work in Washington pass into history without expressing to you the disgust I feel and the hope I entertain that the country will yet recover its moral sense, and vindicate the men and principles that have been overthrown by fraud and *quasi force*, for this last alternative was always in the perspective, and as you know greatly influenced and demoralized good men!

"It is certainly to be regretted, I think, that our friends were ever beguiled into the electoral commission scheme, and though I did my best, within the bounds of my influence, to secure from its action the triumph of truth and justice, I have the satisfaction to know that from the hour we had the returns of the Presidential election my utmost effort was directed to influence the House of Representatives to assert its constitutional prerogatives and elect a President, rather than co-operate in the declaration of a result which is false in fact and which outrages the moral and numerical sense of the country. If such a result was inevitable, I could accept it as well as another; but I would have left its consummation to the conspirators who did the counting in the Southern States and the Federal army at the seat of government, under the immediate direction of the retiring President.

"Until I have the pleasure of a personal greeting, I remain,

Very truly and faithfully,
"Yr. friend and obt. servt.,
ROBT. M. MCLANE."

"*To Hon. S. J. Tilden.*

A. E. ORR TO TILDEN

"BROOKLYN, *Mch. 3d, '77.*

"MY DEAR GOVERNOR TILDEN,—I regret exceedingly that illness has confined me to the house for the past few days.

"I wanted to say to you personally what I feel towards you in my heart.

"Under cover of law—justice has no part in it—a great wrong has been committed, and you are deprived of a position to which all honest-minded men believe you were fairly elected.

"Knowing you as I have had good opportunity of doing, and the earnestness and truthfulness of purpose which were the incentives to your every action, and your courage to carry out what you deemed to be the path of duty irrespective of consequences to party or persons, I am led to deplore the finding of the electoral commission as a national misfortune—an injustice done to the whole country in greater measure, if possible, than to yourself.

"The good seed of reform which you have sown has not fallen on stony places; it has taken deep root in the hearts of the people, and will bring forth its fruit in due season. Time will show you that you are loved, trusted, and appreciated, and although the people have at this time been denied the pleasure of seeing you enjoy the noble gift they had bestowed upon you, depend upon it, my dear sir, this pleasure on their part has only been postponed for a season.

"With unswerving confidence and sincere friendship,

"Believe me very respectfully,
"A. E. ORR.

"*Thirty-seven Tompkins Pl., Brooklyn.*"

HOWARD POTTER TO TILDEN

"*March 3d, '77.*

"MY DEAR MR. TILDEN,—I avail of the leave which you gave me, when we met the other afternoon in the street-car, to urge you, now that the campaign is ended in which the Democratic party has 'lost all but honor,' to give them a few valedictory words of counsel and encouragement, and the country some words of admonition and warning.

"You have been the leader of that party, and it seems to me that you owe it—at least to its 'rank and file'—some such acknowledgment of a support which was in the main everywhere honest, devoted, and given upon grounds such as must be just those upon which such a man as you are would desire to be supported.

"And what an opportunity this is to say something which the country may ponder!

"What to say no one knows so well as yourself—who have been one of the keepers of the true Democratic 'sacred fire'; and you may be sure that everywhere throughout the land whatever you may say will be read attentively by men of all parties.

"But I won't enlarge. It seems to me that it is a great opportunity to do your party and the country a lasting service, and I have not known how to refrain from urging you again to avail of it. I am, with sentiments of the highest esteem and regard,

Yours faithfully,
"HOWARD POTTER.

"*Hon. S. J. Tilden, &c., &c.*"

GEORGE B. MCCLELLAN TO TILDEN

"ST. JAMES HOTEL, BALTIMORE, *March 5, 1877.*

"MY DEAR MR. TILDEN,—I do not doubt that you are overwhelmed with letters just now from your many friends; but I cannot refrain from adding one to the number, to express my intense disappointment that you are not to-day the '*de facto*,' as you truly are the '*de jure*' President of our country. I *did* believe that the justices of the Supreme Court would, in a case of such vital interest, rise high above all party trammels, carefully ascertain the facts of the case, administer the law with equity and consistency, and hold to the doctrine that fraud must vitiate the acts it was employed to accomplish. I am deeply grieved to find that these justices can, after all, be mere politicians—no better than the least patriotic of the tribe. I regret sincerely that your labor of the last four months has met with such a result, but my confidence in your patriotism is such that I am very sure that, so far as personal considerations are concerned, you will feel the disappointment far less than your friends do for you.

"You will not consider it a liberty if I congratulate you—or rather the party—upon the dignified and high-toned course you have pursued in the midst of the difficulties surrounding you.

"I am sure that we agree in the belief that the worst feature of this memorable business is that open fraud should be triumphant, and that through such means the control of a corrupt party should again be fastened upon our country. I do not know that I am capable of judging dispassionately of the future, but it now appears to me that that future is black indeed, when another than yourself—the honestly elected—holds to-day the name and powers of President.

"Under you I thought the future of my country would be bright and happy: now, I do not care to look beyond the evils of the day—for they are sufficient.

"With sentiments of the highest respect,

"I am, sincerely, your friend,
"GEO. B. MCCLELLAN."

HON. CHARLES FRANCIS ADAMS TO TILDEN

(THE STAMP OF FRAUD FIRST TRIUMPHANT IN AMERICAN HISTORY)

"BOSTON, *5th March, 1877.*

"MY DEAR SIR,—On this day when you *ought* to have been the President of these United States, I seize the opportunity to bear my testimony to the calm and dignified manner in which you have passed through this great trial.

"It is many years since I ceased to be a party man. Hence I have endeavored to judge of public affairs and men rather by their merits than by the names they take. It is a source of gratification to me to think that I made the right choice in the late election. I could never have been reconciled to the elevation by the smallest aid of mine of a person, however respectable in private life, who must forever carry upon his brow the stamp of fraud first triumphant in American history.

"No subsequent action, however meritorious, can wash away the letters of that record.

"Very respectfully yours,
"CHARLES FRANCIS ADAMS."

HON. ABRAM S. HEWITT TO THE NATIONAL DEMOCRATIC COMMITTEE

(HIS MOTIVES IN SUPPORTING THE ELECTORAL TRIBUNAL)

"WASHINGTON, D. C., *March 3.*

"GENTLEMEN,—The last act of the executive committee was the announcement to the people of the United States that Samuel J. Tilden was elected President, and Thomas A. Hendricks Vice-President.

"This announcement was followed by a scurrilous pronunciamento from the national Republican committee, claiming the election of Hayes and Wheeler. The power to determine the result resided in Congress; but grave differences of opinion, threatening the peace of the country, existed as to the lawful methods of procedure, and the constitutional rights, and the duties of the two Houses in the premises. Committees were therefore raised in both Houses to consider the question, and to confer with each other as to legislation proper to be adopted in order to secure a declaration of the result without confusion and public disorder. The Senate committee had practically perfected a bill for this purpose before the House committee met with them in conference. This bill had received the assent and approval of the three Democratic Senators serving on the committee.

"To have rejected this settlement would, necessarily, have produced division in the Democratic party, and been fatal to its immediate and future success. On the other hand, the bill itself seemed to be so wisely framed in its main features, that the judgment of the Democratic members of the House committee gradually confirmed the action of the Senate committee, and, with some changes which were deemed favorable to the Democratic position, the Electoral bill was approved by all the Democratic members of both committees, and was duly reported and became a law by the vote of a large majority of the Democratic members of both Houses, and was approved by the general judgment of the country.

"The result has disappointed the hopes of every lover of his country. By decisions abhorrent to the natural senses of justice, all proof of fraud was ruled out, and the States of Louisiana and Florida have been counted for Hayes, although all fair-minded men concede that they voted for Tilden. This grievous wrong and its authors I have denounced on the floor of the House, and I have no hesitancy in declaring that, for the first time in our history, the Presidency has been awarded to a candidate who has no just title to its honors.

"But he comes into office as the result of the operation of a law which received the support of the Democratic party, and any attempt to resist its operation would, it seems to me, only deprive us of the support and sympathy of all conservative and fair-minded citizens.

"Inasmuch as difference of opinion exist in regard to the policy which has been pursued by the Democratic party since the election, and prior to the meeting of Congress, I have only to say that so far as my action is concerned, whatever has been done has received the approval of the executive committee and of the only persons outside of their number who had any right to be consulted.

"An absurd statement has been widely circulated that had declared that 'I preferred the inauguration of Hayes to the shedding of a single drop of blood.' A leading Democratic journalist, who could at any time from his position as a member of the House of Representatives, have ascertained the truth, has circulated this false statement in a letter over his own initials, although it ought to have been known to him that I had contradicted it in a card, widely copied, immediately after its publication. The only remark which I ever made on this subject was in private conversation, not intended to be repeated, and was to the effect that 'I would prefer four years of Hayes' administration to four years of civil war'; and upon this declaration I am willing to stand, because four years of civil war would, in my opinion, utterly destroy constitutional government for this generation at least.

"It has also been insinuated that my course has been affected by the ownership of a large amount of United States bonds. It is enough for me to express the regret that I am not so fortunate as to own any of these desirable securities, and to state that all my means are, as they always have been, used in giving employment to the working-men of this land, suffering so severely from the maladministration of its public affairs.

"I have also been censured for assenting to the completion of the count in accordance with the provisions of the law which I helped to frame, and which received my cordial approval and my vote. As an honorable man, I do not see that any other course was open to me, but if honor had permitted otherwise, my judgment is that it was the wisest course for the country, as well as for the Democratic party, to proceed in accordance with the law to the orderly completion of the count, although we knew that it would result in the installation of Hayes into an office to which he had no honest right, except such as might be deprived from the unjust decisions of a tribunal which we had helped to create. My reasons for this conclusion are as follows: If the count had been defeated, and the bill to provide for a vacancy in the office of President had become a law, a new election would have taken place in November next: meanwhile the office of President would have been filled by a Republican chosen by the Senate. The whole power of the administration would therefore be under the control of the Republican managers. In order to succeed they must hold on to South Carolina and Louisiana, which would necessarily involve sustaining by force the usurping governments of Chamberlain and Packard, with all their unlawful excrescences in the way of unscrupulous returning boards. The patience of the people of these two unhappy States is utterly exhausted. They would break out in open rebellion against a government thus forced on them, and continued in power by the armed forces of the United States. Civil war would result. The Federal government would re-enforce itself with all the troops at its command; the other Southern States would naturally rush to the aid of their suffering sister States; the safety of the colored as well as the white population would be endangered; and a call would be made for volunteers and militia from the Northern States to suppress the rebellion, and thus the flames of civil war would be lighted all over the Union, in the midst of which a free election would be impossible, and a military despotism take the place of civil government. This generation would pass away before the country would recover from the disastrous consequences of such a fratricidal strife.

"In comparison with the evils of anarchy, or of a government of force, which alone could prevent anarchy, four years of usurpation—but usurpation in accordance with the forms of law—seemed to me by far the lesser evil. Besides, we have not yet tested the judgment of the people as to the great outrage upon all justice and right which has been perpetrated. There is no reason to suppose that it will be sanctioned by the popular voice, but if it should be we could not hope to save them from usurpation and despotism by force used against the judgment of a majority of the people.

"To me, therefore, on the one side was anarchy and civil war, inevitable and disastrous of all the hopes of free government; on the other side was peace and order, with free speech, a free press, and the ballot-box still preserved to us.

"Under the circumstances, I could not hesitate as to my course. I felt that, as a patriot and a trusted servant of the Democracy, no other course was left open to me, and I feel sure that its wisdom will be indicated by the early and triumphant success of the Democratic party, standing, as it does, upon the rock of justice and patriotism, from which no amount of passion or provocation has been able to move it.

"For myself, I feel that I have now completed the duty which was assigned to me at St. Louis. The result of the campaign was the unquestionable election of our candidates. That they and the people have been defrauded of their rights is true, but for this result I do not hold myself any more responsible than any other member of Congress upon whom rested the duty of counting and declaring the votes.

"In the course of my very brief public experience, I have already found that my usefulness as a Representative in Congress has been seriously impaired by my position as chairman of this committee, and I had long since determined to ask to be permitted to retire from it as soon as the result of the election was definitely ascertained. The unforeseen complications which arose have necessarily compelled me to postpone the execution of this intention until the present time. Now, however, that all impediments to my retirement are removed, I beg to be released from further service as your chairman, and, thanking you for the honor you have conferred and for the confidence which you have uniformly manifested in my efforts to promote the success of Democratic principles, I have the honor to be,

"Very respectfully, your obedient servant,
"ABRAM S. HEWITT.

"*To the National Democratic Committee.*"

WHAT GRANT THOUGHT OF IT

[*From the New York "Sun," March 7, 1877.*]

"There are some interesting facts connected with the Louisiana election which it does not seem necessary to keep secret any longer.

"When Mr. Hewitt had his celebrated interview with President Grant on the 3d of December last, just before the beginning of the recent session of Congress and before the Returning Board of Louisiana made its final declaration, the President said that in his opinion there had been no fair election in that State, and that the electoral votes of Louisiana ought not to be counted at all upon either side.

"'But,' asked the President, 'are you going to buy the Returning Board?' Mr. Hewitt assured him that the Democrats had no such purpose; that they would not buy the Presidency.

"Grant knew that the Returning Board and the Presidential election were for sale because Wells' agent had told him so; and it was natural for a man of his cast of mind to suppose that where the office of President was to be sold for money there would be an active competition for the purchase."

SENATOR FRANCIS KERNAN TO TILDEN

"WASHINGTON, *March 12th, 1877.*

"MY DEAR SIR,—I expected to get over to New York and have a chat with you last week, and hence did not write you. Moreover, I was not in a frame of mind to write, and am not yet. We have been wronged out of the fruits of the last Presidential election. You were clearly and fairly elected by the people, and Hayes has been counted in. This is hard to bear patiently, and the mass of our party feel deeply aggrieved—indeed, they are so disappointed and irritated that a great many of them are disposed to find fault with what was done, and to believe that something more successful could have been devised. Notwithstanding my disappointment at the decisions of the commission, I am of the opinion that from the standpoint we judged and voted when we supported the bill creating the commission, we acted patriotically and wisely—unless the two Houses came to some arrangement as to 'counting' the electoral votes; it looked then as though they would disagree and come to a dead-lock; and the result would have been that the Senate would, under some form of proceeding, have declared Hayes and Wheeler elected; the House would have declared there was no election by electoral votes, and would have elected you President, and opponents were in possession and would have sustained Hayes and Wheeler, and civil war would probably have been the result. This would have entailed great evils on the mass of the people, and might have destroyed the government it was intended to preserve. My judgment was and is that what seemed then a reasonably fair tribunal to decide the question involved, was better than the risk of evil to our people and our system of government. Civil war is the last remedy of a people for political wrongs, and should not be inaugurated till every peaceful remedy has failed. But I will write no more on this subject; when we meet, I shall want to talk the matter over fully.

"I think we shall get away from here the last of this week or early next. The new administration will try to win popular favor and turn attention from the title by which it came to power by good conduct. I believe it means to reform some of the graver abuses which marked the administration under General Grant. I hope it will succeed in doing so. The country needs peace, and to end self-government at the South, and honesty and economy everywhere. I am not very sanguine, but I hope for the best.

"Very truly yours,
"FRANCIS KERNAN."

LOUISE LIVINGSTON HUNT TO TILDEN

"MONTGOMERY PLACE, *May 4th, 1877.*

"DEAR MR. TILDEN,—I did not go to New Orleans after all, but I have just had a letter from there of which I think I must copy a few lines to send you, because they are so full of genuine heart-felt enthusiasm for yourself. They are from my brother—who, I think I told you, first mentioned at our own table here his conviction that you would and ought to be candidate for the Presidency. I had written him recently an account of the three cheers for Louisiana given by Mr. Hewitt's guests in New York on the day of the withdrawal of the troops. Mr. Bayard told me all about it, and I was touched to the heart at the generous feeling that prompted the cheers from the defeated Democrats—and their *great leader.* I mentioned the circumstance in writing to my brother, and here is his answer. 'I read with much pleasure your account of the entertainment where Mr. Tilden was present. The fact is I have felt so strongly his merit, his services, and his patriotism that I want him to be next President. I was, in the beginning, of the first among his friends, and I remain, after the dread experience of the past, where I commenced. Sometimes I am puzzled to think he did not favor an uprising of the people to seat him. *I did!* Was it because he was wiser that he did not speak when he might have said, *"Vous qui m'aimez suivez moi!"* I hope so.' 'Yes,' he goes on to say, 'God be praised—the men who have so long oppressed Louisiana are gone. Once more the State breathes free, and, filled with hope of the future, trusts to be again happy and prosperous.'

"I know that these sentiments will not be read by you with indifference, although from one you know not at all.

"I am, as you see by my date, in this spot, which I have loved so dearly from infancy. The snow-storm in the far West has made it cold, but the air is sweet with the fragrance of early spring. The events of each day is the newspaper, and how dull the papers seem after the excitement of the past year. Can't you stir up the elements again? If I dared I could point the way, but perhaps you think women know nothing of politics and would not heed the Sybil!

"With great regard, believe me,

"Very truly yours,
"LOUISE LIVINGSTON HUNT."

W. B. LAWRENCE TO TILDEN

"OCHRE POINT, NEWPORT, *May 26, 1877.*

"DEAR MR. PRESIDENT,—I write to remind you, before you contract any engagements elsewhere, of your promise to pass here so much of the summer as may be agreeable to you. I have only my two unmarried sons with me; and I shall be most happy to place my house at the disposition of yourself and friends. If the ladies are willing to encounter the inconvenience of a bachelor's establishment, it would give me great pleasure to receive them. I shall be ready for you at any time that you may name.

"I was glad to learn from a long letter, which I had a few days ago from Judge Field, that the suggestion of which you spoke to Judge Clifford of a submission of the electoral vote to a more impartial tribunal than the Supreme Court, after the recent action of some of its members present, is seriously entertained with a hope of success, and I cannot but flatter myself that Blaine and his adherents, in order to divert the patronage from Hayes to be used against him in 1880, may be willing for such a change in the law of *Quo Warranto* as, through the action of Florida and Louisiana, may enable you to assume the title, with which I have ventured to address you, before the period named by Judge Clifford for the vindication of popular rights.

"I am, yours very truly,
"W. B. LAWRENCE."

THE NEW YORK "WORLD" AND JOHN BIGELOW (1877)

"A correspondent of the *World* called upon Mr. Bigelow at his residence at Highland Falls yesterday, and in the course of his visit the following conversation took place:

"REPORTER. Mr. Bigelow, I understand that you prepared the volume published by the Appletons, in December, 1877, called the *Presidential Counts*, and particularly the analytical introduction prefixed to it, containing what was deemed to be at the time a semi-official Democratic view of the precedents and practice of the government applicable to the counting of the Presidential vote. Also that you were in frequent communication with Mr. Tilden, and in complete possession of his views and purposes during that crisis.

"MR. BIGELOW. You are correctly informed, so far as that publication is concerned.

"REPORTER. You doubtless read the story related recently by Mr. Mines in the *World*, and derived by him from General Woodford.

"MR. BIGELOW. I saw that publication, and glanced over its contents.

"REPORTER. The *World* would like to know whether at any time under the then existing facts of the case, Mr. Tilden entertained any purpose of taking the oath of office as President of the United States?

"MR. BIGELOW. That question seems to me to have been fully answered by the analytical introduction about which you have inquired, and which in its general scope—though, of course, not in every detail nor in its particular expressions—may be supposed to represent the doctrines entertained by Mr. Tilden in common with the most eminent jurists and statesmen of the country. I do not undertake to speak for Mr. Tilden, or in any peculiar sense as his representative, but the very nature of the views expounded in the analytical introduction necessarily defined the cases in which it would have been lawful and proper for Mr. Tilden to have taken the oath of office as President, and by inevitable implication the cases in which it would have been unlawful and improper for him to have done so.

"There were two contingencies in which it would have been lawful and obligatory on Mr. Tilden to have taken the official oath as President:

"*First.* If Congress had performed its constitutional duty of counting the electoral votes, and had declared that Mr. Tilden was chosen by the electoral colleges.

"The two Houses of Congress have all the powers of verification of the electoral votes which the Constitution or the laws supply or allow. Nobody else in the Federal government has any such powers. This exclusive jurisdiction of the two Houses has been exercised without interruption from the beginning of the government. It is known to all those who come in contact with Mr. Tilden at this period that he concurred in this view of the powers and duties of the two Houses of Congress themselves to count the electoral vote. He was perfectly free and unreserving in the expression of his opinions on this subject.

"This contingency, however, never presented itself. Congress, before the time fixed by the law for counting the electoral votes, passed the Election bill wherein they substantially abdicated their powers, and enacted that the electoral commission should in the first instance make a count, and that its count should stand, unless overruled by the concurrent action of the two Houses. The electoral tribunal counted Mr. Tilden out, and counted in a man who was not elected. Congress did not overrule their count; consequently, the false count stood as law under the act of Congress.

"*Secondly.* The other contingency in which it would have been lawful and obligatory on Mr. Tilden to have taken the oath of office was, that the House of Representatives on the failure of a choice of President by the electoral colleges had itself proceeded to make the election, voting by States in the manner prescribed by the Constitution.

"This contingency, like the first one, never occurred.

"The House of Representatives has by the express language of the Constitution, jurisdiction, if no person has a majority of the electoral votes, to make the election itself.

"The right of the two Houses to count the electoral votes, and to declare that any person has a majority, is a matter of implication, precedent, and practice. But the right of the House of Representatives to supply the failure of a choice is a matter of positive and express constitutional provision. It is not only a right, but a duty. The provision is mandatory. The House is a witness in the opening of the certificates. It is an actor in counting the votes by its own tellers and in its presence.

"Having such means of knowledge as to the facts, enabling it to ascertain whether a choice has been made by the electoral colleges, it is also expressly vested with a power and duty to act exclusively and conclusively in the event that no person be found to have been chosen by a majority of the votes of those colleges. The House acquires jurisdiction by the fact specified in the Constitution. The assent of the Senate to the existence of that fact is nowhere prescribed or required. No judgment, certification, or act of any official body is interposed as a condition to the assuming of its jurisdiction by the House. When the House has once acted in such a case, no review of its action nor any appeal from its decision is provided for in the Constitution. It is difficult to see why the House in such a case, like all tribunals of original jurisdiction and subject to no appeal, is not the exclusive judge of the fact and the law on which its jurisdiction rests. It was the fear that the Senate might lead a resistance to the rightful judgment of the House, and that General Grant would sustain this revolutionary policy with the army and navy and the militia of the great States in which the Republicans had possession of the State Governments that deterred the assertion of the rights of the House of Representatives, and induced its vote for and acquiescence in the electoral commission.

"But without speculating upon causes or motives, one thing is certain. The House of Representatives did not elect Mr. Tilden in the manner prescribed by the Constitution. On the other hand, it did concur with the Senate in anticipating and preventing the contingency in which it might have had to act, and in providing beforehand an expedient which was to make its own action in supplying the failure of an election by the colleges impossible. It adopted the electoral law and went through all the forms of the electoral scheme. True, it afterwards passed a declaratory resolution condemning the action of the electoral commission, and asserting that Mr. Tilden had been duly elected. But the Constitution had not provided that a man should or could take office as President on a declaratory resolution of the House of Representatives. If that resolution could have had full effect to abrogate the electoral law which the House had assisted to enact it would have still been a nullity as an exercise of the constitutional power of the House to elect. It created no warrant of authority to Mr. Tilden to take the oath of office.

"I have been somewhat long in answering your question, because the matter is one of importance. I might have disposed of your question more briefly by simply saying that no contingency provided by the Constitution ever existed in which Mr. Tilden could lawfully or properly take the oath of office as President. The idea that Mr. Tilden ever thought of taking the oath of office illegally is, in my judgment, quite as preposterous as is the other idea that he would have omitted to take it if any contingency had arisen in which it was his right or duty to take it, or that any menace would have had the slightest influence in preventing his performing his whole obligations to the people. I will venture to say that if it had been his right and duty to take the oath, he would not have done so at the City Hall in New York surrounded by the forces which, according to Mr. Mines,

General Woodford pictured to his imagination, but at the Federal capital, even though he had known that he would be kidnapped or subjected to a drum-head court martial five minutes afterwards. It is doubtless true that revolutionary ideas were entertained by the hierarchy of office-holders in possession of the government. General Grant did utter menaces in published interviews, and did make a display of military force in Washington to overawe Congress. I presume this was a part of the system of intimidation for which he allowed himself to be used by the office-holders and which was intended to act upon public opinion through the fear of disturbance as well as upon Congress. But it is safe to say that whatever other effects they produced they did not prevent Mr. Tilden from taking the oath of office, which he never had any lawful authority to take, in the absence of such action on the part of the House of Representatives as would have fulfilled the conditions prescribed by the Constitution. The fear that he would do so, inducing the Republicans to swear their candidate into office privately on the Saturday previous to the commencement of the term of office besides repeating the ceremony at the inauguration, was born of a consciousness that causes the wicked to flee when no man pursueth. I was aware that about that time Mr. Tilden's home was besieged by emissaries of the press and the telegraph to know if the rumors to that effect which prevailed in Washington were true. This was a species of curiosity which, I believe, Mr. Tilden did not consider it any part of his duty to relieve."

A TALK WITH MR. TILDEN

[*From a Special Correspondent of the "World," July 17, 18—*]

"SEA GIRT, N. J., *July 16.*

"Governor Tilden, as some time ago announced in the *World*, will sail in the Cunard steamer *Scythia* Wednesday, and is to be accompanied by Secretary of State Bigelow. The trip is purely for recreation, and the travellers will not return until the middle of October. Mr. Tilden, therefore, will be absent from the country and State during what is expected to be the interesting fall campaign. The fact that Mr. Bigelow is to accompany him will perhaps satisfy the politicians and set at rest the question of his renomination as Secretary of State. I have learned while here, authoritatively, that Mr. Bigelow is not and will not be a candidate before the approaching State convention of New York for a renomination.

"Mr. Tilden is looking remarkably well, and declares himself to be very much improved in health by his sojourn at this pleasant resort. He said to me that his trip has no connection whatever with any business enterprise or railroad scheme, as has been announced without authority in some of the papers. As to the events which have happened since the Presidential election and the numerous wild rumors circulated in reference to his political intentions, Mr. Tilden talked very freely. In regard to the electoral commission, he said that he had never had any real confidence in the arbitration of a question where there was so much at stake by a body of that kind. That settlement, he said, involved not only the Presidency, but all the patronage and power of the Federal administration, together with all the schemes, plans, and jobs connected with it. The Republican party and the men who had managed it in the past were too anxious to retain the administration to yield any point in an arbitration. The result of the electoral commission, therefore, was what might have been expected considering the power and influence brought to bear upon the political majority of that body as finally constituted.

He furthermore never liked the scheme as a matter of principle, believing that the true direction of a Democratic appeal was not away from 369 representatives of the people towards fifteen individuals, and still less from fifteen individuals towards one to be selected necessarily with a large element of chance, not to say of trick and device. He thought there should rather have been an appeal from the 369 representatives to the 8,000,000 of voters through a new election. He was distrustful of the secrecy, celerity, and improvidence with which the arrangement was carried through and ushered into being. But the proposition appealed to the hopes of the business classes, which were anxious above all things for a settlement of almost any kind, at almost any price, and as it was presented by the unanimous report of the joint committee, it become the representative, and the only representative, of the public desire for peace.

"The events which are now attracting so much public attention in New Orleans and the disclosures which, perhaps, may follow, Mr. Tilden seemed to consider only as the logical outcome of the revolutionary acts of last fall and winter. 'In a government like ours,' he said, 'such fraudulent practices as were reported from New Orleans last November sooner or later must come to the light, and the guilty parties with their practices must be made known. It was so with the ring frauds in New York; it has been the case to a certain extent in Washington, and a like result will follow in New Orleans. It is against the natural course of events that deeds of this kind should ultimately fail of being brought to light in all their enormities.' All this was said with philosophic calmness and without any heat whatever.

"In regard to his own political future, Mr. Tilden had nothing to say except that he could not see any possible contingency which could induce him to be a candidate for or to seek an election to a seat in the United States Senate. He felt entirely confident of the success of the Democratic party this fall in all the large central States, and especially in New York, by a very large majority, believing that events were all pointing in that direction. To the charge that he has been seeking to control the nominations of the next Democratic State convention of New York, he gave a direct denial, and added that he thought it unwise to interfere in any way as between the numerous friends who are seeking position on the State ticket. His absence abroad during the time for holding the convention and selecting the delegates would, he said, preclude any interference on his part. He thought, however, that the drift of public sentiment was towards a new ticket altogether, with none of the present incumbents upon it. He hoped that the ticket would be so made up as to be recognized as thoroughly able, strong, and upright. He appeared to be specially anxious that the Democracy should secure a majority in the next State Senate, in order that the evils which have been brought about by Republican control of that body might be corrected.

H. C."

Mr. Tilden spent the summer of 1877 in Europe. On his return he was serenaded by the Young Men's Democratic Club, on which occasion he made a brief speech, in the course of which he said, according to the New York *Tribune* of October 26, 1877:

"The increase of power in the Federal government during the last twenty years, the creation of a vast office-holding class, with its numerous dependents, and the growth of the means of corrupt influence, have well nigh destroyed the balance of our complex system. It was my judgment in 1876 that public opinion, demanding a change of administration, needed to embrace two-thirds of the people at the beginning of the canvass, in order to cast a majority of the votes at the election. If this tendency is not arrested its inevitable result will be the practical destruction of our system. Let the Federal government grasp power over the great corporations of our country and acquire the means of addressing their interests and their fears; let it take jurisdiction of riots which it is the duty of the State to suppress; let it find pretexts for increasing the army, and soon those in possession of the government will have a power with which no opposition can successfully compete. The experience of France under the Third Napoleon shows that, with elective forms and universal suffrage, despotism can be established and maintained. In the canvass of 1876 the Federal government embarked in the contest with unscrupulous activity. A member of the Cabinet was the head of a partisan committee. Agents stood at the doors of the pay offices to exact contributions from official subordinates. The whole office-holding class were made to exhaust their power. Even the army, for the first time, to the disgust of the soldiers and many of the officers, was moved about the country as an electioneering instrument. All this was done under the eye of the beneficiary of it, who was making the air vocal with professions of civil service reform, to be begun after he had himself exhausted all the immoral advantages of civil service abuses. Public opinion in some States was overdone by corrupt influences and by fraud. But so strong was the desire for reform that the Democratic candidates received 4,300,000 suffrages. This was a majority of the popular vote of about 300,000, and of 1,250,000 of the white citizens. It was a vote of 700,000 larger than General Grant received in 1872, and 1,300,000 larger than he received in 1868. For all that, the rightfully elected candidates of the Democratic party were counted out, and a great fraud triumphed, which the American people have not condoned and will never condone.

[Prolonged applause and cheers.] Yes, the crime will never be condoned, and it never should be. I do not denounce the fraud as affecting my personal interests, but because it stabbed the very foundations of free government. [Loud cheers.] I swear in the presence of you all, and I call upon you to bear witness to the oath, to watch, during the remainder of my life, over the rights of the citizens of our country with a jealous care. Such a usurpation must never occur again, and I call upon you to unite with me in the defence of our sacred and precious inheritance. The government of the people must not be suffered to become only an empty name." [Loud applause.]

The remainder of Mr. Tilden's address was as follows:

"The step, from an extreme degree of corrupt abuses in the elections to a subversion of the elective system itself, is natural. No sooner was the election over than the whole power of the office-holding class, led by a Cabinet minister, was exhorted to procure, and did procure, from the State canvassers of two States, illegal and fraudulent certificates, which were made a pretext for a false count of the electoral votes. To enable these officers to exercise the immoral courage necessary to the parts assigned to them, and to relieve them from the timidity which God has implanted in the human bosom as a limit to criminal audacity, detachments of the army were sent to afford them shelter. The expedients by which the votes of the electors chosen by the people of these two States were rejected, and the votes of the electors having the illegal and fraudulent certificates were counted, and the menace of usurpation by the President of the Senate of dictatorial power over all the questions in controversy, and the menace of the enforcement of his pretended authority by the army and navy, the terrorism of the business classes and the kindred measures by which the false count was consummated, are known. The result is the establishment of a precedent destructive of our whole elective system. [Applause.] The temptation to those in possession of the government to perpetuate their own power by similar methods will always exist, and if the example shall be sanctioned by success, the succession of government in this country will come to be determined by fraud or force, as it has been in almost every other country; and the experience will be reproduced here which has led to the general adoption of the hereditary system in order to avoid confusion and civil war. The magnitude of a political crime must be measured by its natural and necessary consequences. Our great Republic has been the only example in the world of a regular and orderly transfer of governmental succession by the elective system. To destroy the habit of traditionary respect for the will of the people, as declared through the electoral forms, and to exhibit our institutions as a failure, is the greatest possible wrong to our own country. It is also a heavy blow to the hopes of patriots struggling to establish self-government in other countries. It is a greater crime against mankind than the usurpation of December 2, 1851, depicted by the illustrious pen of Victor Hugo. The American people will not condone it under any pretext or for any purpose. [Cheers.] Young men! in the order of nature, we who have guarded the sacred traditions of our free government will soon leave that work to you. Within the life of most who hear me, the Republic will embrace 100,000,000 of people. Whether its institutions shall be preserved in substance and in spirit, as well as in barren forms, and will continue to be a blessing to the toiling millions here and a good example to mankind, now everywhere seeking a larger share in the management of their own affairs, will depend on you. Will you accomplish that duty and mark these wrong-doers of 1876, with the indignation of a betrayed, wronged, and sacrificed people? [A voice—'You bet we will.' Laughter.] I have no personal feeling, but thinking how surely that example will be followed if condoned, I can do no better than to stand among you, and do battle for the maintenance of free government. I avail myself of the occasion to thank you, and to thank all in our State and country who have accorded to me their support, not personal to myself, but for the cause I have represented, and which has embraced the largest and holiest interests of humanity." [Continued applause.]

SOME OF THE SPECIFIC TEMPTATIONS BY WHICH THE ELECTORS OF LOUISIANA AND FLORIDA WERE DEBAUCHED

[*From the New York "Sun."*]

LOUISIANA

MEN CONNECTED WITH THE RETURNING BOARD.

Names.	*Political Employment in 1876.*	*Office Held Now.*
J. Madison Wells	President Returning Board	Surveyor Port of New Orleans
Thos. C. Anderson	Member Returning Board	Deputy Collector Port of New Orleans
L. M. Kenner	Member Returning Board	Deputy Naval Officer
G. Casanave	Member Returning Board	Brother of U. S. Storekeeper, N. O.
Chas. S. Abell	Secretary Returning Board	Inspector Custom House
York A. Woodward	Clerk Returning Board	Clerk Custom House
W. M. Green	Clerk Returning Board	Clerk Custom House
B. P. Blanchard	Clerk Returning Board	Clerk Custom House
G. P. Davis	Clerk Returning Board	Clerk Custom House
Chas. Hill	Clerk Returning	Clerk Custom House

	Board	
Geo. Grindley	Clerk Returning Board	Clerk Custom House
Jno. Ray	Counsel for Returning Board	Special Agent Treasury Department and Counsel for Mr. Sherman
S. S. Wells	Son of J. Madison Wells	Inspector Custom House
A. C. Wells	Son of J. Madison Wells	Special Deputy Surveyor, N. O.
F. A. Woolfley	Affidavit Taker	United States Commissioner
R. M. J. Kenner	Brother Returning Board Kenner	Clerk Naval Office

STATE OFFICERS AND MANAGERS.

Names.	*Political Employment in 1876.*	*Office Held Now.*
Michal Hahn	State Registrar	Superintendent Mint
A. J. Dumont	Chairman Republican State Com.	Inspector Custom House
J. P. McArdie	Clerk to Republican State Com.	Clerk Custom House
W. P. Kellogg	Governor	United States Senate
L. J. Souer	Kellogg's Agent to Buy Mem. of Leg.	Appraiser Custom House
W. G. Lane	Kellogg's Agent to Buy Mem. of Leg.	U. S. Commissioner Circuit Court, La.
S. B.	Candidate for Governor	Consul to Liverpool

Packard		
Geo. L. Smith	Candidate for Congress	Collector New Orleans
James Lewis	Police Commissioner, N. O.	Naval Officer
Jack Wharton	Adjutant-General of Louisiana	United States Marshal
A. S. Badger	General of State Militia	Postmaster, N. O., $3500; now Collec.
H. S. Campbell	Chief of Affidavit Factory	United States Attorney, Wyoming
H. Conquest Clark	Kellogg's Secretary (knew of forgery of Electoral Certificates)	Private Secretary to Commissioner Internal Revenue
Wm. F. Loan	Chief of Police and Supervisor of Fifteenth Ward, N. O.	Inspector Tobacco Internal Revenue
W. L. McMillan	Canvassed State for Hayes	Pension Agent New Orleans, now Postmaster

ELECTORS.

Names.	*Political Employment in 1876.*	*Office Held Now.*
W. P. Kellogg	Elector at Large	United States Senator
J. Henri Burch	Elector at Large	State Senator
Peter Joseph	Elector	Clerk Custom House
L. A. Sheldon	Elector	Counsel for John Sherman
Morris Marks	Elector	Collector Internal Revenue
A. B. Levisee	Elector	Special Agent Treasury

		Department
O. H. Brewster	Elector	Surveyor-General

SUPERVISORS AND PERSONS CONNECTED WITH THE ELECTION

Names.	*Political Employment in 1876.*	*Office Held Now.*
M. J. Grady	Supervisor at Ouachita	Deputy Collector Internal Revenue
Jno. H. Dinkgrave	Manager at Ouachita	Legislature
H. C. C. Astwood	Manager at Ouachita (knew Garfield)	Deputy United States Marshal
W. R. Hardy	District Attorney at Ouachita	Inspector Custom House
Henry Smith	Sheriff of East Feliciana	Laborer Custom House
Samuel Chapman	Sheriff of East Feliciana	Laborer Custom House
Jas. E. Anderson	Supervisor of East Feliciana	Declined Consulship to Funchal
C. L. Ferguson	Supervisor of De Soto	Captain Night Watch Custom House
J. E. Scott	Supervisor of Claiborne	Money Order Postoffice, N. O.
B. W. Woodruff	Supervisor of Rapides	Box Clerk Postoffice, N. O.
L. F. Baughnon	Supervisor of East Baton Rouge	Laborer Custom House
W. H. McVey	Supervisor of Franklin	Inspector Custom House

L. Williams	Supervisor of 16th Ward, N. O.	Watchman Custom House
E. K. Russ	Supervisor of Natchitoches	Letter Carrier Postoffice
F. A. Desionde	Supervisor of Iberville	Night Watchman Custom House
W. H. Heistand	Supervisor of Tangipahoa	Clerk Custom House
F. A. Clover	Supervisor of East Baton Rouge	Assistant Weigher Custom House
L. C. Lesage	Clerk to Supervisor of East Baton Rouge	Inspector Custom House
Wm. McKenna	Supervisor of Caddo	Postmaster Shreveport
A. D. Cornog	Supervisor of Red River	Inspector Custom House
M. A. Lenet	Supervisor of Lafourche	Laborer Custom House
Victor Gerodias	Republican Manager of St. Tammany	Tax Collector, N. O.
A. J. Brim	Republican Manager of 2d Ward, N. O.	Inspector Custom House
Patrick Creagh	Republican Manager 3d Ward, N. O.	Chief Laborer
R. C. Howard	Republican Manager 4th Ward, N. O.	Laborer Custom House
J. C. Peuchler	Republican Manager 5th Ward, N. O.	Laborer Custom House
W. J. Moore	Republican Manager 7th Ward, N. O.	Gauger Internal Revenue
Thomas Leon	Republican Manager 8th Ward, N. O.	Gauger Custom House

T. H. Rowan	Republican Manager 10th Ward, N. O.	Night Inspector Custom House
A. W. Kempton	Commissioner of the 11th Ward, N. O.	Assistant Weigher Custom House
L. Backus	Manager of 11th Ward, N. O.	Police
Napoleon Underwood	Supervisor of 12th Ward, N. O.	Inspector Internal Revenue
P. J. Maloney	Supervisor of 14th Ward, N. O.	Inspector Custom House
L. E. Salles	Republican Manager of Lafayette	Weigher Custom House
R. A. Herbert	Republican Manager of Iberville	Superintendent Warehouses Custom House
W. B. Dickey	Republican Manager and Tax Collector, Madison	Inspector Custom House
Thomas Jenk	Husband to Mrs. Jenks, who swore for John Sherman.	Clerk Mint

FLORIDA

VARIOUS DOMESTIC OFFICERS AND AGENTS.

Names.	*Political Employment in 1876.*	Office Held Now.
M. L. Stearns	Governor	Commissioner Hot Springs
F. C. Humphries	Elector	Collector Pensacola
S. B. McLin	Member of Returning Board	Associate Justice of New Mexico (not confirmed)

Moses J. Taylor	Clerk Circuit Court Jefferson County	Clerk United States Land Office
Joseph Bowes	Inspector Leon County	Clerk Treasury Department
W. K. Cessna	Judge Alachua County	Postmaster
R. H. Black	Inspector Elections Alachua County	Philadelphia Custom House
Geo. H. DeLeon	Secretary to Gov. Stearns	Clerk in Treasury Department
John Varnum	Adjutant General	Receiver Land Office
Chas. H. Pearce	Elector	
James Bell	Changed tickets, Jefferson County	Timber Agent
Manuel Govin	Republican Manager of Monroe	Consul to Spezia
—— Phelps	Political Manager	Secretary to McCormick at Paris Exposition
E. W. Maxwell	Detective in employ of Republican Visiting Statesmen	Lieutenant in Regular Army
P. G. Mills	Telegrapher who gave news about Democratic dispatches	Treasury Department
W. G. Purman	Republican Member of Congress	Sister in Treasury, dismissed when he said he considered Tilden elected
Dennis	Chairman Republican	Timber Agent

Eagan	State Com.	
L. G. Denni	Republican Manager of Alachua	Treasury Department. Removed and published affidavit
J. W. Howell	Manager false return from Baker	Collector Fernandino

VISITING STATESMEN.

John Sherman	Visiting Statesman, La.	Secretary Treasury
John M. Harlan	Visiting Statesman, La.	Justice Supreme Court
Stanley Matthews	Visiting Statesman, La.	Senator from Ohio
James A. Garfield	Visiting Statesman, La.	Administration candidate for Speaker
Eugene Hale	Visiting Statesman, La.	Offered Postmaster-Generalship
E. W. Stoughton	Visiting Statesman, La.	Minister to Russia
John A. Kasson	Visiting Statesman, La.	Minister to Austria
Samuel Shellabarger	Visiting Statesman, La.	Messrs. Hayes and Sherman's Private Counsel
John Coburn	Visiting Statesman, La.	Commissioner Hot Springs
E. F. Noyes	Visiting Statesman, La.	Minister to France
Lew Wallace	Visiting Statesman, La.	Governor of New Mexico

John Little	Visiting Statesman, La.	Attorney-General, Ohio

The following officers of the Government were in Florida during the Presidential canvass, drawing their regular salaries, looking after the canvass:

Thomas J. Brady	Second Assistant Postmaster-General
—— Peyton	Assistant in Attorney-General's Office
H. Clay Hopkins	Special Agent Postoffice Department
Wm. Henderson	Special Agent Postoffice Department
Z. L. Tidball	Special Agent Postoffice Department
B. H. Camp	Special Agent Postoffice Department

SPECIAL AGENT

Wm. M. Evarts	Secretary of State

The sum total per annum which these men who counted Hayes in receive is $254,115, which will amount in the four years that Hayes must remain *de facto* President to $1,022,460.

STEPHEN J. FIELD TO TILDEN

"WASHINGTON, *Dec. 11, 1877.*

"DEAR SIR,—I did not forget, on my return to Washington, the promise I made in New York to send you the copy I have of Judge Bradley's letter explaining his action on the electoral commission, but for some days I could not find it. Having now found it, I enclose it to you, and also an extract from an article which appeared in the Newark *Daily Advertiser* about the same time, and to which the judge evidently refers in his letter.

"The language of the letter[21] justifies some of the comments of the press upon the change of views which the judge experienced shortly before the vote was taken in the Florida case.

I am, very sincerely yours,
"STEPHEN J. FIELD."

DOCUMENTS REFERRED TO IN JUDGE FIELD'S LETTER

[*Justice Bradley to the Newark "Daily Advertiser" and the Electoral Commission.*]

The *Sun* gives Bradley's letter in full as follows:

"'STOWE, VT., *September 6.*

"'EDITOR "ADVERTISER."

"'SIR,—I perceive the New York *Sun* has reiterated its charge that after preparing a written opinion in favor of the Tilden electors in the Florida case and submitting it to the electoral commission, I changed my views during the night preceding the vote in consequence of the pressure brought to bear upon me by Republican politicians and the Pacific Railroad men, whose carriages, it is said, surrounded my house during the evening. This, I believe, is the important point of the charge. Whether I wrote one opinion or twenty in my private examination of the subject, is of little consequence and of no concern to anybody. The opinion which I finally gave was the result of my deliberations without influence from outside parties. The above slander was published some time since, but I never saw it until recently, and deemed it too absurd to need refutation. But as it is categorically repeated, perhaps I ought to notice it. The same story about the carriages of leading Republicans and others congregating about my house was circulated in Washington at one time, and came to the ears of my family only to raise a smile of contempt. The whole thing is a falsehood. Not one visitor called at my house that evening, and during the whole sitting of the commission I had no private discussion whatever of the subjects at issue with any person interested on the Republican side, and but few words with any persons. Indeed, I zealously sought to avoid all discussion outside the commission itself. The allegation that I read my opinion to Judges Clifford and Field is entirely untrue. I read no opinion to either of them, and have no recollection of expressing one; if I did, it could only have been suggestively, or in a hypothetical manner, and not for committal of my final judgment or action. The question was one of great importance to me, of much difficulty and embarrassment. I earnestly endeavored to come to a right decision, free from all political or extraneous considerations. In my private examination of the principal question, about going behind the returns, I wrote and rewrote the arguments and considerations on both sides as they occurred to me, sometimes being inclined to one view of the subject and sometimes to the other, but finally I threw aside these lucubrations, and as you have rightly stated, wrote out a short opinion, which I read in the Florida case during the sitting of the commission. This decision expresses the conviction to which I had arrived, and which after a full consideration of the whole subject seemed to me a satisfactory solution of the questions; and I may say that the more I have reflected since, the more satisfied have I become that it was right. At all events, it was the result of my own reflections and consideration, without any suggestions from any quarter, except the arguments adduced by counsel in the public discussion and by members of the commission in private consultation. As for the insinuation contained in a recent article published in a prominent periodical by a noted politician, implying that the case was decided in consequence of political conspiracy, I can only say that from the peculiar position I occupied on the commission I am able positively to say that it is utterly devoid of truth, at least, so far as the action of the commission itself was concerned. In that article the writer couples my name with the names of those whom he supposes are obnoxious to the public odium. The decencies of public expression, if nothing more, might well have deterred so able a writer from making personal imputations which he did not know to be well founded.

"'Yours respectfully,
"'JOSEPH P. BRADLEY.'

"NEW YORK, *September 6th.*

"The *Sun* regards Bradley's letter as a confession, and calls for his impeachment.

"JUDGE BRADLEY HEARD FROM

"An explanation has at last been offered in behalf of Judge Bradley respecting his alleged misconduct as a member of the electoral commission. It is found in the columns of the Newark *Daily Advertiser*, a journal with which he is known to maintain relations of unusual intimacy, and is in the following language:

> "'It is just as well that the full fact should be known as a matter of history. Judge Bradley had already decided, in the Florida case, that he could not go behind the returns of the State officials. In the Louisiana case, he finally, and, after anxious thought, held to the same opinion, but of two sets of returns he chose the one he thought most authentic and legal. That elected Hayes. As to the doubt whether Judge Bradley could have prepared a written opinion on one side while he was expressing different opinions orally on the other, the facts are worth telling, and we dare to assert them without any other authorization than our challenge that they cannot be contradicted. The morning before the opinion was given, Senator Edmunds had guessed out Judge Bradley's decision, but he did not know it. Up to that time, as we understand, the opinions delivered had been oral. There may have been one or two exceptions. At the session next day, Senator Edmunds whispered to Judge Bradley that as the opinion he was to give was to be decisive, it ought to be in writing. The argument had not then closed. Bradley accepted the suggestion, and, sitting at his place, dashed down the decision on paper within an hour, in the presence and during the debate of his colleagues. He was subsequently urged to enlarge the argument, but it stands in the printed report just as it was then written. And therefore Judge Field is very correct in saying that Judge Bradley did not, at any time before, "read" to him an opinion.'"

H. F. TYLDEN TO TILDEN

"CUMBERLAND HOUSE, CHILHAM, N. CANTERBURY, *26th March* (*1878?*).

"MY DEAR GOVERNOR,—I sent you the fly-leaf of an old Bible, in my possession, the year after you left England. It was scribbled over with the word 'Catts' in different places, and had the names of several Tyldens—John, Richard, and Henry and a Mary. The Bible was published in 1559. I was sent the accompanying rude verse, which is supposed, in the last line, to refer to the change in the spelling of the name Tylden, and Catts is again mentioned, as if it were the home from which the Tyldens said 'Good-by' when they were going across the water. I have painted the writing over, as it was so indistinct. A man living in Ashford had it in an old receipt-book. I wonder if that house we went to see near Tenterden could have been Catts? There is a farm called Cat's Farm quite close here, but I don't think it can be the one alluded to, though Sir John Fagge, whose palace adjoins Chilham Park originally spelt the name Fogge (or rather his ancestors did), and evidently the book of receipts originally belonged to some one of that name. We hope your party arrived quite safely in New York. Some day I shall ask you to send me all their photographs, as we wish to get all the Tildens and Tyldens in a book together.

"Katie was thought like one of your nieces by some of the people here who saw them walk up the village. I don't know which it was. Dick is still quartered at Woolwich; he was at home for three weeks lately, and Katie much enjoyed riding about with him. We are now having a little winter, snow falling. I am suffering from inflammation of the eyes. The state of Ireland is a great worry to me for many reasons. I can't tell you how we always think of you, and wonder if we shall meet again.

"I should very much like to send you the Bible of which I sent you the fly-leaf. I think it might be interesting to you. Messrs. Morgan were your agents when you were here. I might find out from them how to send it. Katie joins me in love and kind remembrances to your nieces.

"Believe me to be, dear Governor.

"Very sincerely yours,
"H. F. TYLDEN."

(Enclosure.)

"Kentish Tyldens like to ratts
Have crossed water fleeing Catts

Lo, every ratt that said Good-bye
Has turned a tail into an eye.

"J. FOGGE,
1713."

"*Halden.*

GENERAL WILLIAM PRESTON TO S. J. TILDEN

"LEXINGTON, KY., *30 March, 1878.*

"MY DEAR GOVERNOR,—The kindness and interest you have shown towards my son in New York are very deeply felt by me, apart from the great aid you gave him in commencing his life in an untried field. Through your influence he has commenced his career under excellent auspices, but I can readily discern from our correspondence that the social and fashionable attractions of the city can have left him but little time for reading and work. This he tells me very frankly in his letters, but I have indulged in no long admonitions or remonstrances, because you must give a young horse head sometimes to keep him to the course. As I know you have equestrian tastes, you must pardon my illustration. But whilst I observe this plan, I do not wish my son to run with a loose rein nor swerve from the course. I know he has honor, truth, and courage, and I hope he will be a true gentleman and useful citizen in after life. Although wealth and distinction in the intellectual world are desirable, they are not, to my mind, paramount objects. I was brought up with old-fashioned ideas that honest military renown and oratorical distinction were first, and rather inclined to the thought '*Ratio ab oratio sunt arma hominis acutiora ferro*,' but it seems that taste is not hereditary; or, at least, I fear it is not. The course he is pursuing is rather in obedience to my own advice than his inclinations.

"But I sat down to write only a few lines of thanks to you, and I am trespassing on your time. Wickliffe writes me that he will be with you, or at your house, on Monday, and if you can write me a few lines so that I may know how he is getting along in New York, you would confer upon me a great personal favor.

"I pray you to present my kind remembrances to your sister Mrs. Pelton and to the ladies, and to believe me.

"Very truly and sincerely,
"Your friend,
"W. PRESTON."

WHITELAW REID TO S. J. TILDEN

"23 PARK AVE., *April 4, 1878.*

"DEAR GOVERNOR,—I want you to advise me in a matter which interests you, since you have promised to come to my dinner to Bayard Taylor at the Union League Club on the evening of the 10th inst. I invited Mr. O'Conor, and am sure, from the tone of his reply, that he would like to come. He declines, however, basing the refusal on the belief that I cannot, and ought not, keep the entertainment private, and that he is anxious for the remainder of his days to avoid any agency in public displays.

"You know him so well that you can tell me in a word whether it would be discreet for me to write again endeavoring to remove his objection. The dinner is to be limited to about twenty (the table will only seat twenty-five), and I am not going, under any circumstances, to admit any reporter. It will be absolutely as private as it is ever possible to have anything of this sort.

"Mr. O'Conor's letter is so evidently sincere in tone, and I have been so desirous, anyway, to have him present, that I venture to ask your advice as to whether I should try again.

"Forgive the bother, and believe me

"Very truly yours,
"WHITELAW REID."

TILDEN TO HON. CHARLES CAREY

"NEW YORK, WEDNESDAY MORNING, *June 5th, 1878.*

"DEAR MR. CAREY,—I received your telegram late last evening, and answer by mail because the telegraph is leaky.

"My appreciation of Mr. Henderson has been so manifest that I need not say how competent I deem him, or that he may fairly be classed among those from whom a choice is to be made.

"But I am totally uninformed of the views of Governor Robinson. He may, for aught I know, have a purpose already formed; and he is always independent and persistent. I think it would be advisable for you to learn the situation as fully as possible before making our friend a candidate, whom you do not wish to expose to a failure. Perhaps you had better go down to Albany quietly and get what information you can. The attempts of the Republican press, when Governor Robinson first came in, to create an impression (utterly unfounded in fact, as everybody who knows his independent, self-poised, and firm nature must see) that he occupied to me a relation of dependence, was intended to wound him and his friends, as well as to misrepresent me; and induced me to adopt the rule of not recommending anybody, or anything to him, of my own motion, or unless he had occasion to consult me, which he seldom, if ever, has any need to do. Under that rule of delicacy and respect, I am less advised of his ideas than might be supposed.

"Very truly yours,
S. J. TILDEN."

S. S. COX TO TILDEN

"HOUSE OF REPRESENTATIVES,
"WASHINGTON, D. C., *June 17th, 1878.*

"DEAR SIR,—In rummaging over and burning up the documents which have accumulated through twenty years' service, I found your old pamphlet, which gave to me many lessons during our perilous days before and during the war. Thinking that it might be of more interest to you now than to one who has learned it by heart, and knowing how valuable, after many years, are one's own thoughts for memory and suggestion, I cannot refrain from tendering it to you—if only for a retrospect. It may be more useful to you than to myself.

"We are just closing up the long session. You will see by my last vote, all alone from New York—though for one, if alone—I would never consent to quiet bad title, even though technically legal. The worst things that I have ever known in public life have been statutory.

"If ever the devil took a walk upon earth, according to Coleridge's poem, he took more delight in seeing a bad lawyer cheating by *statute* than by any other mode.

"Yours with respect,
S. S. COX."

"P. S.—Excuse the *mutilations*; you can see that I have used the pamphlet in various ways and at various times. The clippings are significant.

"*Vide*: 'Logical result after disunion—'

"P. S.—This is an interesting as well as curious coincidence, and will please you, I am sure; so I have told Mr. Cox to let his friendly and charming letter go to its destination. As I wrote you on Friday, Keith was the only speaker on the right side—but there were some staunch men who stood by him. I shall get to see you Wednesday morning, when I shall hope to be able to make our visit to Mr. O'Conor.

Sincerely,
H. W."

ARPHAXED LOOMIS TO TILDEN

"LITTLE FALLS, *August 4, 1878.*

"HON. S. J. TILDEN,—I write to express to you the gratification I have felt on reading the *exposé* in this morning's *Argus*, by Mr. Marble, of your opinions and course in respect to the memorable arbitration for the Presidency. The common sense of public opinion pointed in the same direction. Moral courage and firmness from the start in the House would most certainly have secured a just result.[22] The perpetrators of the wicked fraud would have cowed. If Grant's military *penchant* had brought in the use of arms, the rash resort and its consequences would be for the other side to answer for. But timid counsels prevailed. Your friends consented to arbitrate whether your coat belonged to you or to Mr. Hayes—they had, moreover, the weakness to confide in the fair professions of the other side, so far as to give them a majority of the arbitrators.

"I am glad to learn by Mr. Marble's *exposé* that you gave no assent to the arbitration, but took your stand upon the true legal and constitutional ground. And in this expression I believe a great many of your friends concur. When the decision was made, by a tribunal appointed by law, it was too late to revolt. Concurrence was then the only manly course.

Sincerely yours,
"ARPHAXED LOOMIS."

TILDEN TO THE DIRECTORS OF THE LOUISVILLE INDUSTRIAL EXPOSITION

"NEW YORK, *Aug. 25, '78.*

"GENTLEMEN,—It would give me the greatest pleasure if I were able to attend the exposition to which you do me the honor to invite me.

"I am not a stranger to the excellence of the agricultural industries of Kentucky. I have derived from them the favorite horses which I have used for out-of-door exercise, and should be delighted to see the best specimens of the Kentucky stock in the beautiful region where they were nurtured.

"Two months ago I returned from a brief visit of rest and recreation to the British Isles. I brought with me a vivid impression of the yet unappreciated value of the cereal products of the Mississippi Valley. I felt thankful that we have a sun in our heavens which, in the season of agricultural growth, pours down daily floods of light and warmth, making the earth prolific, giving abundance and variety of fruits, assuring the wheat crop, yielding cotton in its zone, and ripening corn everywhere, even to the verge of the farthest north. Take, for instance, the single product of Indian corn which forms one of the staples of Kentucky. It is the most natural and spontaneous of our cereal products. It ought to give in our country an annual yield of 1,500,000 bushels, or three times the whole wheat crop. It is little inferior to wheat in nutrition, and costs less than one-half on the seaboard and much less than one-half on the farm. It can be cooked by those who consent to learn how, into many delicious forms of human food. It is the most valuable sustenance of animal life. It ought to become the basis of an immense traffic with the British Isles, where the scantiness and economy of food strikes the American traveller, with the contrast to the immense abundance and wasteful consumption of our own people.

"Almost as I write, I notice a late statement that the exports of our country for the year past have been nearly $250,000,000 in excess of our imports. This result is mainly due to the development of our agricultural industries. It is a cheering indication that amid the pressure and distress we are laying the foundation of a new and real prosperity by the energies of our farmers.

"I regret that involuntary engagements render it impossible that, on the present occasion, I should be a personal witness of the attainments of our agricultural industries."

TILDEN AND A "WORLD" REPORTER

(WHY HE DID NOT TAKE THE OATH AS PRESIDENT)

"*1878-9.*

"Last Friday evening a reporter of the *World* visited Mr. Tilden in his Gramercy Park mansion, and was accorded a brief interview in the commodious and well-appointed library of that distinguished gentleman. Mr. Tilden looked well, and conversed with all his old-time fire and interest.

"'Of course, I have come to see you by instructions respecting the story that General Woodford related to Mr. Mines, and that the latter gentleman has related to the public through the *World*.'

"'I have not read it through. A friend told me of its substance this morning while I was down-town. But I am averse to talking about these insignificant matters.'

"'Nothing can be insignificant, Mr. Tilden, that concerns your relations to the Presidency or its relations to the public. What the *World* mainly wishes to know is whether or not you at any time purposed taking the oath as President.'

"'At any time'—musingly. 'Certainly, if the House had declared me elected. Then I should have had a certificate—a title. But after the electoral scheme, which I always opposed, was complete—although advised that I might so as to raise the question—I never for a moment entertained the idea of taking the oath of office either in Washington or in New York or elsewhere. It would have been ridiculous. I have no evidence of title then—no claim—no warrant.'

"'Then you do not believe General Grant intended to arrest or detain you?'

"'How can I tell what General Grant intended? All I can tell you is what I intended as the representative of the people who, by nearly half a million majority on the popular vote, elected me their President.'

"'Is there anything more in the story you would wish to speak of?'

"'I have not thoroughly read it. Besides, as the pivot of the story is my intention to challenge an issue by taking the oath of office, is not the story substantially disposed of when I tell you that there is no real pivot?'"

WILLIAM ALLEN BUTLER TO TILDEN

"TRINITY BUILDING, NEW YORK, *June 23d, 1879.*

"MY DEAR GOVERNOR TILDEN,—I was very glad to find that no obstacle presented itself in the way of your completing the arrangement for hiring Mr. Waring's place at Yonkers, and the prospect of numbering you and your household among our residents is a very gratifying one to me. I have lived nearly fourteen years in my little suburban home there, and am satisfied that I have warded off serious dangers to my own health and that of my family by the change from city to semi-country life. I believe Yonkers to be in every respect the most desirable suburb of New York, and I trust you will conclude to purchase Mr. Waring's property on which I know a vast sum has been well expended. I hired my house when I first went to Yonkers, but in less than sixty days bought it, in the belief that whether I remained or not it was a safe property, and I have never regretted the purchase.

"Hoping to see you soon in our neighborhood,

"I am, yours sincerely,
WM. ALLEN BUTLER."

For some time previous to the receipt of the foregoing note, Mr. Tilden had been encouraged by his medical advisers to provide himself with a country home conveniently accessible from the city, where he would secure as many hygienic advantages from its situation as possible. He had been assisted by Mr. Trevor, himself an old resident at Yonkers, in selecting a property in that city which was for sale, and bore the name destined to become famous—"Graystone." He leased it at first, but before his lease expired completed the purchase of it. To the original purchase, he added several adjoining properties in subsequent years. The cost of his purchases and improvements at Yonkers may be stated with sufficient precision as follows, and possesses a certain historic interest:

ESTIMATE OF COST OF PROPERTY AT YONKERS

1879.	Original Purchase:		
June 25.	To cash paid Mutual Life Insurance Co	$3,000 00	
Sept. 4.	To cash paid Mutual Life Insurance Co	119,162 26	
Sept. 5.	To cash paid taxes	12,544 77	
Sept. 5.	To cash paid J. F. Waring	3,500 00	
Sept. 5.	To cash paid J. F. Waring	11,792 97	—$150,000 00
Improvement (?)			48,208 91
Baldwin Property, purchase			55,198 40
Baldwin Property, improvements			546 02
Clark Property, purchase			12,266 38
Other plot			10,521 10
Forward			$276,779 81

Carried forward	$276,779 81

Work on Greenhouse:

Lord Hort Mfg. Co.	$49,611 50	
Stewart, mason	635 83	
Plumbing, painting, concreting, etc.	685 12	
Labor, blasting, and digging	4,696 21	
Supplies, chairs, bedding, etc.	102 87	—55,731 53
Wall in front of Greenhouse		945 62
Gardener's Cottage		3,045 88
Farmer's Cottage		6,849 38
Additions to barn		703 27
Plumbing		18,964 55
Allowance Stone Stable		1,500 00
Furniture		19,269 05
Furniture Baldwin House		1,600 00
Plants in Greenhouse	8,901 89	
Plants outside	75 25	—8,977 14
		$394,327 23

JOHN BIGELOW TO HON. WILLIAM H. PECK, EX-SECRETARY OF STATE OF MICHIGAN

"NEW YORK, *Febry. 28th, 1879.*

"MY DEAR FRIEND,—In your last note you ask me if Tilden will be in the field for the Presidency in 1880.

"That is a question which, I presume, no one, not even Tilden himself, could answer categorically at present. I can express to you my own conviction, and you may take it for what it is worth.

"Mr. Tilden has scarcely been in a position at any time, since the election, to consult his own tastes or personal comfort in this matter; if he had been, I think he would have notified his friends immediately upon his return from Europe in 1877 that they must look for another leader. He forbore to take that step, because he shared the popular belief that he was the President-elect of the United States, and that he was thereby clothed with certain responsibilities to his party at least, anomalous and unprecedented it is true, but which were of the gravest character and which it was impossible for him to put off.

"He was still the commander in the midst of a campaign in which he had defeated the enemy, but had not yet realized the fruits of victory. To leave his soldiers in the field and in the presence of the enemy without a leader was a step which would not stand the test of a moment's reflection. Washington could, with equal propriety, have resigned his command after the battle at Yorktown and delivered his sword to Cornwallis, instead of himself taking the sword of the British general.

"Such a procedure on Mr. Tilden's part would have practically disarmed the Democratic party and compelled its surrender at discretion. What in 1877 would have been only compromising subsequent events would now make disgraceful. Conscious that they had come into office by criminal processes, and that Tilden was the choice of the people, the administration has exerted all the powers of the Federal government in the effort to reconcile the country with this result by defaming and maligning the character of Mr. Tilden, and persecuting him, if possible, out of public life.

"In the latter purpose, they would probably have succeeded had Mr. Tilden been a poor man, and dependent upon his profession for his daily bread.

"Mr. Tilden could easily accommodate himself to the choice of any good man for the Presidency, for it is no vulgar ambition which has led him to accept the prominence which his party has given him, but he cannot be expected to make the slightest concession that involves his personal honor. He will defend that as long as he has a drop of blood in his body, whoever may stand by him or desert him. Of this you may feel perfectly assured.

"Now, I do not see how it is possible for Tilden, under the circumstances, to withdraw from the canvass for 1880; and just so far as it seems impossible for him to withdraw, it seems impossible for his party to assent to his withdrawal.

"There are three questions which must take precedence of every other in the next national convention.

"1. Was Tilden elected by the people in 1876?

"2. Was Hayes counted in by corrupt and fraudulent means?

"3. Has Tilden done anything since the election to forfeit the confidence of his party or of the nation?

"Its answer to these three questions will exercise a controlling influence over its final action.

"On the proofs already in the possession of Congress, I venture to say that there could not be found a jury of twelve disinterested and unbiased freeholders in the land who would hesitate to hold—-

"*First.* That Tilden was elected President by the people.

"*Second.* That he was deprived of the office by fraud; and,

"*Third.* That the charges of attempting to purchase electoral votes are not only not proven, but that they are the foul offspring of the most ruffianly and rancorous partisanship.

"To take another candidate in 1880 is to admit that Tilden was never the choice either of his party or of the country, and that he was unworthy of the support of either. It is to sanction the base conspiracy by which the people were defrauded of their choice. It is to lie down under the degrading imputations by which, through Tilden, the conspirators have sought to humiliate and demoralize his party.

"Can you believe for a moment that the Democratic party is or can be reduced to such extremities?

"The calumnies which have been propagated against Tilden will rather strengthen than weaken him as a candidate if renominated. They will be fatal to any other candidate, and for the obvious reason that any other candidate would have to contend with the practical admission of his party that it had presented and supported a candidate at the last Presidential election who was unworthy of its own or the country's confidence, and whom they had in consequence deliberately abandoned.

"Such an admission would be fatal, and the more surely fatal both because it would be an act of the most flagrant injustice to Mr. Tilden, and because the responsibility for such an act of political brutality would be directly traceable to the unreasonable ambition of men whose first duty it should be to sustain and defend him.

"It is, therefore, a vital necessity for the party to vindicate itself no less than Mr. Tilden, while to desert him would be as much more disastrous to the former as the interests of a nation are greater than those of any individual citizen however eminent.

"I do not think there are many people in the Democratic party so dull as not to see this, or so wanting in loyalty to a brave and successful leader as not to feel that they themselves will have to suffer most by deserting the man who has endured three years of unparalleled persecution rather than desert them.

"To you I need not dwell upon other obvious reasons for renominating Tilden—I need not remind you of what he has done for the Democratic party during the last fifty years, and especially since 1874; I need not tell you how he has stood and stands to-day, like Saul in Israel, a head and shoulders above all his countrymen as a statesman and party-leader; of the impossibility of our carrying his native State for any other candidate whose nomination must of necessity be an insult to him and to it; of the vast power and promise treasured up in the political personality, which for several years has enjoyed the distinction of concentrating upon itself the hostility and malignity of all those classes and parties which it has always been the paramount effort and duty of the Democracy to subdue or to exterminate.

"Independent of these obvious, though on that account none the less important, considerations, and looking solely to the special questions which for the first time in our history will confront the next national Democratic convention, I do not see how it can hesitate to renominate Mr. Tilden by acclamation unless he refuses to be a candidate. Nor do I see how, under the circumstances, he can refuse to be a candidate. I have never heard him express any determination upon the subject, but I think it safe to presume that if he had not intended to be a candidate again he would have purchased the peace and repose which such an announcement would have procured him long before this, and when such a step was beset with fewer difficulties than at present.

"That I have not incorrectly interpreted the drift of public sentiment on this subject, I send you a copy of the Albany *Argus* containing five or six columns of extracts from the leading Democratic journals of nearly every State in the Union. They show how much more logically the people generally are reasoning upon the subject than many who aspire to lead them. These journals, as you will see, almost unanimously recognize not only the expediency, but the necessity of renominating Mr. Tilden. Yours faithfully,

JOHN BIGELOW."

"*Hon. William H. Peck.*

The universal conviction that Mr. Tilden was going to receive the votes of the nation for President in 1876 compelled Mr. Hayes, or his official dependents in Washington, to begin, in the fall of that year, a campaign of defamation against the one who promised to become General Grant's inevitable successor.

Mr. Tilden's public services and character, and the expressions of popular favor with which the press was teeming, left the administration no resource but calumny.

The prosperity which he had enjoyed in the prosecution of his profession during the years succeeding the election of Mr. Lincoln to the Presidency inspired the suspicion that he had become a man of far greater wealth than he had yet realized; and through the control which the administration could exert over the machinery of the Federal courts, they hit upon the device of charging him with giving false reports of his income to their officers.

Without any proof except their corrupt suspicions, they directed the United States District Attorney at New York to institute proceedings for the recovery of the income supposed to have been illegally withheld. By such a proceeding they not only expected to subject Mr. Tilden to enormous expense in reproducing records of his professional income reaching back fifteen or twenty years, but to hold him up, in the press, at least, until after the election or his retirement from public life, as a defaulter to the government and as a perjurer in his returns of his professional earnings.

This suit moved along very leisurely, but actively enough to keep the subject and the victim of it before the public during the election. Later on they realized that its partisan uses not only had not been exhausted, but were more important than ever to them; for the fraudulent means by which Mr. Tilden had been deprived of the office to which he was elected made him apparently the inevitable candidate to succeed Mr. Hayes.

In due time the weakness of their machinations could no longer be concealed, and in the winter of 1878 they were obliged to confess that they never had any testimony on which to go to trial in support of their caluminous allegations; but to keep the charge alive in the servile prints of the administration, they filed a "bill of discovery" to extort from Tilden himself proof of their infamous charges. It was in consequence of this aggravating persecution that Mr. Tilden invited Mr. O'Conor to assist in his defence, which led to the following correspondence.

The history of this vexatious and vicious prosecution will be found in ample detail from its initiation, in 1876, to the government's ignominious retreat, in 1882, in the *Biography of Tilden*, p. 225.

O'CONOR TO TILDEN

"*March 20, 1879.*

"DEAR SIR,—As I never accept retainers,[23] you will pardon me for returning the enclosed.

"Yours truly,
CH. O'CONOR."

"*Hon. Samuel J. Tilden.*

MEMORANDUM OF CASE FOR O'CONOR'S OPINION

"*March, 1879.*

"A copy of the draft of the Bill of Discovery intended to be filed in the United States Circuit Court is submitted. It is for discovery merely, and is in aid of a common-law action pending in the district court. The complaint in that action is also submitted.

"Some of the questions on which Mr. O'Conor's opinion is desired in the first instance are the following:

"First.—If to the Bill of Discovery a plea, or an answer in the nature of a plea, should be made denying the right of action of the United States in the suit in the district court, and, consequently, its claim to a discovery on the ground that the quasi judicial determination of the assessor as to the amount of the tax, and the satisfaction of the judgment rendered by him are conclusive against the United States, and if the Circuit Court should overrule that point and grant the discovery, would that decision of the Circuit Court be a final judgment on which an appeal would lie to the Supreme Court?

"Second.—Would that appeal probably be effectual to obtain the rulings of the Supreme Court on the main question of the controversy?

"First.—If to the Bill of Discovery a plea, or an answer the defendant's income was in excess of the amount found by the assessor to be his income, calls on the defendant to state on oath every item of income during ten years, and every item of deductions therefrom and many items of receipts which are not income. There is no proposition between the foundation and the superstructure.

"What are the rules applicable to such a case?

"The interrogatories are not even limited to taxable income, but would involve accretions of value which are not taxable.

"Can the objection (*a*) that there is not any proper foundation for any interrogations? (*b*) that an interrogatory is too broad? (*c*) that an interrogatory relates to a matter in which the plaintiff has no interest or concern, as, for instance, to a subject not within the tax laws—can such objections be taken by way of special plea if we prefer that mode?

"The opinion or advice on the first and second questions is more emergent—the others can be dealt with later."

CHARLES O'CONOR TO TILDEN

"*Monday, Mar. 24, 1879.*

"DEAR SIR,—I have your note requesting me to examine some questions touching a bill of discovery. No papers accompanied it except the original complaint and a copy of the bill.

"This controversy has been some time in the courts. The law case is at issue, and arguments and a judgment have been had in it. The nature and merits of the law case should be understood by any one who would venture to advise in the equity case.

"It is true that I could investigate all this matter from the beginning without aid from any one; but, considering that you have had counsel in the law case, it seems to me that a statement from them, with points referring to statutes and authorities, might be put into my hands with advantage. As this might facilitate my researches, it would expedite my conclusion and you indicate a desire for speed.

"Yrs. respy.,
"CH. O'CONOR."

TILDEN TO O'CONOR

"NEW YORK, *March 25th, 1879.*

"TO CHARLES O'CONOR.

"MY DEAR SIR,—The action of the United States in the income tax case is a common-law action. The complaint has been sent to you.

"The substance of the plea is that the defendant had been assessed by the proper officers of the United States. The tax and penalties fixed and the amount collected by the government. A copy of the plea will be sent to you, but the above is the substance of it.

"The question argued before Judge Blatchford in the district court was on the point raised by the defendant that the action of the government officers was quasi judicial, and their determination conclusive and exclusive.

"The points of the defendant are sent herewith.

"In this state of things the District Attorney proposes to file a bill of discovery to obtain the facts which shall establish the right of action.

"It is understood that the District Attorney desires, if possible, to have the judgment of the Supreme Court on the main question. But that purpose may, perhaps, be regarded as confidential.

"The advance sheets of the bill of discovery intended to be filed, which had been informally furnished to one of the defendant's counsel, have also been sent you.

"The first point upon which your opinion has been asked is whether, in case we plead to the bill of discovery, that the plaintiff is barred as to his right of action by the quasi judicial determinations of the officers, and has no right to discovery by reason of having no right of action, and that plea is overruled by the Circuit Court, the decision will constitute such a judgment as will be appealable to the Supreme Court.

"There are other questions, but this is the most immediate.

"I write this note to give you information at once without the delay incident to getting the counsel together to write out a case for submission.

"Very truly yours,
"(Signed) S. J. TILDEN.

"Hon. Charles O'Conor."

TILDEN TO GEORGE W. CLINTON

"August 26, 1879.

"DEAR JUDGE,—I thank you for your kind letter.

"The life I am leading with out-door exercise and physical activity alternated with rest has left me little time for correspondence after I get through with other calls upon my attention. But I none the less appreciate intercourse with such men as yourself. Nor do I forget that there are three generations since my ancestors were first allied to the great founder of your family, amid the trying scenes which attended our national independence, and the formation of a genuine government of the people.

"You are quite right in the impression that I would not think it fit for me to run for *Governor* at the coming election. The reasons against it are conclusive.

"In the first place, I don't want to add to the burdens I have had and now have connected with public affairs.

"In the second place, although I do not expect to be installed in the Presidency to which I was elected, I deem it due to the four and a quarter millions of voters who have been defrauded of the fruits of their suffrages, that I should not, during the term for which I was chosen, do anything inconsistent with their moral right.

"In the third place, I should not like to be a convenience to the dictation to the Democratic State convention that they must surrender their choice if it be Governor Robinson, whose administration has deserved so well of all good citizens.

"I have not time to dilate on these topics, but I do not doubt that you and I will think the same things concerning the Republic.

"It will give me great pleasure to hear from you whenever you find time to write me, and I hope to have the pleasure of seeing you personally.

"Very truly yours,
"(Signed) S. J. TILDEN."

TILDEN TO JOHN GILL, JR., CHAIRMAN

"NEW YORK, *September 27, 1879.*

"GENTLEMEN,—I have received the letter of the Democratic executive committee in the city of Baltimore inviting me to attend a mass-meeting at the Maryland Institute on the 29th inst.

"It would give me great pleasure to meet so respectable a representation of the Democracy of Maryland, but my engagements will deprive me of that gratification.

"I concur with you in regarding the issue created by the subversion of the election of 1876 as the most transcendent in our history. The example of a reversal of the votes of the people after they have been deposited in the ballot-box, if successful and followed by prosperity to the wrong, would be fatal to the system of elective government. *The hierarchy of office-holders would maintain their possession indefinitely, and every effort of the people to change the administration would be nullified. The government, elective in form, would become imperial in substance precisely as did that of Rome.*[24] Such an issue, involving the very existence of our free government, is not to be belittled into a personal grievance. It is to be dealt with as a great public cause.

"With assurances of my cordial esteem for yourself personally,

"I remain, very truly yours,
"(Signed) SAMUEL J. TILDEN."

S. J. TILDEN—INTERVIEW WITH "SUN" REPORTER

(Draft.)

"*Dec. 19, '79.*

"A *Sun* reporter called on Mr. Tilden, showed him a copy of the *Sun* of Sunday last containing an article copied from the *Star*, and asked if it would be agreeable to him to say whether there was any, and, if so, what foundation for the statements there made about negotiations with him to obtain the electoral vote of the State of South Carolina for $30,000.

"Mr. Tilden took the paper, ran his eyes over it, and then said: 'I have no objection to answer your question if my friends of the *Sun* think the publication worthy of such notice.

"'I do not see, on looking this article over, any statement concerning me personally which is not a mere fiction.

"'The substance of the story is that I was visited at my house by a gentleman from South Carolina, who told me that the vote of the State had been given to me, but that the Returning Boards had determined to count it against me unless they were paid $30,000; that after declining the proposition, I recalled this agent by a letter addressed to him at his hotel; that on the second interview I referred him to a gentleman in this city; that that gentleman gave him a package containing $30,000, which was sent to Charleston; that the letter had scarcely left the wharf when the agent received another letter from me requesting him to call at my house immediately; that I then insisted upon the immediate return of the package unopened, and that it be restored to the person from whom it was received; that the agents remonstrated, saying:

"'"The corrupt men in Columbia and in the State generally have not tried to count Hampton out. They know perfectly well that both you and Hampton are elected and have received a majority of the votes of the people, but they can afford to count you out, but not to count Hampton out, because he and his friends will not stand it."

"'That notwithstanding this remonstrance, I persisted in requiring the package to be restored to the person who handed it to the agent.'

"Mr. Tilden: 'Every one of these statements is totally false; no one of the three pretended interviews ever happened. I never sent either of the two letters attributed to me; I never referred any agent bearing such a proposition to Mr. Brown or to Mr. Anybody else. All the details concerning the package of money being sent and recalled and my conversations respecting it also are wholly destitute of truth. They are simply a fabrication from beginning to end.'"

GEORGE L. MILLER TO S. J. TILDEN

"*Personal and Confidential.*

"'HERALD' OFFICE, EDITORIAL DEPARTMENT,
"OMAHA, NEB., *Dec. 26th, 1879.*

"HON. SAMUEL J. TILDEN.

"MY DEAR SIR,—Pardon a preliminary statement before I reach the main object of this letter.

"Since I last saw you I have met the slanders circulating against you, to the effect that you were seeking a second nomination to the Presidency by corrupt and other means, by saying in my paper, as a matter of my own opinion, that you would neither seek nor accept such nomination. I have also said, on my belief in Governor Seymour's sincerity, that *he* would not accept a nomination to the Presidency. I now want to give you some news for your special information.

"I have a letter from a leading Democrat of Oneida County who has peculiar facilities for getting at the 'true inwardness' that Horatio Seymour will not decline a nomination to the Presidency. He will not write any letters forbidding the use of his name, and if he is interviewed at all the result will be uniformly that which was recently seen in the New York *Times*. He will not change front exactly. No one will be authorized to say he will consent to run, but it will appear that the Governor's health is greatly improved, and that he was never better in his life, and nothing authentic will be got from him to show that he would not accept a nomination.

"I said this is sent to you as *news*. It may not be such to *you*. But the information I get is such a great surprise to *me* that I could not rest without sending it to you.

"I am, most truly yours,
"GEORGE L. MILLER."

JOHN A. McCLERNAND TO TILDEN

"SPRINGFIELD, ILL., *Jany. 27th, 1880.*

"EX-GOVERNOR SAMUEL J. TILDEN.

"DEAR SIR,—There is no other motive for this communication than a patriotic one. Its purpose is not to intrude counsel or to invite confidence. A common interest upon a subject of vital public concern is its only warrant.

"The fundamental right of the people to choose, according to constitutional forms, their Chief Magistrate has been violated in your person. This fact devolves upon every true Democrat and, no less, upon you as their representative, the solemn and binding duty of redressing the wrong. In no other way can that duty be so effectually performed as by renominating and re-electing the old ticket. The masses are emotional and sentimental rather than metaphysical. They feel that the old coach stands ready to be hitched to, and that, that done, a safe and prosperous journey is before them.

"If anything like a concerted appeal to the country had been sustained by its leading Democratic press, the renomination and reelection of the old ticket would have resulted by an overwhelming vote. Nor is it too late now to amend the omission, notwithstanding the supervening complication of the late New York elections. Putting the latter upon a salient issue of *principle* and *faith*: whether, indeed, the organization and voice of the Democratic party in that State shall prevail, or whether a predatory faction of bolters shall be allowed to dominate both. Such an appeal ought and, I think, would meet with an approving response from true and tried Democrats.

"The bolters failing to retrace their steps, what else is left but for a strong and emphatic demonstration to be made declaratory of the above issues. Pardon my boldness. I deem it advisable, nay, necessary, for you to lead the way in a speech or paper couched in such form and terms as you may consider appropriate, and as will be effective to ring throughout the land. A leader who is demonstrative will always find followers.

"Very respectfully,
"Your obt. sert.,
"JOHN A. MCCLERNAND."

JOHN BIGELOW TO G. PITMAN SMITH

"58 E. 34TH ST., NEW YORK, *March 10, 1880.*

"HON. G. PITMAN SMITH.

"DEAR SIR,—Mr. Tilden has shown me your favor to him of the 25th ult., and desires me to thank you for its friendly counsel. In complying with his wishes, I will take the liberty of adding a few words on my own account for which I trust my cordial sympathy with the manifest objects of your communication will be a sufficient apology.

"There is no one in this country, I suppose, who can suffer more from a popular misunderstanding of his motives than Mr. Tilden, but circumstances constrain him, no less now than heretofore, to leave the vindication of his conduct as the leader of his party in the last Presidential contest to its good sense and its love of justice. There has been no time when he could participate in any public discussion of the methods finally adopted for counting the electoral vote, without appearing to criticise the conduct of statesmen standing high in the confidence of the Democratic party and whose patriotism is above suspicion. That alone would be a sufficient reason with him for maintaining silence, and for declining to make of what might seem to some a personal grievance a provocation of unprofitable party dissension.

"But in my judgment he had another and a better reason. He knew that whenever, if ever, it should become necessary for the people of the United States to pass judgment upon his conduct during and subsequent to the canvass of 1876 they could not fail to acquit him of any responsibility for its final result.

"The logic of nations is far more rigorous than that of the individuals composing it, and it would be doing the understanding of the American people great injustice to suppose they cannot see that there was no time when Mr. Tilden could have taken any step towards seizing the Presidency with any color of right or with any prospect of success. There were just two contingencies, and only two, in which it would have been lawful and obligatory on Mr. Tilden to take the oath as President of the United States.

"The first one would have been presented if Congress had performed its constitutional duty: had counted the electoral votes, and declared Mr. Tilden the chosen of the electoral colleges. The duty of verifying the electoral votes is given by the Constitution to the two Houses of Congress and to them only; it has always been exercised by them at the choice of every previous President from the foundation of the government. It was known to all who came in contact with Mr. Tilden—for he was unreserved in the expression of his opinion upon that subject—that in his view this power and duty of Congress was lodged nowhere else.

"The two Houses of Congress, however, did not see fit to exercise that power nor to discharge that duty, and as a consequence this contingency in which it would have been proper for Mr. Tilden to take the official oath never presented itself. Before the time fixed by law for counting the electoral votes, Congress passed the electoral bill by which they practically abdicated in favor of a tribunal unknown to and, in my judgment, unknowable by the Constitution, and enacted that the electoral commission should in the first instance make the count, and that its count should stand unless overruled by the concurrent action of the two Houses. This electoral tribunal counted Mr. Tilden out, and counted in a man who was not elected. Congress did not overrule their count, in consequence of which the false count stood as law under the act of Congress.

"The only other contingency in which it would have been obligatory, or even lawful, for Mr. Tilden to have taken the oath of office was in case of a failure in the choice of President by the electoral colleges, the House of Representatives had itself proceeded to make the election, voting by States in the manner prescribed by the Constitution and pursued in the election of John Q. Adams.

"This contingency, like the first, never presented itself, and, both failing, any attempt on the part of Mr. Tilden to seize the Presidency by violence would have been not statesmanship, but simply brigandage.

"Courage is too common a virtue among Americans for any one to make a boast of it, and the lack of courage too rare to explain the conduct of any body of representative men. At the same time, there is no doubt that if there was any place where a special display of heroism could have prevented the defeat of the popular choice and installed the elect of the people in the Presidential chair, that place was the floor of Congress. I suppose I say nothing which any Democratic member of that Congress will be disposed to dispute when I state that it was the fear that the Senate would lead a resistance to the rightful judgment of the House, and that President Grant would sustain this revolutionary policy with the army and navy, and with the militia of the great States in which the Republicans had possession of the State governments, that deterred the House of Representatives from the assertion of its rights, and induced its vote for and acquiescence in the electoral commission.

"But without speculating upon the causes or motives for such vote and acquiescence the facts are beyond dispute. The House of Representatives did not elect Mr. Tilden in the manner prescribed by the Constitution or in any other. On the other hand, it did concur with the Senate in anticipating and preventing the contingency in which it might have had to act, and in providing beforehand an expedient which incapacitated it for supplying a failure of an election by the colleges. It adopted the electoral law, and went through all the forms of the electoral scheme. True, it afterwards rebuked itself by passing a declaratory resolution condemning the electoral commission, and asserting that Mr. Tilden had been the choice of the people. But the Constitution had not provided that a man should or could take office as President on a declaratory resolution of the House of Representatives. If that resolution could have had full effect to abrogate the electoral law which the House had assisted to enact, it would still have furnished Mr. Tilden with no warrant of authority for taking the oath of office. Had Mr. Tilden been declared President-elect by either of the constitutional methods, no one who knows him can doubt that he would have taken the oath and the office or sealed the people's choice with his blood, as he was in duty bound to do.

"I do not weary you with the recapitulation of these facts, because I suppose any of them new to you. On the contrary, they are all now matters of history. It is because they are of public notoriety, and because they point so directly to the one and inevitable conclusion that Mr. Tilden's responsibility in the late canvass terminated at the ballot-box, that I recall them here to justify in your eyes his silence upon the subject referred to in your letter, and his perfect faith in the good sense and justice of his countrymen.

"I need hardly say that in what I have here written in explanation of Mr. Tilden's attitude before the country I have written as his friend, not for him.

"Very truly yours,
"JOHN BIGELOW."

TILDEN TO JOHN A. McCLERNAND

"*Confidential.*

"GRAMERCY PARK, NEW YORK, *March 16, 1880.*

"MY DEAR GENERAL,—I thoroughly appreciate the motives which prompted your note of the 27th of January, and it is not from any want of consideration for your suggestions that I have not sooner acknowledged it. I thank you cordially for your friendly counsels. I agree with you entirely as to the danger to the elective system of government liable to result from the subversion of the popular will as manifested in the election of 1876.

"I also concur with you in the opinion that the dissension which exerted a temporary power in this State in 1879 cannot be continued or repeated with success in 1880.

"I regret the narrow limits to which a letter confines the interchange of sentiments between us, but I need hardly assure you that I shall always be happy to hear from you, and that your counsel, whenever you are disposed to favor me with it, will not be wasted upon me.

"With high esteem, I remain,
"Very truly yours,
"(Signed) S. J. TILDEN.

"*Hon. John A. McClernand, Springfield, Illinois.*"

THEODORE P. COOK TO S. J. TILDEN

"UTICA, *April 6th, 1880.*

"MY DEAR MR. TILDEN,—The Seymour movement is assuming a shape which must draw from him, in a few days, a more positive declination than he has yet made—unless he is really looking for a nomination, and I am positive that he is not. I think he talks with me more, and more plainly, than he does with anybody else. The misunderstanding of his position (which perhaps you share) grows partly out of the talk of his family and friends, and partly out of the impression that he leaves on the minds of those with whom he talks, that he is not particularly friendly to you. He is fully and firmly resolved to go out of public life and remain out. But he would like to take his contemporaries out with him. That is all there is to his opposition. I have made a careful study of this matter, and I am very confident that I am not mistaken in my conclusions. A few days, however, will show. Our district convention will probably adopt a resolution urging Governor Seymour for President. A letter from him, defining his position, will then be in order. The *Observer* is floating in the local current, hopeful of directing it when the time comes. Mr. Spriggs will probably go to the State convention. He is with us, as you know. Mr. Grannis, of the State committee, and Mr. Birt, of Bridgewater, are talked of for the other two places. Of these three, Spriggs will be the controlling spirit.

"Faithfully yours,
"THEO. P. COOK."

BENJAMIN H. HILL TO TILDEN

"*Private.*

"UNITED STATES SENATE CHAMBER,
"WASHINGTON, *April 12th, 1880.*

"HON. S. J. TILDEN, NEW YORK.

"SIR,—I have not the pleasure of knowing you personally. I have never sought to make myself consequential in your estimation, nor have I annoyed you with visits or opinions. I am no politician, nor given to tricks nor to pretentiousness. Without asking your pardon for doing so, I take the responsibility of writing this letter.

"The crime in the Presidential count of 1877 was not against you, nor was it against the Democratic party. It was a crime against the American people and against popular government. If the American people are worthy of popular government they will visit their wrath upon the authors and abettors of that crime. The most effective way to do so is by your re-election. You have no right to deny them the opportunity of doing so. You have no right to deny to the Democratic party the privilege of presenting your name to the people, nor have you the right to relieve the party from the shame of refusing to present your name to the people.

"For three years the Republicans have been laboring to destroy your good name in order to avoid the issue the presentation of your name will make. Certain Democrats aided them in committing the great fraud, and they have been aiding them to destroy you for the same reason. They say they have succeeded. They seek to impress the public that you are not available. I do not believe the American people are idiots or knaves, nor are they ready to consummate their own degradation at the bidding of this coalition of Republican and Democratic politicians.

"I was a new man here in 1877 and was myself entrapped. If I had known certain men then as I know them now, I am almost vain enough to believe the electoral bill would not disgrace our history. Be that as it may, I feel anxious to atone for the wrong I helped to consummate by that bill.

"Some very recent events have added to my information, and strengthened my convictions in regard to motives, persons, and things potential in the wrongs of 1876-7.

"I have spoken frankly because I feel deeply, and expect your favor only because I have spoken briefly.

"With highest regards, I am, yours very truly,

"BENJ. H. HILL, of Georgia."

R. T. MERRICK TO TILDEN

"*Private and personal.*

"WASHINGTON CITY, *June 11th, 1880.*

"MY DEAR MR. TILDEN,—It may be desirable that you should know something of what transpired at the Maryland convention, in order to determine correctly the character and sentiments of those by whom its proceedings were directed.

"Maryland is, as you are aware, the theatre for the operations of a ring not unlike that which you hate in New York.

"This ring is under the control of Gorman, Colton, and two or three others, with Governor Carroll as a subordinate but confidential copartner.

"Carroll is violent in his hostility to you, and equally violent and unreasoning in his devotion to Bayard.

"These gentlemen, though at one time committed to you, came over to this city last winter and 'pledged' the State to Bayard.

"Bayard himself, I have occasion to know, designated some of the delegates and advised the defeat of others. Five days before the convention assembled he visited the residence of Governor Carroll, where about a hundred and fifty men of that particular Congressional district were invited to meet him.

"Carroll resides in the same county in which I reside—viz., Howard.

"I was a candidate in that district for the position of delegate against a ring ticket. I carried the district and secured, of my friends in the convention and others not known to me, but *instructed* to vote for me by the conventions that appointed them, more than enough to elect me.

"But Carroll and his associates induced a sufficient number of those who had been instructed openly to violate their obligation of good faith and personal honor to defeat me. I confidently believe that of the *people* of the district I had two to one in my favor as against the *Bayard ring ticket.*

"Bayard and his friends seem to cherish a personal bitterness to you and those interested in having justice done to you, which is as blind as it is stupid.

"There are some few good men in the delegation, but it is completely under Gorman's control, who will do everything he can to secure Bayard's nomination, but directs his efforts *principally* to *appear* on the successful side. I beg leave to suggest that you intimate to such of your friends at Cincinnati as may have your confidence, and be in possession of your views and wishes, to be on their guard in any consultation or interview they may have with this gentleman or the members of this delegation.

"I presume Mr. Blair has written—he carried his county, though not his district, and for reasons similar to those indicated above is not a member of the delegation.

"With most profound respect,

"Sincerely your friend,
"R. T. MERRICK."

As introductory to the following letter, I quote the following from my diary under date of May 12, 1880:

> "Mr. Tilden has finally determined, I believe, to be a candidate for the Presidency before the Cincinnati convention.
>
> "I have no responsibility for advising him to expose himself to such an ordeal in his present state of health, though I rather congratulate myself that he has taken that responsibility for himself. He has been so abominably calumniated that nothing but a renomination and re-election can fully vindicate him and his friends. Should the exposure cost him his life, could it be spent in a better cause for him? As long as he can make himself heard, he is capable of making a better President than any man besides him that either party is likely to nominate.
>
> "While the Terre Haute and Alton suit was pending against him, I think he was fully determined to withhold his name from the convention. He complained to me, as we were riding one day, of his want of the requisite strength to prepare his defence, though sure of winning if the case were promptly presented. He then added, 'If I have not strength enough to prepare a case for trial I am not fit to be President.' In saying this he turned to me as if it were in answer or as a remonstrance against pressure to

run. I said to him: 'Governor, I am the last one to ask you or to urge you to run. No one has a right to ask you to accept a burden like that at the risk of your life, and there is no disguising the fact that there is nothing from which you have so much to apprehend as from excitement of any kind, and especially of the kind and degree to which a canvass for the Presidency, and the first six months' service in that position, would inevitably expose you.' It was on that ground that I advised him to settle the Terre Haute and Alton suit without reference to the cost in money. It was fretting the life out of him.

"Then just before the State convention for the election of delegates to Cincinnati the income tax suit was noticed for trial. This completely unsettled him for several weeks, so completely that I was again confirmed in the conviction that any increase, or even continuance, of excitement like that under which he was laboring would soon destroy him."

Mr. Tilden's brother Henry took with him to Cincinnati Mr. Tilden's letter to the Democratic national convention in 1880 declining a renomination to the Presidency, and this letter pictures the confusion into which the convention was thrown by it.

SMITH M. WEED TO S. J. TILDEN

"FRIDAY, *June 25, '80.*

"MY DEAR GOVERNOR,—I have not had a moment's time to write until now, and I have very little to write except what you have already read in the papers.

"It was very apparent to any one that it was not possible to have nominated you even if you would have taken it, as I know you would not. The element that sold you out in Washington in 1877, with those who were *honestly* fearful you could not win, were enough to defeat you under any circumstances, and yet the fear that we meant to try to do it prevented our being able to.

"This feeling was kept alive by earnest but injudicious friends of yours from New York and elsewhere, and this and the action of our own delegation absolutely destroyed our influence in the convention. The Brooklyn people did not want you, and Jacobs, Pratt, and others told people they would not go for you or be transferred by you. Had they been absolutely with us, and had Manning spoken your wishes, we could have nominated Mr. Payne. M. seemed to fear the Brooklyn people, and I don't wonder, for I never saw any set of men act so very ugly as they and the Fox-Shay New York gang.

"Randall also acted bad, and talked bad, and yet, under your advice, or what I took to be your advice, I acted with the Brooklyn and Fox gang and named him as our second choice. I did not like to do so, for I feared Hancock's nomination, but did not fear it so early.

"Had your letter been there Saturday morning, and had *we* all acted together—*i. e.*, your friends—we could have nominated Payne. I don't think we could have nominated Randall.

"The South and Southwest and New Jersey were represented by a bad lot, and the convention was nothing to compare with the convention of 1876. So far as I was concerned, I was good for nothing, for it took about all my time to keep our delegation from kicking over the traces in some way.

"I cannot write in detail, but will talk it all over with you if you want to know anything more of the disgusting subject. I do not think it an easy victory for any one, and am confident that the ticket is a fairer representation of *that* convention *than you would have been.* The fact is that in the talk and action the old dictation of the South was prevalent without the old intellect.

"I cannot express my contempt for New York's and Brooklyn's acts.

"Barnum will tell you of the talks with Hancock people. I hope he (H.) will make it apparent that he is to be your friend, and if so that you will help him through. I am about dead, as I have not slept over two hours a night since I came.

Yours very truly,
"SMITH M. WEED."

CASSIUS M. CLAY TO TILDEN

"*June 26, 1880.*

"MY DEAR SIR,—Though personally unknown to you, my devotion to your interests, I think, warrants me in giving you my sincere sympathy in your unjust defeat.

"I sent you, soon after your count out, the original resolutions carried by me in county convention of Madison, which was made the basis of the Louisville convention, and which caused me to be made its president, without my solicitation, being myself for a constitutional count without compromise. I was a candidate for delegate for the State at large, and was only beaten by your opponents and the Greenback element, after I vindicated you in a speech which united all the opposition against me. But as alternate of our mutual friend, General William Preston, as directed by the convention, I stood for you—till your letter of declension, which left me free to defeat those who defeated you and me. The position of Payne overshadowed by Thurman, with him, Jewett, and Foster candidates, I foresaw that Payne could not lead; and Randall had the opposition of all your opponents, handicapped with the high tariff record, which is more and more hateful to all Democrats. Under these circumstances, I deemed Hancock the man of destiny. I brought over seven of our delegation, and through my friend, General W. C. C. Breckinridge, who was not a Hancock man, pressed a vote on Wednesday, against all attempts of the opponents of Hancock, and placed him in the lead, thus insuring his selection on the second ballot Thursday, as we anticipated. I had a great respect for Bayard, but told General Wade Hampton and his other friends that his war records and his action in the eight to seven commn. were fatal objections; and now we have a man who is bound to win, as it seems to me, as you could have done but for your want of health, as set forth in your letter. I spoke several times in your behalf before our commn. at Lexington, and I honestly believe you were the choice of seven-eighths of the people of Kentucky. But the Congressmen defeated you—almost all of whom were against you—first, because of your Southern-claims letter, and that other principle of our weak human nature, never to forgive those whom we have injured.

"General Preston grows old, has lost an eye, and is very deaf: which sets him back in oratory—but he made with me the only two speeches in your behalf in our Jefferson convention. He was the first to leave Bayard for H—and is a true gentleman and patriot. His speech in your behalf was very able.

"I close by assuring you that your letter is one of the ablest State papers of our annals; and brough[t] with all intelligent and patriotic men conviction of your wrongs, your ability, and your patriotism.

"Please accept assurances of my sincere respect.

"C. M. CLAY.

"*Hon. S. J. Tilden, New York, &c.*"

LETTER FROM H. A. TILDEN (NED) TO S. J. TILDEN

"GRAND HOTEL, CINCINNATI, MONDAY, 9 O'C. A. M., *1880.*

"I reached here at twelve; found Weed and Green at station. Every one expected a letter, and a rush was made to know all about it. I gave it to Mr. Manning as soon as I could, and he read it over and had a copy—the original he has and will keep—and deliver up to you on his return. He wanted to do this. I yielded.

"On my way I had a room at one end of the car, and was not disturbed, and saw no one till the last hour but Judge Parkerson, and we only talked about last fall. He wanted some explanation, which I gave, and relieved some wrong impressions. I found that Tim Campbell admits that Robinson was cheated out of over 20,000 votes. Pasters were rubbed off, and the ballot counted for Cornell. The cheat is estimated at enough to have elected Robinson. The delegation had adjourned till Monday 10 A.M. I advised holding the letter till then, and not make it public till read in convention. This was intended, but the pressure was so great that Weed, Manning, Barnum, and all hands wanted it as early as possible, that it would be of benefit on the Payne effort, &c., and they called a meeting of the delegation, read it, and gave it to the press. I stayed up till three this morning to see that the proof was all right. The sentiment it has created is good, the antagonism all gone out, and regret takes its place. Now they have no one to grumble about and fight. There are three classes: those who are against us accept it as final; the moderate men, who have doubted if we could carry the State, want it reserved and not acted upon as final; then there are our friends, who say it shall not be regarded, and must come before the convention for final action.

"As the day wears on the sentiment in favor of the old ticket will increase, and we cannot tell where it will end. I don't believe any man can be picked up and get through the convention. I think perhaps Whitney, Weed, and Faulkner rushed Payne too sharp—did not do it in a suggestive form—and they have got up a feeling with the Brooklyn delegation. The Brooklyn people have started Pratt lively, and, clashing with Payne men, got up considerable feeling, and I hear Hughes has been deputed to charge you with not having explained to him, as fully as you should, the Payne relations. I have had no chance to talk with Hughes, but shall quiet this sentiment. I can remove it.

"MONDAY, *5.30 P.M.*

"I have just left Manning. We construe your despatch about P. to Randall as positive instructions to force a fight on Payne, and M. is unwilling to modulate it, because he greatly fears disaster.

"I have had a talk with Henderson and Babcock, and they say the Standard Oil monopoly is so very unpopular that they can't see their way clear to go P., and are anxious to do all they can, and go with Manning, and fear the effect in these elections. The Oil Company has ruined so many men in this locality that it is impossible to get up a sentiment for any one directly or indirectly in it; the same feeling exists in Pittsburg, and those delegates will not go for Payne. There is no Payne sentiment from any States but New York and Ohio that I can hear of. I have sent you the enclosed despatch, somewhat reduced, which Manning dictated.

"I send you a list of delegates as they stand at this hour. The discussions are lively. Tilden men are cheered and have all the sentiment.

"Faulkner is sour; thinks he is not fully consulted. Manning is managing him best he can. There is little to consult about. There is so much jealousy, and so many statesmen, I am glad you are out. *Hewitt is in.* Green thinks lightning may strike him. So we go. Have not heard from Randall. Barnum was to see him, but has been so engaged did not yet. One of the Illinois delegation says he cried when he read the letter.

NED.

"The Pratt movement dates back a long way. Fowler intent on securing delegates to represent certain interests, and explains now how McL. declined to go as delegate at large, and Jacobs came in and got from Manning a word that any one satisfactory to McL. would be satisfactory, and then put forward Pratt. Weed says that the Pratt movement is made up of the mining speculating class, who have made money, and brag they have more to put up for him than Tilden would put in.

"Will close for mail. Will send full memorandum by mail and telegraph important points.

NED.

"Strong objection to P., because of Oil Company in our delegation; also because Brooklyn is aggressive for Pratt. Thurman holds Ohio firmly; how long, uncertain. Steadman has gone over to Jewett. Manning thinks it will never do to push P. upon Ohio; she must act first. Several States voluntarily agree to follow our lead.

"Shall we make fight now for anybody, or wait for developments? Answer, yes or no."

General Winfield S. Hancock was nominated for the Presidency by the Democratic convention at Cincinnati on the 23d day of June, 1880. A short time after, Mr. Tilden received the following note from General Hancock at the hands of General W. G. Mitchee, to which Mr. Tilden suggested the addition which follows it.

GENERAL W. S. HANCOCK TO TILDEN

"GOVERNOR'S ISLAND, N. Y., *July 27th, 1880.*

"MY DEAR SIR,—I introduce my friend, General W. G. Mitchee, who will hand you a copy of the lines of acceptance which I have resolved to issue.

"Will you have the kindness to read it and give me any suggestions in regard to it which may occur to you? I intend to issue the letter before the 1st of August.

"I also send for your perusal a copy of a letter which I addressed to General Sherman under date of December 25th, 1876, which will no doubt be published a week or so after my letter of acceptance.

"With best wishes for yourself, and pleasant remembrances of your hospitality which I so much enjoyed last week,

"I am, very truly yours,
"WINF'D S. HANCOCK."

[Enclosed card.]

"General W. G. Mitchee, who would like to see Mr. Tilden for a few minutes to deliver a package to him.

"W. S. H., Governor's Island.

"If Mr. Tilden is in the country General M. will go there."

DRAFT OF ADDITION FOR LETTER OF ACCEPTANCE OF GENERAL HANCOCK

"*July, 1880.*

"It is time we should enjoy the benefits of that reconciliation and restoration of fraternal feelings which has cost so much blood and treasure. As one people, having a common interest, the welfare and prosperity of all would be advanced, a generous rivalry would be stimulated for the growth of our merchant marine which has been destroyed by the policy of the party in power. The extension of our foreign and domestic commerce with nations naturally tributary to us, and the further development of our immense natural resources would result. A wise and economical management of our governmental expenditures should be maintained in order that labor may be lightly burdened, and that every individual may be protected in his natural right to the immediate fruits of his own industry."

TILDEN TO MRS. W. C. BRYANT

"NEW YORK, *Sept. 17th, 1880.*

"MY DEAR MRS. BRYANT,—After I left the city two weeks ago, thinking not so much where I would go as where I would not remain, I found in my pocket a note which I supposed had been left to be sent to you. It was designed to aid an article which has doubtless appeared in your household in explaining its own advent—a friendly office, which, although too long delayed, must still be fulfilled.

"I could not resist the impulse to supply what you had, one day when I last had the pleasure of visiting you, casually mentioned as your *only want.* It may never again happen to me—if I lose that opportunity—to be able to fill the measure of a housekeeper's contentment; and I am anxious, if you will permit me, to procure for myself the gratification of witnessing such a novelty, as well as the sense of having contributed to produce it. Perhaps I ought to acknowledge a still more selfish motive. If the example of so much moderation shall have the influence to which it is entitled, I shall, doubtless, at some period not yet distinctly foreseen, share its benefits; and, notwithstanding all I can now do to signalize my appreciation of it, be reminded that I am forever your debtor. In the mean time, I remain, very truly,

"Your friend,
"S. J. TILDEN."

MRS. WILLIAM CULLEN BRYANT TO TILDEN

"*Monday Evening.*

"MY DEAR TILDEN,—If I said, 'A bamboo settee is my only want,' I had forgotten it long before your present arrived, which certainly fills most commodiously a vacant space in my hall or on my piazza, as the weather may be; and for which I make you my very best acknowledgments. I do not think I was a 'discontented housekeeper' before I had it, but I admit I have much more reason to be contented now.

"I wish I could as easily send you in return the thing you most want for your future household, or even tell you where to obtain it. But permit me to say that I have observed that people become more fastidious and less enterprising the longer they postpone the acquisition of what, we are told by high authorities, was the only thing wanted to make the first man happy in paradise.

"Your lilies, I am happy to say, are all alive and doing nicely. The first leisure you have come and look after them.

"Yours most truly,
"F. F. BRYANT.

"ROSLYN, *Monday Evening.*"

TILDEN TO YOUNG MEN'S DEMOCRATIC CLUB

"GREYSTONE, *October 26, 1880.*

"GENTLEMEN,—I have received your invitation to be present and address a meeting of the Young Men's Democratic Club of the city of New York at Chickering Hall this evening.

"My voice is not yet sufficiently restored to make it prudent for me to address a large meeting. My cordial sympathy with your efforts to elect General Hancock has already been conspicuously expressed.

"As the canvass advances every day renders more manifest the duty to promote that result incumbent upon all who believe in the traditions of free, constitutional, representative self-government as illustrated in the better days of the Republic.

"One Presidential election, as made by the people, has been subverted by a false count of the votes cast by the Presidential electors founded on a substitution of votes known to be fraudulent or forged.

"If the next Presidential election should be controlled by corrupt influence exercised by the government upon the voters in particular States, opening a vista of third terms, and an indefinite series of terms, and the undisputed mastery of the office-holding class in the successive elections, our government will be degenerated into a bad copy of the worst governments of the worst ages."

ALEXANDER T. McGILL TO TILDEN

"THEOLOGICAL SEMINARY,
"PRINCETON, N. J., *Nov. 27, '80.*

"HON. SAML. J. TILDEN.

"MY DEAR SIR,—I cannot refrain from writing to you, as I often desired to do in times past, to testify my respect and admiration alike, when you were covered with merited honors and persecuted with unmerited obloquy. I am an old man, senior professor in this institution since the death of Dr. Charles Hodge. Mr. J. F. D. Lanier first made me acquainted with your character, and my wife met you once at his residence near Lenox, where she was on a visit to her particular friend, Mrs. Lanier. I am a native of western Pennsylvania, and was professor in the Theological Seminary of Allegheny until 1854, when the Presbyterian General Assembly transferred me to this seminary as successor to Dr. Archibald Alexander.

"I am indebted to you for the surpassing ability and probity with which, in connection with Lanier, you saved my savings, which I had invested in the Pennsylvania and Ohio, now 'The Wayne' Railroad. It was therefore my duty, when you were abused by various lying papers on every occasion, to tell my own personal knowledge of the rare integrity with which you secured to a multitude of poor men what we thought was lost in the bankruptcy of that great road. My son, a lawyer in Jersey City, 'Prosecutor of the Pleas' for Hudson County, was vastly more efficient, of course, in using the information I gave him. I have now three sons in Jersey City, professional men, who would rejoice exceedingly to have the opportunity of yet voting for you if you ever consent again to a nomination for the Presidency.

"We all rejoice in the downfall of that wicked and treacherous conspirator, John Kelly. His vindicative antipathy to you now meets a recompense in the just indignation of Providence. It is the signal overthrow of this bad man which prompts me to write these lines at this time, to congratulate you that your faithful and distinguished life is illustrated by that detestable enemy in the foil of his nature coming to the notice of all men sooner than we expected.

"Pardon me for tasking you to read so long a letter. I think it is due to you from me to inform you a little more how deeply you are esteemed and loved for your integrity, pureness, patriotism, and moral courage. Not one in a thousand of our best public men would have relinquished the Presidency when it was fairly in his grasp, and that, too, for the sake of peace. History will do you justice. A memorial unique and grand, better far than the actual Presidency, showing to all generations the moral sublimity of an American citizen, will be yours. May your precious life and health be long preserved.

"With great respect and true friendship,

"Yours,
"ALEXR. T. MCGILL."

TILDEN TO MONTGOMERY BLAIR

"GREYSTONE, *Nov. 29, 1880.*

"DEAR MR. BLAIR,—If I seem slow in replying to your letter of the 10th inst., you must ascribe it to the difficulties presented by its chirography which have not been surmounted until this morning. As your productions always repay a real perusal, a third and successful attempt to read that letter was persisted in.

"In this connection I must tell you a story. Mr. Cambreling wrote Mr. Van Buren a long and argumentative letter in favor of the annexation of Texas while the latter was preparing his letter upon that subject. It was written in an ink which stuck the pages together, and Van Buren was foiled or gave up in the attempt to decipher it. I have a vague impression that he afterwards thought that letter might have modified his own view. Possibly it might have changed the course of events.

"Mr. Smith has brought up some photographs of three sorts. I send herewith three of each kind.

"If a man can afford the slightest pleasure to friends who have been so partial, so kind, and so faithful by a photograph, it is a real delight to comply with their wishes.

"I have not yet gone down to the city for the winter, and probably shall not until next week.

"My health is gradually improving, and I intend to persevere in living a purely physical life, alternating between out-of-door exercise and rest until the experiment shall have been fairly and fully tried.

"With best regards to Mrs. Blair, and to the other members of your family,

"I remain, very truly yours,
"(S'g'd) S. J. TILDEN.

"I return Mr. Fox's letter."

JOHN C. THOMPSON TO TILDEN

"BOSTON, MASS., *Dec. 25, '80.*

"DEAR SIR,—The night before Mr. James F. Starbuck, of Watertown, New York, deceased, he completed an article intended for the Albany *Argus* entitled 'Political Cowardice,' a copy of which (the original being retained by his family) I am requested by his daughter, Miss May Starbuck, to place in your hands, with the request that if upon perusal you recognize the power and logic of the intellect that penned the article, you will please forward the same to the Albany *Argus* for publication.

"I am the son-in-law of Mr. Starbuck. Will you do me the honor to acknowledge receipt of this and oblige, with great respect,

"Your obt. servant,
"JOHN C. THOMPSON."

JAMES F. STARBUCK TO TILDEN

("POLITICAL COWARDICE")

"The following facts are instructive:

In 1876 Tilden majority was		32,818
In 1879 Robinson's vote was	375,790	
and Kelly's vote was	77,566	
Total Dem. Vote in 1879	453,356	
Cornell's Vote was	418,567	
Democratic Majority	34,789	
But the votes for Cornell being		418,567
and Robinson's Vote		375,790
gives Cornell his plurality of		42,777

"The following table shows the number of votes cast for Kelly in 1879 and the Democratic loss in 1880, as compared with 1876 in each of the counties named:

	Kelly	Loss in 1880
Cayuga	712	557
Duchess	673	2,171
Kings	5,788	9,179
Monroe	2,088	1,749
New York	43,047	12,640
Niagara	574	861

Onondaga	1,468	658
Orange	980	762
Oswego	1,327	678
Queens	1,586	783
Rens'	1,144	1,313
Saratoga	452	1,317
Ulster	1,666	1,882
Westchester	1,755	1,985
	63,260	36,535

"The following table shows the same facts as to the counties therein named:

	Kelly
Franklin	16
Jefferson	86
Otsego	74
St. Lawrence	35
Schoharie	16
Tompkins	35
Warren	83
Wyoming	65
	410

In these 8 Counties the Democratic loss was only 684.

"These eight counties, having a population of about 350,000 and nearly 100,000 voters, gave to the Kelly bolt in 1879 only 410 votes, and in 1880, as compared with 1876, they lost only 684. If only this ratio of loss had obtained throughout the State, our candidates would have succeeded by more than 25,000 majority.

"But political cowards lacked the courage so to bear themselves as to command success. At the behest of the malcontents, who only one year before had fatally conspired against the Democratic party and its principles, they committed the cowardly act of calling the Saratoga convention for the avowed purpose of reinstating the traitors of 1879, and restoring them to influence and power. Being thus restored to position and power, the figures above presented are useful as tending to show how that power was used.

"This, however, is by no means the only act of political cowardice connected with the late canvass. In 1876 the people elected Mr. Tilden to the Presidency. There is not at this day an intelligent, fair-minded man in America who doubts it. He was cheated of his rights, and the people were defrauded of their choice of President by the most atrocious crimes known to civilization. The time arrived to select a candidate for 1880. Mr. Tilden still lived, and, though his physical powers were somewhat impaired, he was conceded to be one of the ablest statesmen living. He was reluctant to enter upon the canvass, and asked the people to relieve [him] of so great a burden. Those by whom the crimes referred to were committed, impelled by the desire for self-protection, had devoted themselves for years to unprecedented efforts to destroy him. The logic of the situation, and the exercise of a manly courage, pointed to one single line of duty. That duty was to refuse to accede to Mr. Tilden's request, and to move forward with united voice and action to right the great wrong that had been done by placing him in nomination and electing him to the office from which he had been excluded only by the high crimes of his adversaries. Instead of doing this, men forgot their courage, and took counsel only of their fears. They listened to the clamor of the criminals by whom this great man was maligned, and allowed themselves to be intimidated even by the malcontents who defeated the party only one year before. Mr. Tilden was abandoned, and another candidate was selected. That abandonment was a most conspicuous act of cowardice! And who shall say it has not borne just such fruit as might have been expected?

"The selection made was undoubtedly an excellent one. General Hancock is a true, pure, and able man, and eminently worthy of the high place for which he was named. His nomination was, however, the outcome of a great act of cowardice, and there is not a State in the Union in which multitudes of men did not experience a feeling of disgust at the manifest lack of courage to stand manfully and do what clearly ought to have been done.

"JAMES F. STARBUCK.

"This was completed Dec. 9th, 1880. Mr. Starbuck *died* Dec. 11, 1880."

TILDEN TO CHAUNCEY F. BLACK

"NEW YORK, *January 27, 1881.*

"HON. CHAUNCEY F. BLACK.

"MY DEAR SIR,—I have received your letter notifying me of my unanimous election as the first honorary member of the Jefferson Democratic Association of New York.

"I accept the distinction thus conferred, in order to testify my approval and commendation of the objects of your association.

"Thomas Jefferson has a title to the esteem and gratitude of the American people, even greater than that which he derived from being the Author of the Declaration of Independence, and from being the Author of the Statute of Religious Freedom by the State of Virginia.

"During all the bloody conflicts of the American Revolution, and the civil struggles out of which our system of government emerged, and the controversies through which was impressed upon it the character of a government 'by the people, for the people,' he was the apostle of human freedom, and the greatest leader of that beneficent philosophy which was embodied in our institutions.

"At a time when powerful tendencies are at work to subvert the original character of our government—to break down the limitations of power established by the Constitution—to centralize the action and influence of official authorities—to create a governing class, using the machinery of government as a corrupt balance of power in the elections, and then shaping legislation and administration in the interests of the few against the many—the precepts and example of such a man as Mr. Jefferson cannot be too often invoked.

"The formation of societies which can act as centres of discussion, and as agencies for the propagation of the pure principles of the fathers of the Republic, is a measure capable of great service to the people and to mankind.

"With assurances of sympathy and esteem—to the members of your association and to yourself, I have the honor to be

"Your fellow citizen,
"(Signed) SAMUEL J. TILDEN."

TILDEN TO BIGELOW

(HIS HEALTH FIVE YEARS BEFORE HIS DEATH)

"15 GRAMERCY PARK, NEW YORK,
"*Monday evening, January 31, 1881.*

"DEAR MR. BIGELOW,—I have just received and read your letter of the 18th, and resolve to answer it on the spot. I seem to be free from all engagements and obstructions, and am desirous to atone as far as possible for delinquencies in respect to your two former letters. At the end of two lines, however, I was compelled to refuse to admit a caller. With John's help, to whom I am dictating, both of us sitting before the wood-fire in the dining-room, I will ramble through a few of the many things I would like to say.

"I was not without hope that you had heard of me through Poultney. Mrs. Bigelow gave me a charge to take some care of the desolate members of the family remaining in America, and I have been doing a little to entertain Poultney.

"In respect to my personal health, I cannot make a very decided report, although, on the whole, I think I am improving. I am taking no tea and rarely any coffee. I substantially take no medicine internally. For a month past I have been trying electricity—the continuous current from a galvanic battery—with some apparent advantage. When you consider that the latter period of my work was passed under the aid of the borrowing power of the will, and with some help from medicine to hold my own—when these are withdrawn, is in itself a gain. The later impression is that I have taken rather too much exercise; that the malady is an exhaustion of the central nervous force by overwork and overwear, and that rest rather than physical activity is indicated. It is a problem to avoid fatigue, and yet take exercise enough to keep in order the general functions and particularly the digestion. You will see the situation does not favor very active travel or overmuch sight-seeing or sociable festivities—but I am going too much into detail and yet imperfectly. It is better to reserve opinions for a month or two longer.

"Whether I can go over early enough to do much in Italy is not easy now to say. My disposition is to cross the ocean at some time in the spring. I am snugging up my affairs, and getting out of the way all business matters. Indeed, that is substantially done.

"I should like to know what your own plans are for the spring and summer, or, if they have not taken definite shape, what your contemplations are.

"I am not troubling myself much about business, but perceive a tendency in little things of my own and everybody else to come in and occupy the vacancy. I do not propose to indulge this tendency.

"I thank you for your suggestions in regard to the acquisition of works of art. They seem to me judicious. As to the bust of Cicero of which you sent a photograph, the important question is the authenticity of the bust.

"If you can find satisfactory evidence on that point and think the purchase judicious, you may make it for me.

"The fact is I have really had very little to do with the political movements which you mention—perhaps nothing at all. I do not think I have done more than to express an opinion.

"There are many more things about which I would like to say, but I must reserve them until some future occasion.

"Present my regards to Mrs. Bigelow and the girls, and accept them for yourself.

"Very truly yours,
"S. J. TILDEN."

G. W. SMITH TO W. A. WILKINS

"NEW YORK, *Feb. 21, 1881.*

"MY DEAR SIR,—Mr. Tilden requests me to acknowledge the receipt of your two notes, and to say that he gives them the earliest attention in his power.

"It is a settled policy of Mr. Tilden to abstain from all transactions which may impose upon him any future care. What he can afford to do he gives outright. In addition to claims upon him from kinship or other special relations, every day brings to him more applications by letter and by personal appeal than is possible for him to grant.

"Mr. Tilden has every disposition to be kind to you, and, as a token of his good-will, sends his check for two hundred and fifty dollars, which he will not expect you to repay, and which he hopes will be more serviceable to you than the loan suggested.

"Very truly yours,
"G. W. SMITH."

FROM THE NEW YORK "HERALD," MARCH 5, 1881

(MR. HAYES GOES OUT)

"A rough Republican wit remarked, the other day, that 'Mr. Hayes came in by a majority of one and goes out by unanimous consent.'

"We are not certain that this is quite accurate. A good many people will remember that Mr. Hayes gave the country peace and rest for four years, and that, while he did not make the unimpeachably 'clean' administration of which some of his favorites boast, and did continually, and as may be justly said, brazenly violate his repeated pledges for civil service reform, he managed to avoid great scandals. Most of his Southern appointments were disgraceful; they were worse even, for they did great harm, and there is no denying the truth of the accusation that he put, or kept, corrupt and base men in office—not a few, but dozens upon dozens—to reward them for political and personal services of a kind which no decent public man would recognize. But he passed two or three years in the White House in constant terror of threatened disclosures which would compel him to leave the Presidency a disgraced man, and he probably regarded the improper appointments he made as necessary in self-defence.

"The very general contempt and dislike of Mr. Hayes, felt and openly expressed by public men of both parties, rests, we believe, on a sound basis. That he took the Presidency, knowing he was not elected to it, forms but the smaller part of the ground for this feeling; for, after all, he took it on the decision of a high court of arbitration which was final. His real offence is that he took office at the hands of his party, having carefully deceived it up to the last moment as to his purposes when he got what they only could give him. That great and, in a free government, criminal act of deceit has rightly called down on him the lasting dislike and contempt of his party's leaders and of honest men in both parties."

W. R. MARTIN TO TILDEN

"*March 9, 1881.*

"HON. S. J. TILDEN.

"DEAR SIR,—In reading this article in the *Herald*, I feel with greater force the duty you owe to yourself, and to all, to gather your materials to fix your place in the history of the country. I once spoke to you of this, and you said you would recur to it.

"If you had filled an administration, the records of it would have marked your influence on the progress of the country, but you did not.

"You must gather them, under your own supervision, collect, select, and arrange them, and give the general outline of your positions and purposes yourself.

"It is what the French call, '*Memoirs pour Servir*.' There are many passages where autobiographical sketches will be very valuable.

"You run this great risk of the future: that, while in one light your action after the election may be regarded as in the highest sense patriotic, in the other it may be said that your failure to be President was because of something you lacked.

"It depends upon who your biographer may be. He must be well supplied with all materials, on your arrangement, and informed with your ideas.

"The time that you may devote to this, will it not be the best use you can make of it?

"Yours very truly,
"WM. R. MARTIN."

STILSON HUTCHINS TO TILDEN

"WASHINGTON, *March 18, 1881.*

"MR. TILDEN,—The article which I wrote and published in the *Post* on the morning of the 4th of March, the day on which Mr. Hayes took his leave of his usurped office, you may not have seen, and hence I take the pains to cut it out and enclose it to you. I think few persons—not even your most intimate and immediate friends—have pursued the great fraud or denounced it with more consistency and pertinacity than myself. I have never forgotten for a moment, nor have I allowed an opportunity to pass, to remind the beneficiary or his supporters of the great wrong they have inflicted on the people and the country and the institutions which have endeared it to us. And yet, had you taken your seat, I do not suppose there was one of the four millions who worked for you who would have less to ask than myself.

"With great respect and great regret,

"Yours,
"STILSON HUTCHINS."

TILDEN TO HON. STILSON HUTCHINS

"15 GRAMERCY PARK, NEW YORK, *March 26, 1881.*

"MY DEAR SIR,—I had seen the article, a slip of which you have kindly sent me, and also another similar article of yours largely copied.

"You are entitled to great credit for your faithful vindication of the rights of the Democratic party, and the interests of the people in respect to the election of 1876.

"I never considered the question as at all personal to myself. It seemed to be a duty cast upon me by events to represent the public grievance until the Democratic party and the people had an opportunity to take the matter into their own hands. That duty was very onerous, and certain to be prolific of nothing but sacrifices; and though I would not retire from it, I was glad when it was completed, and I was discharged of responsibility for all consequences of the violation of the elective principle, whatever they made hereafter prove to be.

Very truly yours,
"S. J. TILDEN."

J. S. BLACK TO TILDEN

"BROCKIE, near YORK, PA., *April 5th, 1881.*

"MY DEAR SIR,—At Washington last week I took a tentative look at the business you wot of. The Attorney-General was made to understand the whole affair. He is anxious to be amiable, and, I think, would stop this dirty persecution at once but for Blatchford's decision, which I cannot help but admit is an embarrassing fact, though seen to be perfectly lawless. He proposes that a memorial or formal application be made which he will refer to the local authorities for their report, and he promises to do whatever he can to accomplish the object. He is, of course, not fool enough to believe that the proceeding against you is justified by law. He thinks you had better give a final judgment for any amount that the District Attorney wants, coupled with a protest, and trust to a writ of error.

"The thing looks badly. An appeal to the magnanimity of these people will be so humiliating that I don't see how you can go through it. It will have to be discussed officially and unofficially by the inside and the outside of the administration—in public and in private, and I do not know when it will be ended. Speeding to-day, it may be put back to-morrow, and be lost at last. On the other hand, if you give a *pro forma* judgment, your chances of reversal will be in inverse proportion to the amount of it for certain reasons which I need not now give.

"I think Blaine would have manhood enough to do right, disregarding all other considerations, and sense enough to see that he would make more politically than he would lose, if the responsibility rested entirely upon him, but he is not in a situation to force his advice upon the others.

"The President is not at all equal to such an occasion. He will probably think it a kind of duty to repeat wrongs upon a man whom he has already injured.

"Please to think over all this at your leisure, and decide whether it is not best to defy these devils to their worst.

"I am, yours truly,
"J. S. BLACK."

TILDEN TO DAVID DOWS

"*Personal and confidential.*

"NO. 15 GRAMERCY PARK, NEW YORK, *April 22, 1881.*

"DEAR MR. DOWS,—I recollect that some time ago you casually mentioned that you were a considerable holder of N. Y. Elevated R. R. bonds, and I replied that I held all I ever had; whereupon you reminded me that you knew how many I collected interest on in January.

"It seems to me appropriate to the cordial friendship existing between us that I should tell you that my situation in respect to that investment has changed. I desired before I should go into the country, and especially if I should decide to go abroad, to revise my knowledge in respect to that investment; and before I had completed my investigation it seemed prudent to reduce my interest or dispose of it altogether. I have substantially done the latter.

"I called at your home last evening, but not finding you, and not liking to leave word asking you to call upon me this morning, I send you this note.

"Very truly yours,
"S. J. TILDEN."

DAVID DOWS TO TILDEN

"*April 22d, 1881.*

"DEAR GOVERNOR,—Your note of this date rec'd. I am very much obliged to you for it.

"I think you have acted judiciously, not that I think the bonds unsafe, but I think the chances are that they will decline in price.

"Your note will be regarded as you request and again thanking you for it,

"I am, y'r friend,
"DAVID DOWS."

S. J. TILDEN TO GEORGE BANCROFT

"GREYSTONE, YONKERS, N. Y., *July 11, 1881.*

"DEAR MR. BANCROFT,—I thank you for your kind attention to Mrs. Rummel's[25] request. She is the same lady whom you knew in Berlin.

"I presume that you read other things in preference to the newspapers. That is often the taste of retired statesmen and men of letters. Notably it was of Mr. Jefferson. To mention little things with large, it is my own.

"You remind me that it is five years since I have had the pleasure of seeing you. I hope the interval may not be so long hereafter. In the mean time, I am always glad to hear of your health and happiness.

"With remembrances to your family, and with assurances of cordial esteem for yourself, I remain,

"Very truly yours,
"S. J. TILDEN."

RESOLUTIONS DRAWN BY MR. TILDEN FOR A MEETING OF THE CITIZENS OF YONKERS ON THE OCCASION OF THE DEATH OF PRESIDENT GARFIELD

"*September, 1881.*

"The citizens of Yonkers, convened in public meeting, on the invitation of the Mayor and Aldermen of the city, and presided over by the civic authorities, resolve:

"*First*—That the death of the President of the United States by the individual crime of a private assassin is a deplorable event in our national history; that the evil example is intensified by the occurrence of such an event a second time within about sixteen years; that such treason against the elective sovereignty of the people tends to encourage future attempts to subvert the Chief Magistracy of the Republic by criminal violence, under the influence of progressively increasing temptations to personal resentments and private malignity, which are incident to the ever-growing power and patronage of the executive office; and that all good citizens ought to join in every wise measure for limiting these temptations, and for restoring and strengthening every moral security which heretofore surrounded the First Citizen of the Republic as he moved without guards among the people.

"*Secondly*—That to Mrs. Garfield and the other members of the bereaved family of the heroic sufferer and illustrious victim is given our heart-felt sympathy and condolence."

S. J. TILDEN TO HON. WILLIAM PURCELL

"GREYSTONE, *October 3, 1881.*

"MY DEAR SIR,—I have received your letter stating you intended to call on me and your inability to do so.

"I should have written to you earlier except for an illness, and the pressure of claims upon my attention during my convalescence.

"It would have been agreeable to me to have seen you, and to have treated you with that frankness and courtesy you have always experienced from me.

"In respect to your assurance that you would not be a candidate for nomination, if your nomination 'would be disagreeable to me and be discountenanced by me,' I have to say that I cannot assume any such position. I have neither the right nor the wish to exclude you from a legitimate and honorable competition for any public trust. My practice, when I was at the head of the party organization, was not to become a partisan of any particular candidate, but to confine myself to such advisory suggestions as might seem fit and useful during the deliberations of the convention; to defer largely to the judgment of the best men of the counties, formed at the convention, in view of immediate action on the complex considerations which enter into the formation of a collective ticket. I need not say that I have not undertaken any such function on the present occasion, and have not possessed myself of the information to make me competent to such a work. I assume that you have not given credit to the idle fictions of Republican and other newspapers which ascribe to me a desire to control the nominations and canvass for the present year with a view to becoming a candidate for Governor next year. The truth is, I ran for Governor in 1874 simply for the purpose of sustaining the reform movement to which I had given the three preceding years, and I should not have continued in the office for a second term in any possible event; nor would I now entertain the idea of returning to it, even if I flattered myself that I would receive a unanimous vote of the people.

"All I desire for the Democratic party in the coming canvass is, that it shall make the best possible choice of candidates, and do everything to advance the principles of administration to which I have devoted so many efforts and sacrifices.

"With cordial good wishes, very truly yours,

"(Signed) S. J. TILDEN.[26]

"*Hon Wm. Purcell.*"

TILDEN TO GEORGE W. SMITH

"GREYSTONE, *October 26, 1881.*

"DEAR MR. SMITH,—Will you see Mr. Cooper and communicate to him the following:

"The view which I took of the matter talked about between Mr. Cooper and myself yesterday is unchanged. If nothing can be raised in New York for the State committee, the best way is frankly to communicate the fact. It could scarcely be expected to foray on one man for the whole supplies desired. I am subject to a continual running fire of contributions. To deal with them, and with the applications now before me, or sure to come, will be as much as ought to be expected from me.

"When I was at the head of the committee I stopped the practice of distributing funds from the State committee to the localities; and nothing of the kind was done in any campaign which I directed, or in which I was a candidate. I doubted the system, and can scarcely be expected to renew it single-handed on my individual account.

"Of course, nobody will give or take any trouble to collect money, if all that is necessary is to ask one man for it.

"I do not just now feel very affluent. I have given away so much this year, and have been led into such large expenses that I am trenching upon my capital, and do not feel as indifferent to unnecessary extravagance as I might under other circumstances.

S. J. T."

HARRIET F. TYLDEN TO TILDEN

"CUMBERLAND HOUSE, CHILHAM, N. CANTERBURY, KENT,
"*3d Decr. 1881.*

"MY DEAR GOVERNOR,—In looking through the books in the library at Chilham Castle yesterday I came across four ponderous volumes of Halsted's *History of Kent*, published about one hundred years ago. In referring to the index of the second and third volumes, I found several entries of the name of *Tilden* as holding possession of manors in the reign of King Henry the Second. There was a parish called Tilden also, but, in the reign of Charles the First, the names of Tilden and Tylden seem to be used indiscriminately to designate the same individual. This carries out my husband's often-disputed assertion that there were family records in existence when he was a child proving that Tilden was the original name; but that, in the reign of Charles the First, the family divided into two branches, one following the fortunes of King Charles, calling themselves Tylden, and the other who sided with Cromwell, keeping to the old spelling, *Tilden.* And it seems to me that the Puritan names in your family, 'Samuel,' 'Solomon,' goes far towards proving the truth of the statement. We, while adopting the 'Y' in the surname, have kept fast to the Christian names of Richard and of John, but especially Richard. Nearly every Tilden in Halsted's History for centuries past has borne this Christian name. I think it likely you may have seen the book or have had extracts from it made for you. Should such *not* to be the case, I shall be *only too pleased* to copy out everything relating to your ancestors from the history at Chilham Castle. A lady in Kent is busy on a genealogy of the Tyldens, but as yet I have not seen it, and no doubt she differs from my husband in thinking the Tildens dropped the 'y' and inserted an 'i' in the time of Cromwell when they are supposed to have emigrated to America.

"I hope you continue in good health. We have seen your name prominently brought forward during the elections. The weather was dreadfully rough here after your nieces sailed. I hope they got safely back.

"I expect Dick to spend his Christmas with me. Katie is staying with a friend, but I expect her home next week. Mr. Parnell has done great harm in Ireland: six hundred ladies are in the Unions (parish work-houses), owing to non-payment of rent.

"Believe me to be,

"Always sincerely yours,
"HARRIET F. TYLDEN."

C. A. DANA TO TILDEN

"'THE SUN,' NEW YORK, *Feb. 23, 1882.*

"DEAR MR. TILDEN,—I have been slow in thanking you for the box of Steinberger Cabinet, because I only wish to taste it in the most adequate society; and now, having had a suitable opportunity, I am prepared to say again that the wine is one of the very noblest products of nature, and that I am, as ever,

Sincerely yours,
"CHARLES A. DANA."

"This shows that two men at least knew Steinberger Cabinet of 1868, which cost $84 a case—gold—in 1870.

"G. W. S."

The following letter was in reply to a gentleman in Texas, who proposed to start a newspaper at Floresville, Wilson County, Texas, with Mr. Tilden's name at the head of its editorial columns as its candidate for the Presidency. It was dated May, 1882. The answer was written at Mr. Tilden's request by George W. Smith, then his secretary.

"GREYSTONE, *July 8, 1882.*

"DEAR SIR,—Mr. Tilden thanks you for the kind sentiments expressed towards him in your volume of poems, a copy of which you so kindly sent to him.

"In respect to your starting a newspaper and keeping his name 'at the masthead as the Democratic nominee for President in 1884,' I would say that Mr. Tilden started in life and passed almost through the allotted time of human existence, on the theory of performing all the duties which a citizen of the Republic owes to the State without ever entering upon an official career. His entrance into public life was a deviation from his plan, made for a temporary period and for a special purpose. He has no desire, I think, to again quit his home, his books, and his private pursuits.

"Very truly yours,
"G. W. SMITH, Secretary."

GEORGE CARY EGGLESTON TO TILDEN

"797 GREENE AVENUE, BROOKLYN, *2 Aug. 1882.*

"MY DEAR SIR,—May I trespass upon your attention, briefly, in behalf of a literary undertaking in which I think you will feel an interest? The facts are these: Mrs. Charlotte M. Clarke, who has won a very decided success as a novelist while writing under a pseudonym, has now in press a novel of a good deal more than ordinary breadth and power, in which she treats the social and political history of this country during the period immediately preceding the late war and later. It is now her purpose to carry the review forward in another novel to be entitled *The Theft of an Empire*, and to concern itself with the events of 1876.

"From the character of the work now in press, which I have had occasion to read in proof, I am satisfied that in the hands of this writer the story of the election frauds of 1876 will have such a dramatic setting forth as will command respect and attention in quarters where the facts are now misconstrued. I need not suggest to you the potency of fiction to impress truths of this nature upon minds which receive such truths in no other way, but I may assure you that I know of no author likely to make so effective use of this material as Mrs. Clarke.

"The lady already has possession of very valuable materials, and in making further collections she will have the active assistance of some of the most prominent editors and public men of the country, who are her friends; but she is especially anxious to get possession of certain facts which you can doubtless furnish at once, but which it would be difficult to get elsewhere. In her eagerness to get full and accurate information for this purpose, she asks the privilege of an interview with you at your own convenience, and my own interest in the due performance of this necessary work induces me to make this request for her. With respect to myself, and the sincerity of my interest in the establishment of historic truth in this connection, I beg to refer you to my friend Mr. Parke Godwin, under whom I served upon the editorial staff of the *Evening Post.*

"Mrs. Clarke is staying for a few days at the Hotel Branting, Madison Avenue and Fifty-eighth Street, and, if you are willing to grant her request for a brief interview, she will call upon you at any time you may name, and will trespass as little as may be upon your time.

"Very respectfully, your obt. servant,
"GEO. CARY EGGLESTON."

D. B. HILL TO TILDEN

"MAYOR'S OFFICE, ELMIRA, N. Y., *Sept. 2, 1882.*

"HON. SAMUEL J. TILDEN.

"MY DEAR SIR,—I would very much like the Democratic nomination for Lieutenant Governor, and, if you can consistently aid me in securing it, I shall be under renewed obligations to you. I think I am as much entitled to it as either of the other gentlemen mentioned for the place. My district has been solid for 'our side' ever since you asked me to take hold of it and make it right, which was early in 1875. I have had to fight strong men—such men as Arnot, McGuire, Walker, and McGee, who have all been combined against me, and who started a newspaper to crush me out, and I have come out ahead every time. It has, however, been a hard struggle for many years.

"If I could receive this nomination, I should be greatly gratified. The party leaders on our side—such men as Messrs. Manning, Faulkner, McLaughlin, Thompson, Whitney, Weed, and others—will accept your suggestion on this subject, and be glad to adopt a course which will meet with your approval.

"If you will speak a good work for me for this nomination, it will settle the question. If there is any plan or arrangement agreed upon, which renders my candidacy embarrassing to you or our friends, or makes it inexpedient or impolitic, I should like to be advised of it.

"I trust you will see your way clear to do this for me.

"I remain, faithfully yours,
"D. B. HILL."

PARKE GODWIN TO TILDEN

"ROSLYN, *Oct. 3d, '82.*

"MY DEAR TILDEN,—I am one of the committee appointed to raise subscriptions for the Statue of Liberty to be placed on Bedloe's Island, and we propose, this fall, to go to work earnestly to raise the necessary money. I should like very much to put down your name as the first, in a good sum—and my own as the first successful applicant. Evarts, the head of our committee, has been dilatory, but there is no doubt we shall succeed. It is an important object, in which I have interested myself from the first, and am still interested. I know that applications of this kind are often made to you—and, if you have the least reluctance, just burn this up, and consider it unwritten.

"Yours truly,
"PARKE GODWIN."

PARKE GODWIN TO TILDEN

"MURRAY HILL, 19 EAST 37TH ST., *Oct. 12th, 1882.*

"MY DEAR TILDEN,—It seems to be the general opinion of our committee on the Statue of Liberty that we ought to have the name of an ex-President and ex-Governor of New York on the list of our subscribers. I concur in that opinion, and hope you will be induced to lend us a helping hand. The subscriptions range thus far from $1 to $5000, and we shall try to get $10,000 from Vanderbilt and Astor each. I should like to see one great representative of Liberty, in all the best senses of the word, at the head of the poll.

"Yours very truly,
"PARKE GODWIN."

MARY TILDEN TO S. J. TILDEN

"ST. OLAVE'S, TRINITY CRESCENT, FOLKESTONE, *Oct. 12, 1882.*

"DEAR SIR,—Some few years back I heard that you came to England to look up some of your relations. I so much regret that I did not have the pleasure of making your acquaintance, as we are the old family of Tildens of Ifield Court in the parish of Northfleet.

"I have always heard my husband say that there were three branches of the Tilden family: one lived at Milsted (Sir John Tylden), they altered the spelling of the name; one branch went to America, and the other to Ifield Court. My husband was the fourth John Tilden who had lived at the old place; we were married in 1838, and I lived there with him thirty-four years, as he died in 1872 at the age of seventy-six. He was twenty years older than me; we have three children—my eldest son John still has Ifield Court. My daughter Lucy married, in 1868, Captain Miller, of the Royal Engineers; he died of typhoid fever at Gibraltar in 1876, leaving his wife and four children—three girls and one boy; they are now living with me. William, my youngest son, is a major in the Sixtieth Rifles; he has just engaged himself to be married to a Miss Bell, a lady of good family and connections.

"If you should visit England again, I hope I may have the opportunity of meeting you. I have long wished to write to you, but did not know where to address you. This summer I was spending a few weeks at Thonne in Switzerland, and an American gentleman and his wife were staying at the hotel. They were struck with my name and asked if we were related to you. I asked if he would give me your address, which he did, and I made up my mind to write to you as soon as I returned home.

"There is a church not far from here called Lynne, where Canon Jenkins took me to see where some of our ancestors were buried, spelling their names as we do, *Tilden.* My dear husband was very proud of his family; his brothers are all dead; he has only three sisters living; there *were* twelve in the family. I hope you will pardon my writing to you, but I feel you would like to know something of the Ifield Court, Tildens.

"My daughter unites with me in kind regards to her kinsman, and believe me,

"My dear sir, yours very truly,
"MARY TILDEN."

TILDEN TO MRS. LOWELL

"GREYSTONE, YONKERS, N. Y., *November 15, 1882.*

"DEAR MRS. LOWELL,—I received, on Saturday evening, your letter dated November 3d, and take the first time at my command to answer it.

"You do not overestimate the influx of communications which you are pleased to term 'begging letters.' They count by thousands. It is only in rare and exceptional cases that they can be answered. To comply with their requests would overmatch the journalistic exaggerations of the income and fortune which, in the mind of each applicant, is compared with a single want, presented as most meritorious, and as very inconsiderable in amount.

"I had occasion to tell the principal of a college, who tried to tempt my vanity with the offer to call an edifice by my name, that I should regard it as a calamity to be published as a philanthropist—having discovered that a dim suspicion of that character is scarcely consistent with the repose of a retired life.

"Nevertheless, I am open to consider the case to which you call my attention. Would it be convenient to you, some day when I am in New York, to call upon me, or to send some well-informed person to explain to me your scheme—what it needs and what your plans are? If so, I will make an appointment not earlier than next week.

"Very truly yours,
"S. J. TILDEN."

TILDEN TO MRS. LOWELL

"January 2, 1883.

"DEAR MRS. LOWELL,—I have received your note containing some account of the subscriptions for the Charity Organization Society.

"Herewith is the speech which I promised to send.

"My subscription, which was to be paid after the beginning of the New Year, will be ready whenever you may come, in person, to collect it. Since almost seven years elapsed without my having the pleasure to see you, I do not like to throw away this occasion.

"Very truly yours,
"S. J. TILDEN.

"*Mrs. J. S. Lowell.*"

TILDEN TO CHARLES A. DANA

"YONKERS, N. Y., *January 2, 1883.*

"DEAR MR. DANA,—I reciprocate your good wishes for the New Year for both yourself and Mrs. Dana.

"I fear there is some danger that the unsettling of the established system in regard to the canals may lead to projects for enlargements which will be of no real utility, but mere pretences for a renewal of abuses.

"I send herewith a copy of my speech on the canals in the convention of 1867, which, I think, you once expressed a wish to see; and also a copy of my first Message which contains a passage on the same subject.[27]

"It is sad to think of Louis Blanc and Gambetta, who have just passed away. In September and October, 1877, when Mr. Bigelow and I were in Paris, we saw something of them. Louis Blanc was an intelligent, mild man of gentle manners, and with the air of a scholar or professor. Gambetta seemed to be an impersonation of great forces. I brought back a magnificent photograph of him, which I have been examining with fresh interest to-day. Both knew enough of American politics to sympathize with the view you take of the electoral transaction of 1876-7.

"Very truly yours."

TILDEN TO PARKE GODWIN

"GREYSTONE, *January 11, 1883.*

"DEAR MR. GODWIN,—I intended to answer your first letter in respect to the foundation of the Statue of Liberty, although it expressly waived a reply. My thought then was to have a conference which should explain to me the scheme proposed; but, in the progress of time, that result came about of itself....

"My impression has been, and still remains, that other objects ought to have a preference; and those will suffice to consume all I shall at present devote to such purposes.

"With my best wishes for the health, prosperity, and happiness of yourself and family, I remain,

"Very truly yours."

HENRY ADAMS TO TILDEN

"1607 H STREET, WASHINGTON, *24 Jan., 1883.*

"DEAR SIR,—Your kind letter of the 12th, acknowledging the receipt at some past time of a copy of *New England Federalism*, reached me yesterday. I am forced to confess that I have equally forgotten sending you the book, and can recall nothing except the fact that I sent you my *Life of Gallatin* in consequence of assistance which you rendered me in regard to it. Probably the other book was sent in the same connection. I am quite sure that while in Europe, where I went for papers after the *Gallatin* appeared, I received a letter of acknowledgment from you for the volume.

"To do justice to Gallatin was a labor of love. After long study of the prominent figures in our history, I am more than ever convinced that for combination of ability, integrity, knowledge, unselfishness, and social fitness Mr. Gallatin has no equal. He was the most fully and perfectly equipped statesman we can show. Other men, as I take hold of them, are soft in some spots and rough in others. Gallatin never gave way in my hand or seemed unfinished. That he made mistakes I can see, but even in his blunders he was respectable.

"I cannot say as much for his friends Jefferson, Madison, and Monroe, about whom I have been for years hard at work. In regard to them I am incessantly forced to devise excuses and apologies or to admit that no excuse will avail. I am at times almost sorry that I ever undertook to write their history, for they appear like mere grasshoppers kicking and gesticulating on the middle of the Mississippi River. There is no possibility of reconciling their theories with their acts, or their extraordinary foreign policy with dignity. They were carried along on a stream which floated them, after a fashion, without much regard to themselves.

"This I take to be the result that students of history generally reach in regard to modern times. The element of individuality is the free-will dogma of the science, if it is a science. My own conclusion is that history is simply social development along the lines of weakest resistance, and that in most cases the line of weakest resistance is found as unconsciously by society as by water.

"I am very truly y'rs,
"HENRY ADAMS."

JOHN BIGELOW TO TILDEN

"THURSDAY MG., *April 19* (*1883*).

"MY DEAR GOVERNOR,—Referring to the request of L. Smith Hobart, of New Haven, in regard to your collegiate residence at New Haven, I find myself only partially prepared to answer his questions, and though I had it on my mind when I saw you Tuesday morning to question you of other matters, I left without bethinking me of that duty.

"Your correspondence shows that you entered Yale College a third-term Freshman in the year 1834, and left at the close of that term never to return, for in December you were settled in New York. I find no evidence of your having returned to college in the fall.

"But there is nothing in your correspondence to show what *room* you occupied. As you ate at Commons, I infer that you had a room in the college.

"If you will have the goodness to supply the information about the number of your room and the name of the college building that you occupied, I will be prepared to answer Mr. Hobart.

"If I am not right in assuming that you were a Yale third-term Freshman in 1834, and no longer, please correct me.

"Yours faithfully,
"JOHN BIGELOW.

"P. S.—If you did not room in the college, please tell me where or with whom you had lodgings."

TILDEN TO BIGELOW

"GREYSTONE, *April 20, 1883.*

"DEAR MR. BIGELOW,—I entered Yale College in the third term of the Freshman class, in June, 1834. I had no room in the college building, but I had a room in the house of a Mr. Goodman, which was situated below the Tontine, in a street at right angles with the front of the college buildings. At first I took my meals at Commons, but soon found that the diet would not answer for my delicate stomach. I left the college at the end of the Freshman year, expecting to return after the long vacation, but found myself unable.

"As Mr. Hobart seems to desire more particulars, I enclose herewith two copies of the *Courier Journal* Biography. Would it not be well for you to open communication with Mr. Hobart, saying that his letter had been referred to you?[28]

"Very truly yours,
"S. J. TILDEN."

TILDEN TO MRS. MARY TILDEN

"GREYSTONE, *June 19, 1883.*

"DEAR MRS. TILDEN,—Your kind and interesting letter of October 12, 1882, has ever since awaited an opportunity for me to answer it, which, with the best intentions, has not been accomplished until now. I regret that I did not have the pleasure of making your acquaintance when I was last in England in 1877.

"My grandfather's name was John, which seems to have been a favorite name in that branch of the family. The ancestor who migrated to this country was Nathaniel; he came from Tenterden, of which he and several of his kinsmen had been Mayor.

"I am interested in the particulars which your letter contains in respect to your family.

"I send a photograph of myself. Please present to your daughter and accept for yourself my best regards.

"Very truly yours,
"(Signed) S. J. TILDEN."

MARY E. BLAIR TO TILDEN

"FALKLAND, MONTGOMERY COUNTY, MD., *June 26th.*

"MR. TILDEN.

"DEAR SIR,—Mr. Blair was much touched by your kind note of sympathy received a few days since. When I wrote Mr. Bigelow I was anxious and hurried, fearing the fatigue of the drive to the country on Mr. Blair. The change has been most beneficial, and his improvement since we came very decided, though our city papers will contrive to say that he is very ill. We are all greatly encouraged. He has less pain—is stronger and sleeps better. I follow your advice, and only present the most agreeable topics for his thoughts. The arrival of a young Holstein or Jersey calf—the Silo well filled—and a touch of the New York *Sun's* sarcasm often diverts his attention from himself and interests him. He desires me to remember him kindly to you. I hope the papers report truly when they say your own health is so good.

"Very truly yrs.,
"MARY E. BLAIR."

TILDEN TO MRS. BLAIR

"GREYSTONE, YONKERS, N. Y., *July 28, 1883.*

"DEAR MRS. BLAIR,—I am deeply afflicted by the sad intelligence concerning Mr. Blair which comes to-day. I share with you and his children in the great bereavement, lamenting that I am so impotent to lessen your sorrow while mingling with it my own.

"Tendering you my heart-felt condolences, I am,

"Very truly yours."

WILLIAM ALLEN BUTLER TO TILDEN

"TRINITY BUILDING, 111 BROADWAY, *Sept. 10, 1883.*

"MY DEAR GOVERNOR,—I am asked to write you a line about the law school of the New York University whose work and wants have, I understand, been brought to your attention. While the early plans of my father and his associates, Judge Kent and Mr. David Graham, Jr., were not carried out according to their full intention in its foundation, the later years of the school have been full of encouragement, and it is now prospering under good management. The class of young men who avail of its instruction is largely drawn from those students who must make their way in the profession for themselves; and the training they get is, I believe, exceptionally thorough and conscientious. I have no right to make any suggestions on the subject; but you will, I am sure, appreciate my interest in the school and my motive in saying what I have said in regard to its merits.

"Yours very truly,
"WM. ALLEN BUTLER."

W. P. SCOTT TO TILDEN

"*Personal.*

"NEW ORLEANS, *Sept. 16th, 1883.*

"DEAR SIR,—There come times in men's lives when, it matters not how carefully they have builded, how deep the structure strikes its foundations, or how critically material shall have been selected, all fail if the keystone be not placed skilfully, in season, and well.

"In these States, your sagacity, ability, firmness, and all that pertains to stamp the man as leader, is recognized to such an extent that it renders success impossible to any but yourself. The scheme of politicians may succeed in party conventions, but when candidates nominated by the party appear 'in the fierce light that beats around the throne,' the Democracy will soon find that the voters have discovered that a stronger element has been discarded than won, if you be not nominated.

"In 1880 success was impossible without your name for President, and the case applies with equal vigor at this moment. Since your resignation of its command, drift has been its policy, blunder its action.

"In '74, when nominated for Governor of your State, a Republican majority of 50,000 stared you in the face; your former efforts in the interests of reform nominated you; you had builded well.

"The 14th of September, '74, in this city, drew aside the full curtain and allowed the American people to view the workings of Republican reconstruction in the South; showed how hollow the Republican State government was, and committed the general government to the 'bayonet policy' more absolutely than ever. The people of Louisiana appealed to the nation, through the mouths of cannon, to free her of her oppressors, who were at the moment attempting to deny the right of citizens to keep and bear arms. The leader of that movement was Fred N. Ogden whom C. A. Burke is now vigorously opposing for the Governorship of this State, which nomination takes place in a few months and the election in April, '84. When the convention meets it will in all probability elect delegates to the national convention.

"Two years before your nomination the Democratic party was not able to place a candidate in the field for President, and in '76 elected a President. Louisiana contributed her eight votes to yourself, and maintained, through Fred N. Ogden, on the 9th of January, '77, the genuineness of her vote by destroying every opposition to the Nicholls government, and compelling Hayes to stamp his election as fraudulent without recourse.

"When your election for Governor took place the people were not disappointed, and your reforms heightened the enthusiasm engendered by the campaign of '74, and made your nomination certain for the highest office in the gift of the people. You know much better than myself the causes of its end, and suffice to say that, in my opinion, your patriotism came to me in a stronger and purer light than ever before by your action in not precipitating a civil war of unknown consequences.

"At this moment the situation of the Democratic party is this, in my opinion:

Electoral votes South		153
New Jersey	9	
Connecticut	6	
New York	36	—51
		204
Majority		3

"You are the only man who can carry New York and fill the void that her loss would incur.

"Now, I ask you, Mr. Tilden, to ponder well the refusal of yourself through friends for the candidacy of President.

"Have you not placed yourself so high that you cannot refuse; cannot even afford to deny the right of your friends to run you for your just vindication?

"Let your friends announce that you will accept the responsibility if nominated, however great the sacrifice, and your nomination is assured and your election certain.

"With other candidate I fear the usual result: 'defeat.' You have builded well; your ability will not allow you to cease at the moment of your triumph. You stand upon the banks of Rubicon. Empire is beyond, wilderness behind.

"Enemies delight in publishing your unalterable determination not to be a candidate; your friends cannot even say that you will accept the position if nominated.

"In the past, as in the future, I will trust in your patriotism; and in your own due season, when the fruit be ripe, I trust and know that you will not fail to gather the harvest properly, honestly, and well.

"Your obt. servant,
"W. P. SCOTT."

TILDEN TO WILLIAM ALLEN BUTLER

"*Oct. 11/83.*

"DEAR MR. BUTLER,—You are right in supposing that I do not fail to appreciate the motives of your suggestion in respect to the law school, but I am not prepared to say anything on the subject.

"Very truly yours,
"S. J. TILDEN."

M. W. FULLER[29] TO W. H. BARNUM, CHAIRMAN OF NATIONAL DEMOCRATIC COMMITTEE

"CHICAGO, *December 23, 1883.*

"MY DEAR SIR,—It is clear to demonstration that Mr. Tilden should be our nominee, and if he would consent to run, that he would be again elected, this time by an overwhelming electoral as well as popular majority. From the moment of the nomination to the close of the polls, the canvass would be a triumphal progress. We should be obliged to do some hard fighting, but always under the influence of assured victory by fighting. The nomination and election would not simply vindicate Mr. Tilden, but the right of the people to elect their own officers. Nor is this all. If Mr. Tilden would accept the nomination, that would relieve the Democracy of all jealousy and heart-burning—all controversy between rival candidates, all difficulty in the convention or after the convention. Again, the platform could be carefully drawn before the meeting of the convention, and ought to be by Mr. Tilden himself. Since the days of Jefferson and Franklin, this country has not had a statesman whose pen could delineate so accurately and so simply a principle, a policy, or a line of conduct. What the people need is somebody who can tell them with accuracy and simplicity just what they themselves think. This is the secret of Mr. Tilden's great popularity with the masses, the existence of which eminent jackasses in our party have often denied, and do not seem to comprehend now that they are beginning to be driven to concede it. There are always political prophets (I don't mean to speak irreverently) looking for power in the wind, or the earthquake, or the fire, instead of the still, small voice. Now, the question of Mr. Tilden's health presents itself about which I know absolutely nothing. His age is no objection. Cato learned Greek at eighty, and Goethe completed 'Faust' after he had passed eighty. Taney and Shaw delivered judgments when nearly ninety. Look at John Quincy Adams and Gladstone and 'old Palm.' Why, Lord Palmerston at the age of eighty saved his administration by a masterly practical speech delivered without a note in the early hours of the morning. And, speaking of him, McCarthy, in his *History of Our Own Times*, commences the chapter on the death of Lord Palmerston with the quotation, 'Unarm, Eros, the long day's task is done and we must sleep.' Mr. Tilden's day has not been so long by eleven years. Is his task done? The unfinished window in Aladdin's tower must not remain unfinished. The art of prolonging life lies in an object to be attained. I admit that various things are to be taken into consideration as assisting in sustaining health, and in that way prolonging mere existence; but all these, while mere adjuncts to vegetation, really amount to nothing if there be not a sufficient object for living outside of keeping one's self on this side of the river. I can conceive of no higher object than the attainment of the Chief Magistracy with the view of benefiting the people of this Republic. Here I do Mr. Tilden justice. He is now at an age when he doubtless feels that merely being President is in itself vanity. That doll is stuffed with saw-dust, just as all other dolls are found to be by all men, children of a larger growth. But if he can, by being President, benefit this people by saving their institutions, now in utmost peril, by reforming the methods of administration, by teaching both the great parties, and, in an especial degree, his own, that adherence to principle is as desirable in a party as in an individual, &c., &c., is that not an object worthy the attainment of any man? And is it not an object that would prolong life, and not bring it to termination? I am very much mistaken if renomination, and election, and administration would not do Mr. Tilden good. Of course, as the returns came pouring in, there might be some hours of excitement which possibly would lead to a reaction; but I think not, as what is to be done would still lie ahead. The election would simply give him the certificate, but his duty would commence after the 4th of March. And here consider that what hurried Harrison into his grave was probably office-seeking; but that a man who could lug Roman consuls into his inaugural address probably thought it necessary to listen to every tide-waiter—a kindly but fatal error. I have seen a suggestion in the papers which, by the way, might have come from Mr. Tilden himself, which assigned to others selected by the President the burden of administrative detail. Certainly, in such particulars, my opinion is that Mr. Tilden knows who to choose to carry out his ideas. The difference between one man and another lies a good deal in the ability to do work through others, and the sagacity to select them. So far as the canvass or the administration is concerned, Mr. Tilden would be benefited by both, and injured by neither. As to the second place on the ticket, I think it should be given Governor Hendricks. Napoleon said, 'Imagination rules the world,' and you may depend upon it that sentiment cuts no inconsiderable part in all elections. It must be taken in solution, it is true, but it is a necessary ingredient. Apart from the necessity of the 'old ticket,' it has great strength because it *is* the old ticket. There is a certain sense of justice that has gone unsatisfied since March, 1877, and you blunt its edge if you change the ticket. Undoubtedly Mr. Hendricks made a great mistake in 1880, but such mistakes are often inevitable, and ought never to be irretrievable. That he should now be in favor of the old ticket simply shows that he wishes to reattain his old position in politics. His error threw him out of the line, as everybody knew it would. That he should desire to get back again is natural enough. I thought yesterday you were entirely wrong in attributing another motive entirely foreign to his character. Assuming that the old ticket is to be nominated, and by acclamation, as it would be, this would as readily happen at Chicago as anywhere else. It is much better to have it done here than in any Eastern city. The only doubt is, would it not be better, partly as a matter of sentiment, to select St. Louis, and have the same temporary chairman, committees, and so on, as in 1876, and the same platform, corrected by Mr. Tilden so as to adapt it to the changes produced by lapse of time, and to shape it on the subject of the defeat of the people's will in 1876-7? So far as any other ticket is concerned, Chicago is the place, and so far as the old ticket is concerned, it is the place, except upon the ground above indicated.

"I have but little doubt that Mr. Tilden could carry this State. It would need a good State ticket to ensure it. But if it were known that the old ticket was to run, I think we should get a good local ticket.

"Excuse the length of this letter and, if you can write me, I wish you would.

"The compliments of the season to you and yours.

"Very truly yours,
"M. W. FULLER."

CYRUS H. McCORMICK TO TILDEN

"CHICAGO, ILL., *April 7th, 1884.*

"MY DEAR SIR,—I had a meeting of a few friends at dinner at my house last Friday, some mention of which, I trust, may not be entirely without interest to you. The gentlemen present were Senator McDonald, of Indiana; Mr. W. C. Goudy (member of National Democratic Committee); Mr. F. H. Winston; Mr. Henry G. Miller; Mr. Commissioner Mattocks; Mr. Perry H. Smith, Jr., and my son, all of this city. Judge Shepard, Mr. C. C. Copeland, and Mr. Melville Fuller were invited but could not attend.

"My letter of the 27th of March addressed to yourself was read to the gentlemen present and unanimously approved. I had had a call from Senator McDonald the day before, and had shown him a copy of my letter to you and discussed the subject with him to some extent. He seemed to think that 'the old ticket' (Tilden and Hendricks) would take better in this State than *Tilden and McDonald*, seeming, himself, not inclined to antagonize Hendricks on a ticket headed by yourself; but, at the same time, he stated unhesitatingly that, as a politician, in the ranks of the Democracy, he felt himself subject to the orders of the party.

"There was a striking unanimity of sentiment between the gentlemen present (except Senator McDonald) as to the contents of my letter referred to, while our family physician (a prominent Republican) remarked to me that the ticket mentioned would suit him precisely, and that it would give him pleasure to vote for it. An editorial article in the *Chicago Times*, in speaking of the prospective Democratic candidates, remarked that 'nobody wanted Mr. Hendricks.'

"Since the date of my letter to you, I have observed in the papers very favorable comments by Horatio Seymour on the subject of your health and ability to stand for a Presidential nomination; and I have also observed sundry reviews, by other parties, of the same character—perhaps in all which it may be said that, while you are disinclined to deprive yourself of your home comforts and enjoyments, you have in no case been found to say positively that, if nominated by the convention, you would not accept.

"I may add that Senator McDonald agreed heartily with the other gentlemen present at our dinner party that *no other name could command the support of the Democrats of the country that yours would.*

"Under the circumstances, I beg to ask whether it would be agreeable to your feelings or wishes that I should say anything publicly in regard to the momentous issues briefly referred to in this correspondence.

"I remain, my dear sir,

"Your friend and servant,
"CYRUS H. MCCORMICK."

HENRY C. SEMPLE TO TILDEN

"GILSEY HOUSE, NEW YORK, *April 23d, 1884.*

"DEAR SIR,—I regret that your business engagements make it inconvenient for you to receive me for a few minutes, as I am obliged to set out for home on Thursday evening, and came on from Washington (where I have been in attendance on the Sup. Ct.) principally to see you.

"You must be aware that the Democratic party will not even consider the question of selecting among candidates for the Presidency, unless satisfied that you will be incapable of entering on the discharge of the duties of the office when elected.

"Sensible men in the party will not ask that you *consent* to be a candidate, nor will they regard the fact that you decline to become a candidate.

"Those who wish to see the Republican party maintained in power till we shall cease to have a Republican *government* try to persuade the people that your health renders it *impossible* for you to discharge the duties of the office. Those in our own party, who look to their own interests rather than to the good of the people, would also have us believe this.

"Though comparatively a young man, I acted in 1848 as secretary of a meeting of distinguished men in the Senate who, indignant at Cass' answer in the question of slavery in the territories, proposed to bring out another Democratic candidate, so as to insure his defeat and teach the majority of the party a lesson.

"They selected Littleton Waller Tazewell, of Virginia, and addressed him a letter, asking that he should become a candidate. I, as secretary, preceded this letter to him with a private letter, assuring him that in addition to the names of Yancey and others composing the committee, that the movement would be supported by Jefferson Davis and other leaders who would also write to him to urge his candidacy.

"Mr. Tazewell replied at once, saying substantially that, while entertaining the same opinions, and cherishing the same hopes expressed by the committee, he must decline to allow the use of his name as a candidate, and that no additional numbers, however respectable, would alter his views.

"He advised them to select a candidate from another class; that the Priams of the party said that he could only hope to last *telum imbellisim ictu*, etc., etc.

"In his private letter to me he said that, recognizing me as the son of an old friend, he would say that, while old and infirm (upwards of eighty, I think), he regarded it as the duty of the citizen to serve the State when called on. That Coriolanus had admitted this. That any man could say he would not become a *candidate*, but no one could say he would not *serve* the State.

"I am one of the few survivors of the patriotic but mistaken associates who addressed that letter to Tazewell thirty-six years ago. On his declination no further steps were taken, and the matter was kept quiet. Some of them have since filled high offices—one was afterwards a justice of Supreme Court, New York, others Senators in Congress—places which they would never have filled had this affair become public. Had it become public it is possible that Yancey's influence would have been so far impaired that he would not have possessed the power, in 1860, to 'precipitate the South into a revolution.'

"I thought that a history of this matter might be interesting to you, and that I might draw some inferences from its discussion with you which might enable me to render a valuable service to the country. I believe that Hon. John A. Campbell is the only man now living who could be compromised in any manner by what I have said as to the correspondence with Mr. Tazewell in 1848; but can rely, of course, on your discretion for the preservation of a curious bit of political history.

"Resp'y and truly yours,
"HENRY C. SEMPLE."

D. MAGONE TO DANIEL MANNING

"*Confidential.*

"OGDENSBURG, *Apl. 24th, 1884.*

"DANIEL MANNING, ESQ.

"MY DEAR SIR,—Permit me to advise that whatever your individual opinion is, as to the propriety of Mr. Tilden's candidacy for the Presidency, he should not authoritatively decline until after the election of the delegates to our State convention.

"His name will greatly aid in securing honest delegates. Please give me any point you can, as I only wish to know what may better enable me to second you in the hard work that I know you have to do.

"Truly yours,
"D. MAGONE."

LYMAN TRUMBULL TO TILDEN

"CHICAGO, *June 7, 1884.*

"HON. SAMUEL J. TILDEN.

"MY DEAR SIR,—The Republicans have now made their nominations for President and Vice-President of men who are fair representatives of the Republican organization. Their election means a continuance of the partisanship, abuses, corruptions, and centralizing tendencies of the last twenty years which you and I both believe dangerous, and, if continued, in the end destructive of Republican liberty. It seems to me the patriotic duty of all men so believing to sacrifice all personal considerations for their country's good. The Democracy all over the land are looking to you as the one person above all others to lead them in the coming political contest. The only question seems to be: will you consent to be the candidate? I know nothing of your determination, except what may be gathered from the conflicting statements of the press, and I do not expect or ask a reply to my letter. My only object in writing is to urge upon you the *duty* of yielding to the united demand of the Democracy. There are times when patriots must not hesitate, if necessary, to take their lives in their hands for liberty's sake. I know not your physical condition, but mentally you are all that your friends require; and even at the hazard of your life, I believe it your duty to listen to the united voice of the friends of constitutional liberty. I *know* that you were once fairly elected President. I feel confident that you can be again. Whether any other Democrat can be is uncertain. I fear not. It was a great mistake not to have nominated you four years ago. I felt it at the time. The country now sees it. With the highest regard for you personally, I beg of you to let us make you President in fact.

Yours very truly,
"LYMAN TRUMBULL."

Memoranda made by Charles O'Conor in conference with Mr. Tilden and myself about Mr. Tilden's will, which his brother Henry's death had made it necessary to remodel. It was the last professional consultation O'Conor ever held. He left New York the following day to return to Nantucket (Thursday), and on Monday lay down upon the bed from which he never rose alive. Before leaving New York, however, he posted the following notes to Mr. Tilden:

"Trusts cannot be created to receive and accumulate rents or income of real or personal estate for any of the purposes you have in view.

"You will be obliged to set off at once their shares or allowances to your kindred out of your *capital.*

"The residue can be appropriated to such public purposes as you may name to be created by the legislative allowance within two specified lives after your death."

PATRICK FORD TO TILDEN

"OFFICE OF 'IRISH WORLD,'
"PARK PLACE, NEW YORK, *May 13, 1884.*

"ESTEEMED SIR,—One with whom your name is sacredly linked is passing away—a private telegram informs us that Chas. O'Conor can live but a few hours. As Americans first, as likewise of the race upon whose name his genius and character shed lustre, we desire to fittingly honor his memory. If you will say a few words to our representative as to the public worth and services of Mr. O'Conor, that we may give to the *Irish World* readers as your personal estimate of the man, it will be a favor that we shall heartily appreciate.

"Very faithfully yours,
"PATRICK FORD,
"Per A. E. FORD, Man. Ed."

MR. TILDEN'S REMARKS ON THE DEATH OF CHARLES O'CONOR

"In my judgment, Mr. O'Conor was the greatest jurist among all the English-speaking race. He carried the best spirit of philosophical inquiry into every professional investigation.

"In variety of resources, in every form of experience, participating in every important legal controversy during fifty years, with unexampled power of discrimination and memory, he had a vast mass of information on every professional subject.

"He was a man of lofty integrity and honor, and scorned all idea of making his professional abilities the means of acquiring money.

"His character is worthy of a more elaborate tribute than I have the opportunity to pay to him in the brief time of your call."

JOHN A. McCLERNAND TO TILDEN

"SPRINGFIELD, ILL., *June 5th, 1884.*

"To His Excellency, SAMUEL J. TILDEN, President-Elect.

"DEAR SIR,—The crime which defeated the will of the people in 1876, and kept you from exercising the Presidential office needs to be avenged.

"Time and your example have subdued and conciliated all factious opposition to you in the Democratic party. The opponents of former years are now your most noisy partisans. Your nomination in July will follow as a spontaneous and consentaneous act unless you prevent it.

"Preventing it calamitous consequences must ensue. The Democratic party will be left to fall into strife, anarchy, and impotency. The Old Guard and your old friends—what will become of them? The barriers to latitudinous construction will be broken down, and license given to public extravagance, official corruption, and the greed of unscrupulous and powerful monopolies.

"Your declination is inadmissible. Accept the nomination, even if death should overcome you during or after the fight. If I know myself, I would, in the present extremity of country and party, suffer the martyrdom for you vicariously if it was possible to do so.

"Excuse the freedom and energy of these remarks. They proceed from a sense of duty. I have done.

"Very truly your obt. sert.,
"JOHN A. MCCLERNAND."

JOHN A. McCLERNAND TO TILDEN

"SPRINGFIELD, ILLS., *June 6th, 1884.*

"To His Excellency, SAMUEL J. TILDEN, President-Elect.

"DEAR SIR,—Respectfully reiterating everything I wrote yesterday, I write again to-day to deprecate, if possible, still more emphatically, but with all courtesy, any purpose on your part to decline a renomination.

"I am aware that the question of acceptance has a personal, as well as a political, aspect. I have given consideration to both, though it may be not without prepossession. The wish is often father to the thought. The grave matter of health has already received my attention. Life, even comfort, may well challenge our solicitude and care; still, I am of opinion that both may be dutifully staked upon a transcendent issue involving the welfare of a people. *Dulce et decorum est pro patria mori.*

"What is the situation? The ruling party has overridden the voice of the people, usurped their sovereignty, oppressed the laboring classes by discriminating and unjust taxation, and that as a means of perpetuating its domination and enriching political adventurers. It would be worth the life of the greatest and best man in the land to expel it from its ill-gotten and abused places of power.

"In saying this, I am not unmindful of the memories of the past: of the shameful persecution which the same party wreaked on you, and of its unhesitating readiness to return to its habitual vomit; nor of the ungrateful return formerly made by recusant Democrats to your steadfastness and devotion, but such has not unfrequently been the lot of other public men of positive and decided qualities. Jefferson and Jackson, your illustrious predecessors, did not escape it; yet it is known and admitted that it detracted nothing from their energy, usefulness, or merited renown. Persecution and ingratitude are often the price paid for envied eminence and superiority. But may I not say that the march of events and opinion has raised you above the reach of harmful malice: that it has reformed the sin of recusancy?

"I am persuaded that the rank and file of the Democracy are with you, and are eager and resolute, under your leadership, to vindicate their violated electoral rights and the sanction of the ballot-box.

"Lately I was in Missouri, Arkansas, and Texas, where I sought and conferred with a number of leading men, who assured me on my representation that the Northwest was almost, if not quite, unitedly in favor

[of] your nomination; they would heartily co-operate to effect it, and, indeed, while I was in Texas, several districts passed instructions in favor of it.

"As to the 'Old Guard,' although its ranks are thinned and time has stricken it with age; although it can scarcely hope to survive much beyond the impending contest, yet its spirit is unbroken. It asks not office or emolument: it covets only the post of duty and danger. It never surrenders: it will stand by you whether for a nomination or an election—for both it will keep the faith to the end. Will you not lead it, as its tried, trusted, and honored chief, to deliverance from the humiliation of unceasing contumely and proscription?

"Upon the whole your refusal to lead the Democratic masses would fall on them as a stunning and bewildering blow. It would balk their welling expectations and overwhelm them with disappointment. Would it not provoke a reaction of feeling and opinion injurious—seriously injurious—to both you and the country? I candidly think so.

"In conclusion, I assume, as I believe, that your nomination would be followed by your election.

"Your obt. sert.,
"JOHN A. MCCLERNAND."

In spite of the earnest and almost oppressive urgency of friends to whose counsels he was always anxious and usually ready to defer, Mr. Tilden's consciousness of his lack of strength for the work that would be expected of him if elected President and ought to be required of him, did not permit him to weaken in his purpose. It even hastened his official termination of these importunities before the meeting of the State convention, which had seemed to him the appropriate occasion for any announcement that the four preceding years had worked no change in the views previously expressed of retiring from public life. The circumstances which led him to anticipate by a few weeks what he regarded as the fit time for such an announcement, I hope I may be excused for giving, as I set them down at the time in my diary, premising that delegates from every part of the State to the national convention were already appointed with instructions, or with the understanding that they should support Mr. Tilden for the nomination.

D. MANNING'S APPEAL IN BEHALF OF CLEVELAND TO HAVE TILDEN FORMALLY DECLINE BEING CONSIDERED A CANDIDATE IN 1884

"On or about the 8th day of June, 1884, Mr. Daniel Manning, chairman of the New York Democratic State Committee, called at my house in New York and asked me to accompany him to Greystone to see Mr. Tilden. The motive he assigned for his visit there, and for wishing me to accompany him, was to persuade Mr. Tilden, if persuasion should be necessary, to no longer delay the formal announcement of his intention, well known to Mr. Manning and myself, not to accept a renomination to the Presidency.

"Mr. Manning said while there was a hope, but no certainty of Mr. Tilden's consenting to run, his friends, embracing a large majority of the Democratic party of the State, were getting divided as to their second choice, and there was danger, when he came to withdraw, that the party would be hopelessly distracted, and its influence in the convention dissipated. He had been so impressed by a sense of this danger, he said, that on the Sunday previous he called on Governor Cleveland, laid the whole case before him, and pressed upon his attention the necessity of doing something immediately to prevent the friends of Mr. Tilden from getting pledged to other candidates as their second choice.

"On the following day we repaired to Greystone. Mr. Manning then repeated to Mr. Tilden substantially what he had said to me of his interview with Governor Cleveland and of his mission, except that in regard to the cabinet. I think he said, 'You can name any member of the cabinet you please—an unobjectionable man, of course, like ——, for instance' (naming a gentleman whom he knew Mr. Tilden would regard as such a man).

"Though the general import of the conversation was that the cabinet would be selected in harmony with Mr. Tilden's wishes, I did not hear him state distinctly to Mr. Tilden, as I understood him to state to me in New York, that the cabinet in its entirety should consist of men whose selection Mr. Tilden should approve of. During that part of the conversation with Mr. Tilden which I overheard, he said that Mr. Tilden might name any member of the cabinet he pleased, which might mean many or only one. This statement was reinforced by the remark that Governor Cleveland would do anything that he (Manning) should advise him to do, for he was conscious that his only hope now was from and through Mr. Tilden. The letter to Mr.

Manning declining a renomination appeared in the morning prints the second or third day following the interview.

"He at the same time expressed his conviction that the only way of securing the result was for Mr. Tilden to signify at once and before the election of any more delegates to the State convention, which were in the main to be chosen during that week, that he would not be a candidate.

"Mr. Manning went on to say that Governor Cleveland promptly and unhesitatingly authorized and expressed the desire that Mr. Manning would go at once to Greystone, represent the situation to Mr. Tilden, and give him any assurances he required in regard to the naming of the cabinet, and of his disposition and purpose to regard Mr. Tilden's friends as his friends, and, if elected, to have as nearly as possible a thoroughly Tilden administration.

"I said that I approved entirely of an early publication of Mr. Tilden's intention not to allow himself to be made a candidate. I believed a manifesto to that effect was already written, but was withheld partly out of deference to the wishes of some of his friends in Washington, and partly for what seemed to be the more obvious and appropriate occasion—the assembling of the State convention that was to choose the delegates to the national convention; and finally I promised to accompany him to Greystone."

TILDEN TO DANIEL MANNING

(DECLINING A RENOMINATION FOR THE PRESIDENCY)

"NEW YORK, *June 10th, 1884.*

"TO DANIEL MANNING,
"*Chairman of the Democratic State Committee of New York.*

"In my letter of June 18th, 1880, addressed to the delegates from the State of New York to the Democratic national convention, I said:

"'Having now borne faithfully my full share of labor and care in the public service, and wearing the marks of its burdens, I desire nothing so much as an honorable discharge. I wish to lay down the honors and toils of even *quasi* party leadership, and to seek the repose of private life.

"'In renouncing renomination for the Presidency, I do so with no doubt in my mind as to the veto of the State of New York, or of the United States, but because I believe that it is a renunciation of re-election to the Presidency.

"'To those who think my renomination and re-election indispensable to an effectual vindication of the right of the people to elect their rulers—violated in my person—I have accorded as long a reserve of my decision as possible, but I cannot overcome my repugnance to enter into a new engagement which involves four years of ceaseless toil.

"'The dignity of the Presidential office is above a merely personal ambition, but it creates in me no illusion. Its value is as a great power for good to the country. I said four years ago in accepting nomination:

"'" Knowing as I do, therefore, from fresh experience, how great the difference is between gliding through an official routine and working out a reform of systems and policies, it is impossible for me to contemplate what needs to be done in the Federal administration without an anxious sense of the difficulties of the undertaking. If summoned by the suffrages of my countrymen to attempt this work, I shall endeavor, with God's help, to be the efficient instrument of their will."

"'Such a work of renovation after many years of misrule, such a reform of systems and policies, to which I would cheerfully have sacrificed all that remained to me of health and life, is now, I fear, beyond my strength.'

"My purpose to withdraw from further public service, and the grounds of it, were at that time well known to you and to others; and when, at

Cincinnati, though respecting my wishes yourself, you communicated to me an appeal from many valued friends, to relinquish that purpose, I reiterated my determination unconditionally.

"In the four years which have since elapsed, nothing has occurred to weaken, but everything to strengthen, the considerations which induced my withdrawal from public life. To all who have addressed me on the subject, my intention has been frankly communicated. Several of my most confidential friends, under the sanction of their own names, have publicly stated my determination to be irreversible. That I have occasion now to consider the question is an event for which I have no responsibility. The appeal made to me by the Democratic masses, with apparent unanimity, to serve them once more, is entitled to the most deferential consideration, and would inspire a disposition to do anything desired of me, if it were consistent with my judgment of duty.

"I believe that there is no instrumentality in human society so potential in its influence upon mankind for good or evil, as the governmental machinery for administering justice, and for making and executing laws. Not all the eleemosynary institutions of private benevolence to which philanthropists may devote their lives are so fruitful in benefits as the rescue and preservation of this machinery from the perversions that make it the instrument of conspiracy and crime, against the most sacred rights and interests of the people.

"For fifty years, as a private citizen, never contemplating an official career, I have devoted at least as much thought and effort to the duty of influencing aright the action of the governmental institutions of my country, as to all other objects. I have never accepted official service except for a brief period, for a special purpose, and only when the occasion seemed to require from me that sacrifice of private preferences to the public welfare.

"I undertook the State administration of New York because it was supposed that in that way only could the executive power be arrayed on the side of the reforms to which, as a private citizen, I had given three years of my life.

"I accepted the nomination for the Presidency in 1876 because of the general conviction that my candidacy would best present the issue of reform which the Democratic majority of the people desired to have worked out in the Federal government as it had been in that of the State of New York. I believed that I had strength enough then to renovate the administration of the government of the United States, and at the close of my term to hand over the great trust to a successor faithful to the same policy.

"Though anxious to seek the repose of private life, I nevertheless acted upon the idea that every power is a trust, and involves a duty. In reply to the address of the committee communicating my nomination, I depicted the difficulties of the undertaking, and likened my feelings in engaging in it to those of a soldier entering battle; but I did not withhold the entire consecration of my powers to the public service.

"Twenty years of continuous maladministration, under the demoralizing influences of intestine war, and of bad finance, have infected the whole governmental system of the United States with the cancerous growths of false constructions and corrupt practices. Powerful classes have acquired pecuniary interests in official abuses, and the moral standards of the people have been impaired. To redress these evils is a work of great difficulty and labor, and cannot be accomplished without the most energetic and efficient personal action on the part of the Chief Executive of the Republic.

"The canvass and administration which it is desired that I should undertake would embrace a period of nearly five years. Nor can I admit any illusion as to their burdens. Three years of experience in the endeavor to reform the municipal government of the city of New York, and two years of experience in renovating the administration of the State of New York, have made me familiar with the requirements of such a work.

"At the present time, the considerations which induced my action in 1880 having become imperative, I ought not to assume a task which I have not the physical strength to carry through. To reform the administration of the Federal government; to realize my own ideal, and to fulfil the just expectations of the people, would indeed warrant, as they could alone compensate, the sacrifices which the undertaking would involve. But, in my condition of advancing years and declining strength, I feel no assurance of my ability to accomplish those objects. I am, therefore, constrained to say, definitely, that I cannot now assume the labors of an administration or of a canvass.

"Undervaluing in nowise that best gift of Heaven—the occasion and the power sometimes bestowed upon a mere individual to communicate an impulse for good; grateful beyond all words to my fellow-countryman who would assign such a beneficent function to me, I am consoled by the reflection that neither the Democratic party, nor the Republic for whose future that party is the best guarantee, is now, or ever can be, dependent upon any one man for their successful progress in the path of a noble destiny.

"Having given to their welfare whatever of health and strength I possessed, or could borrow from the future, and having reached the term of my capacity for such labors as their welfare now demands, I but submit to the will of God in deeming my public career forever closed.

"SAMUEL J. TILDEN."

This letter of Mr. Tilden insured the nomination of Grover Cleveland for the Presidency, and the adoption of the following resolutions by the convention:

> *Resolved*, That this convention has read with profound regret and intense admiration the statesmanlike and patriotic letter of Samuel J. Tilden expressing the overpowering and providential necessity which constrains him to decline a nomination for the highest office in the gift of the American people.
>
> *Resolved*, That, though fraud, force, and violence deprived Samuel J. Tilden and Thomas A. Hendricks of the offices conferred upon them by the Democratic party of the nation in 1876, they yet live, and ever will, first in the hearts of the Democracy of the country.
>
> *Resolved*, That this convention expresses a nation's regret that this same lofty patriotism and splendid executive and administrative ability which cleansed and purified the city and State governments of the great Empire State, cannot now be turned upon the Augean stable of national fraud and corruption so long and successfully maintained by the Republican party at the national capital.
>
> *Resolved*, That copies of these resolutions be suitably engrossed, and that the chairman of the convention appoint a committee whose duty it shall be in the name of the convention to forward or present the same to the Hon. Samuel J. Tilden and the Hon. Thomas A. Hendricks.

When these resolutions were presented to Mr. Tilden by the committee named for that purpose by the convention, Mr. Tilden sent them the following reply:

"GREYSTONE, *Oct. 6, 1884.*

"*Mr. Chairman and Gentlemen of the Committee*:

"I thank you for the kind terms in which you have communicated the resolutions concerning me adopted by the late Democratic national convention.

"I share your conviction that the reform in the administration of the Federal government, which is our great national want, and is indeed essential to the restoration and preservation of the government itself, can only be achieved through the agency of the Democratic party, and by installing its representative in the Chief Magistracy of the United States.

"The noble historical traditions of the Democratic party, the principles in which it was educated, and to which it has ever been in the main faithful; its freedom from the corrupt influences which grow up in the prolonged possession of power, and the nature of the elements which constitute it, all contribute to qualify it for that mission.

"The opposite characteristics and conditions which attach to the Republican party make it hopeless to expect that that party will be able to give better government than the debasing system of abuses which, during its ascendancy, has infected official and political life in this country.

"The Democratic party had its origin in the efforts of the more advanced patriots of the Revolution to resist the perversion of our government from the ideal contemplated by the people. Among its conspicuous founders are Benjamin Franklin and Thomas Jefferson; Samuel Adams and John Hancock, of Massachusetts; George Clinton and Robert R. Livingston, of New York; and George Wythe and James Madison, of Virginia. From the election of Mr. Jefferson as President, in 1800, for sixty years the Democratic party mainly directed our national policy. It extended the boundaries of the Republic, and laid the foundations of all our national greatness, while it preserved the limitations imposed by the Constitution and maintained a simple and pure system of domestic administration.

"On the other hand, the Republican party has always been dominated by principles which favor legislation for the benefit of particular classes at the expense of the body of the people. It has become deeply tainted with the abuses which naturally grow up during a long possession of unchecked power, especially in a period of civil war and false finance. The patriotic and virtuous elements in it are now unable to emancipate it from the sway of selfish interests which subordinate public duty to personal greed. The most hopeful of the best citizens it contains despair of its amendment except through its temporary expulsion from power.

"It has been boastingly asserted by a modern Massachusetts statesman, struggling to reconcile himself and his followers to their Presidential candidate, that the Republican party contains a disproportionate share of the wealth, the culture, and the intelligence of the country. The unprincipled Grafton, when taunted by James the Second with his personal want of conscience, answered: '*That is true, but I belong to a party that has a great deal of conscience.*'

"Such reasoners forget that the same claim has been made in all ages and countries by the defenders of old wrongs against new reforms. It was alleged by the Tories of the American Revolution against the patriots of that day. It was repeated against Jefferson and afterwards against Jackson. It is alleged by the conservatives against those who, in England, are now endeavoring to enlarge the popular suffrage.

"All history shows that reforms in government must not be expected from those who sit serenely on the social mountain-tops enjoying the benefits of the existing order of things. Even the divine Author of our religion found His followers not among the self-complacent Pharisees, but among lowly minded fishermen.

"The Republican party is largely made up of those who live by their wits, and who aspire in politics to advantages over the rest of mankind, similar to those which their daily lives are devoted to securing in private business.

"The Democratic party consists largely of those who live by the work of their hands, and whose political action is governed by their sentiments or imagination.

"It results that the Democratic party, more readily than the Republican party, can be molded to the support of reform measures which involve a sacrifice of selfish interests.

"The indispensable necessity of our times is a change of administration in the great executive offices of the country. This, in my judgment, can only be accomplished by the election of the Democratic candidates for President and Vice-President.

"SAMUEL J. TILDEN.

"*To R. H. Henry, Chairman; B. B. Smalley, and others, of the Special Committee of the Democratic National Convention.*"

W. H. BARNUM TO TILDEN

"*Telegram.*

"CHICAGO, ILL., *July 4, 1884.*

"HON. SAMUEL J. TILDEN, YONKERS, N. Y.

"There is much thought here about nominating you by acclamation. Will you accept an unanimous nomination from the convention?

"W. H. BARNUM.

"(Rec'd 6.30 A.M., July 5th.)"

DANIEL MANNING TO S. J. TILDEN

"*Telegram.*

"CHICAGO, ILL., *July 4th, 1884.*

"HON. SAMUEL J. TILDEN, YONKERS, N. Y.

"It seems absolutely necessary that you should answer Barnum's telegram of this evening as soon as possible.

"DANIEL MANNING.

"(Rec'd 6.30 A.M., July 5th.)"

TILDEN TO WILLIAM H. BARNUM

"*Telegram.*

"GREYSTONE, *July 5th, 1884.*

"TO HON. WILLIAM H. BARNUM, CHICAGO, ILLINOIS.

"I have received your telegram informing me of the disposition to nominate me for the Presidency and asking, 'Will you accept an unanimous nomination from the convention?'—and also a telegram from Mr. Manning saying, 'It seems absolutely necessary that you (I) should answer Barnum's telegram as soon as possible.'

"Your inquiry was explicitly answered in the negative by my letter of June 10th to Mr. Manning.

"S. J. TILDEN."

Attached to these telegrams was the following pencil memorandum in a strange handwriting, and presumably a suggested modification of the despatch actually sent:

> "If the convention should nominate me, I should consider it as intended merely to acquit the Democratic party of any shortcomings in respect to the fraudulent possession of the government in 1876, and with the knowledge that I would not accept the nomination."

CHARLES A. DANA TO TILDEN

(WISHES TO STUDY MR. TILDEN'S PERSONAL AND POLITICAL HISTORY)

"'THE SUN,' NEW YORK, *July 18, 1884.*

"DEAR MR. TILDEN,—In the desperate situation in which presumption and incompetence have involved the Democratic party, I feel a natural desire to study more closely and to know more thoroughly the model of genuine Democratic statesmanship.

"Could you put me in possession of the facts and records of your own personal and political history, so that I may examine them at such leisure times as I may be able to rescue from my absorbing daily occupations?

"I wish for this not alone for my own instruction and gratification, but that I may be enabled, as occasion requires, to present the truth accurately to the public, and to discuss the principles involved with knowledge and effect.

"I remain, dear Mr. Tilden,

"Faithfully yours,
"CHARLES A. DANA."

TILDEN TO CHARLES A. DANA

"*July 22d, 1884.*

"DEAR MR. DANA,—I could not but feel much gratified at the interest in my career manifested in your note of the 18th inst.

"It will afford me pleasure to collect such materials for your purpose as I can procure. It may be necessary to have a personal interview to define more exactly what you desire. That will be an occasion for an additional pleasure.

"In the mean time, with assurances of my regards and esteem, I remain,

"Very truly yours."

CHARLES A. DANA TO TILDEN

(PROJECTS A POLITICAL HISTORY)

"'THE SUN,' NEW YORK, *July 24, 1884.*

"DEAR MR. TILDEN,—What I wish is to enlarge my studies of the politics of the last fifty years by going over it all in your relations to it, and in its relations to you.

"Perhaps the best beginning would be made if you could lend me your printed letters, speeches, reports, messages—in short, your published documents of whatever nature and character. I would keep them in my safe and only take out one at a time, so that they would be very little exposed to accident.

"When I have thoroughly studied these papers a great deal will have been accomplished, and I shall then be ready for the next step. My ultimate purpose is to put myself in a situation to write the political history of this half-century between 1835 and 1885.

"It seems to me that in our day there have been three statesmen who have had the genius to rule men through their intellects. I mean Bismarck, Disraeli, and Tilden.

"I remain, dear Mr. Tilden,

"Faithfully yours,
"C. A. DANA."

SMITH M. WEED TO S. J. TILDEN

"PLATTSBURG, N. Y., *July 28, 1884.*

"HON. S. J. TILDEN, GREYSTONE, YONKERS, N. Y.

"MY DEAR GOVR.,—I found, in talking with Manning yesterday, that Govr. C. [Cleveland] had offered to go down and see you about his letter, and had, through M., asked you to name a day, and was anxiously waiting for you to do so.

"I thought I would write you by the very first mail, as I thought that you did not understand it as they do. The Govr. is expecting to come into this country on the 7th or 8th and wants his letter issued before. I write in haste. I did not see Govr. Cleveland, but learned the above from Mr. Manning.

"In haste, yours truly,
"SMITH M. WEED."

DANIEL S. LAMONT TO TILDEN

"STATE OF NEW YORK, EXECUTIVE CHAMBER,
"ALBANY, *Aug. 1, 1884.*

"DEAR SIR,—I am directed by Governor Cleveland to say that, if agreeable to you, he would be glad to call on you at Greystone in company with Mr. Manning on Tuesday next, the 5th instant.

"He takes the liberty of naming the day, because he has engagements which compel his presence here every other day previous to his departure for the woods.

"Very respectfully, your obedient servant,
"DANIEL S. LAMONT, Private Secretary."

SAMUEL J. RANDALL TO TILDEN

"BERWYN, PA., *Aug. 28, 1884.*

"HON. SAM. J. TILDEN.

"MY DEAR SIR,—Allow me to make a suggestion. On the 3rd of September a committee appointed by the unanimous vote of the recent Democratic convention will call upon you with an honorable message from the representatives of the American Democracy. I urge you take this occasion to address yourself to the American people, covering the issues of the coming struggle. No man in the United States knows better than you do just how to do this. The country will listen, the influence of your utterances will be great, and I cannot overstate the importance of such action. It is of the highest moment, and may make success certain. You can take your own time to do this, and can tell the committee you will answer in full in a few days if you are not yet ready for such course.

"An appeal from you for administrative reform will be accepted by the Democrats as conclusive as to their duty at this time, and will determine the doubting and the estranged to fall into line.

"Yours truly,
"SAM. J. RANDALL."

TILDEN TO J. P. TOWNSEND AND OTHERS

"GREYSTONE, *October 13, 1884.*

"GENTLEMEN,—I have just received your letter on behalf of the New York Produce and Maritime, Independent Merchants' Cleveland and Hendricks Club, and representing, also, several other classes of business men, inviting me to be present at the Business Men's Mass-meeting, to be held at the Academy of Music on Wednesday the 15th inst., in aid of the election of Cleveland and Hendricks to the offices of President and Vice-President of the United States.

"I regret that the delicate condition of my health compels me to forego the pleasure of joining with you on that interesting occasion.

"I remember gratefully that when it was my duty as Governor to engage in a grapple with the Canal Ring, which then swayed all the administrative, legislative, and judicial powers of the State, a majority of the local organizations of the Democratic party and all the organizations of the Republican party, the New York Produce Exchange rallied to my support, and stood by my side throughout a prolonged appeal to public opinion until that gigantic power was completely overthrown.

"I cordially concur in your opinion that the election of Cleveland and Hendricks is demanded by the best interests of the country. I believe that their election will be a substantial victory for the cause of good government; that it will assure a safe and prudent administration of the Chief Magistracy of the Republic in all our relations with other countries; that it will restore simplicity, economy, and purity to the Federal government so far as that result depends upon the Executive; that it will give to business men immunity from sudden changes of policy, and enable them to repose under the shelter of a stable, moderate, and equitable administrative system free from favoritism to particular interests or classes and from the injurious fluctuations to which such favoritism always leads.

"SAMUEL J. TILDEN."

GEORGE HOADLEY TO TILDEN

"STATE OF OHIO, EXECUTIVE DEPARTMENT,
"COLUMBUS, *November 22, 1884.*

"MY DEAR SIR,—On the occasions of my last two visits to New York, I was unable to command the time to go to Greystone, so that I did not, during the canvass, have the pleasure of expressing my hopes and anticipations to you with reference to its progress in Ohio, or of exchanging congratulations with you upon its apparently favorable prospects. Now, however, we may rejoice over results, and you are especially to be congratulated. At last a Democratic administration takes possession of power: most fortunately, one whose chief has been trained in New York and has sat at your feet and studied his Democracy in the school of Van Buren and Silas Wright. Your judgment that Ohio was not to be trusted is vindicated. I confess I thought differently. I underrated the forces of corruption, and especially of the money that could be brought to bear. You judged more wisely, and the event proves it. Indeed, I saw this before the Chicago convention, and with my full approval my friends there labored for Governor Cleveland's nomination, and by dividing Ohio made it possible.

"I was asked by telegram during that convention if I would accept the Vice-Presidency. I answered in the negative, my ambition being in the line of our profession and to be a busy man, not an idle man. As I said to you when we last met, I should like to be Attorney-General. If that cannot be, I am content to remain as I am or return to private life.

"There are some other facts connected with this matter which I should be glad to lay before you in person had I the opportunity, but which cannot well be committed to writing.

"I take it for granted that your wishes will have great weight with the President-elect. I should esteem it the success of my life, more valuable than the office itself, to know that you approve, or do not disapprove my ambition, and wish my appointment. I would rather be *your* Attorney-General than hold any office in the Republic short of the highest, and as the value of that lies in being *your* choice and having your confidence in a place wherein something may be done to give effect to your principles an equal importance attaches to your recommendation to your successor. But while I am ambitious, I am not greedy or insubordinate. Your disapproval of my ambition would be law to me. You are the honored head of our party, and I am ready as a loyal soldier to submit to my commander in this, not grudgingly, but cheerfully.

"Please take this matter into consideration, and at your convenience let me know your thoughts.

"With great respect, yours, &c.,
"GEO. HOADLEY."

TILDEN TO GOVERNOR HOADLY

"*Confidential.*

"GREYSTONE, *December 5, 1884.*

"DEAR GOVERNOR HOADLEY,—The present is the earliest opportunity I have had to acknowledge your letter.

"I notice that you mention that there are some things fitter to be discussed in personal interview than by letter.

"You will not doubt my high estimate of your abilities and your character, or of the strong personal regard I feel for you.

"I do not know to what extent or in what cases, if any, I shall be consulted by Mr. Cleveland in respect to the constitution of his cabinet. I do not intend to intrude upon him any advice unasked, or to volunteer any recommendations or requests.

"If consulted I shall not act as a partisan of any of my numerous friends who would like to enter his cabinet, but shall endeavor, with judicial impartiality, to canvass the personal merits and other considerations which ought to influence the choice.

"I am anxious that he should do the best thing possible for the country and for his administration, and shall desire rather to help him in his official task than to add to his embarrassments.

"The formation of a cabinet is a piece of mosaic in which each element may be affected by the size, texture, and color of the others entering into the combination; and it is impossible to foresee how much an individual element may be affected by the cast of the whole.

"In the event that you should be wanted for some other post than the one you prefer, do you mean to say that you have an invincible repugnance to every other post, even though not inferior in dignity or importance?

"Very truly yours,
"S. J. TILDEN."

GEORGE HOADLY TO TILDEN

"EXECUTIVE CHAMBER, COLUMBUS, O., *December 13, 1884.*

"MY DEAR SIR,—Your letter of the 5th inst. was received in due course of mail, and I embrace the first opportunity to reply.

"While my ambition, and I think my qualifications, for public service are in the line of my profession, I should not feel at liberty to refuse any duty consistent with my personal dignity and self-respect which the President might assign me. I am well aware that he must have a wider survey of the situation than I can have, and that he must bear the chief responsibility of failure. As I said in my former letter, I am too good a soldier not to take orders cheerfully and obey them ungrudgingly.

"My dear Mr. Tilden, if I had had the least doubt of your esteem and regard I should not have written you as I did or as I do.

"You intimate a doubt whether you will be consulted by President Cleveland with reference to his cabinet. This disturbs and distresses me. To begin by ignoring you, especially if the men whose timidity and self-seeking sacrificed you and the cause in 1877 are taken into confidence, would be a sad prophecy of disaster to come. A statesman can get along, sometimes, by selfishly disregarding considerations of gratitude to the elements that made him—in other words, by kicking down the ladder by which he has climbed; but if he add to this the closing of his ears to the wisest and most far-seeing of his counsellors he is lost. The new administration may perhaps safely throw Ohio overboard, although our fight here in October made success in November possible, as the national committee has fully acknowledged to our State committee; the new President may perhaps safely turn his back upon the men who risked their own political lives to save his at Chicago, but it will be a sad day for him and for his government if he ignore you and do not seek your counsels.

"The circumstances to which I alluded as not to be written are well known to Mr. Smith M. Weed and to Mr. William L. Scott (I think) and possibly to Mr. Daniel Manning.

"I have the honor to be,

"Very truly your friend,
"GEO. HOADLY."

SAMUEL J. RANDALL TO TILDEN

(SENATOR BAYARD'S PLANS)

The following Associated Press despatch appeared at about this time:

> "When Senator Thomas F. Bayard came to Albany and paid his respects to President-elect Cleveland, it is understood that he left for home with the assurance that he could make his choice of any position in the cabinet, and he would receive the appointment. It is said on good authority that, after having duly deliberated over the matter, the Delaware Senator sent a note to the Governor, which was received yesterday, indicating his preference for the portfolio of Secretary of the Treasury. It is rumored that he will be accordingly appointed."

"HOUSE OF REPRESENTATIVES, U. S.,
"WASHINGTON, D. C., *Dec. 17, 1884.*

"MY DEAR SIR,—Unless you interfere at once and with determination, I apprehend Mr. B. will be selected as Secretary of Treasury. That means an end of your friends.

"Yours truly,
SAM. RANDALL."[30]

ROBERT M. MCLANE TO TILDEN

"EXECUTIVE MANSION, ANNAPOLIS, MD., *Dec. 29th, '84.*

"My dear Governor,—I wish you a happy New Year, and I would be delighted if I could offer my greeting in person. I would do so if I knew when you were to be in the city, or if it would be quite convenient to drop in on you at 'Greystone,' as I am going to pay a New Year's visit to my sister, Mrs. Hamilton, at Poughkeepsie.

"I have not heard from any of my New York friends since the election, and I can see little from the bottom of my well here. I saw Mr. Randall in Washington on Saturday just as he was starting for Kentucky, and was sorry to hear from him that he had expressed the wish that his name should not be associated with any cabinet appointment, for though I appreciate his disinterestedness, no man in the country is better able than he to dispel all distrust in Connecticut, New York, New Jersey, and Indiana when we come to deal practically with the revision of the tariff. He could and would easily reduce duties and increase revenue, ridding us forever of excise taxation! We are, it seems to me, in very nearly the same fix we were in under Jackson and Polk, when we drove the high Protectionists and Free Traders into one camp in opposition to a revenue tariff! Under Polk, Governor Marcy brought from New York the experts employed by Mr. Walker in the Treasury, who gave the maximum revenue duty upon every article imported under the Whig Tariff of 1842. We could raise now over $300,000,000 by applying the same principle, greatly increasing the revenues, and to the advantage rather than to the injury of our industries. Mr. Randall is able to do this, and none of the doubtful States would distrust him. If we do not find such a solution of this question our victory will turn to ashes on our lips! Once more wishing you a happy New Year, and many returns thereof, I remain,

"Very sincerely yours,
"ROBERT M. MCLANE."

TILDEN TO MR. GROSS

"GREYSTONE, *December 29, 1884.*

"DEAR MR. GROSS,—I regret that the temporary obstruction to your hearing, and the weakness of my voice, made the interview which I accorded you of so little utility.

"I have felt obliged to adopt a rule, thus far adhered to, to write no letters to Mr. Cleveland making any recommendations or requests in regard to appointments which may come within his gift. I intend not to volunteer any advice to him on that subject, and, if consulted in any case, I do not design to become a partisan of any one of my numerous friends who may desire his favor, but only to communicate with judicial impartiality such information as I may possess, and such opinions as I shall have formed concerning each of the competitors.

"It seems to me that your prospects of being selected for some such office as you desire will depend mainly upon the extent and character of the support which you may receive from your own locality.

"It can better be judged of, when the cabinet shall have been formed, whether and to what extent you may require extrinsic help.

"I need not say that I regard your connections with great esteem and respect and as entitled to high consideration, and I do not doubt that your qualifications are of a peculiarly excellent character.

"With cordial good wishes, I remain,

"Very truly yours,
"S. J. TILDEN."

TILDEN TO GOVERNOR CLEVELAND

"GREYSTONE, YONKERS, N. Y., *January 2, 1885.*

"DEAR GOVERNOR CLEVELAND,—When you shall relieve yourself of the urgent duties of your present office, if it will be agreeable to you to take a few days' repose at Greystone, it will give me great pleasure to welcome you, and make you as comfortable as possible. I shall be happy to invite Mr. and Mrs. Manning at the same time—which intention, I believe, has already been communicated to you.

"With cordial regards, I am,

"Very truly yours,
"(Signed) S. J. TILDEN."

TILDEN TO HUGH McCULLOCH

"GREYSTONE, YONKERS, N. Y., *January 24, 1885.*

"DEAR MR. MCCULLOCH,—I have received the reports which you were kind enough to send me, and for which please accept my thanks.

"I note your remark that you hope to have the pleasure of meeting me in Washington. I presume you have seen the rumor in the public journals that I have taken rooms in Washington. That rumor is unfounded. I have a disorder of the nerves of motion, which is aggravated by the fatigue and exposure of travel. I therefore forego all such pleasures.

"This note will be handed to you by Mr. C. N. Jordan, formerly cashier of the Third National Bank and an intelligent financier, whom I beg leave to introduce to you and commend to your confidence.

"He is requested, while in Washington, to obtain information which may enable me to guide my judgment as to what measures are necessary, and will be effectual to preserve the faith and honor of the government of the United States, and a sound currency for the people.

"I desire that such voice as a private man in retirement may have should be given in the right direction.

"With my best wishes for Mrs. and Miss McCulloch and yourself, I remain,

"Very truly yours.

"As I write this note, I am reminded that at the last time I was in Washington you were Secretary of the Treasury under the Johnson administration."

DANIEL MANNING TO TILDEN

"Confidential.

"ALBANY, N. Y., *Jan'y 24, 1885.*

"My dear Governor,—Ever since my return home in December, the cashier of our bank has been absent—ill of pneumonia—and I have been doing double duty. Until he returns, I cannot leave the city. We expect him at his desk early next week.

"Mr. Cleveland intends to go to New York on, or about, the 1st of February, to remain a week, for the purpose of giving everybody who wants to see him an opportunity to call on him. Either before, or after, that time (probably after) he will go to Greystone, and he wants me to go there with him.

"No committals have been made, nor will any be made, until after those visits have occurred. The situation remains just the same as when I was last with you.

"Will you want to see me before we make our proposed call?

"M."

SMITH M. WEED TO GEORGE W. SMITH[31]

"*Personal.*

"PLATTSBURG, N. Y., *Jany. 25, 1885.*

"GEO. W. SMITH.

"MY DEAR GOVERNOR,—I saw C. (Cleveland) on Saturday (yesterday) A.M., and talked from 10.30 to 12.30 with him. He was just as he was when I saw him last, and talked very *freely* to me. He is absolutely with *our* friends in sentiment. Has some queer ideas, which can all be talked out of him, I think. I told him what you said about his civil service letter, and it pleased him immensely. I told him about your financial work and talked over that subject with him, and it made an impression, and he seemed very anxious about it and thankful that you sent J. on to W. He spoke of anticipating seeing you in N. Y., but I did not say anything about his going to visit you. He will not give B. (Bayard) anything but Secretary of State, and, I think, *thinks he better stay in the Senate at that.* He is very set on *Whitney,* and I think has no one else but that could be changed. He spoke of regretting both B.'s and G.'s leaving the Senate. He talked very freely and frankly, and I do not think it has hurt him to let him alone for a couple of weeks, as he has been.

"I saw Manning a moment and told him he nor C. had acknowledged your invitation. He seemed surprised, and said he understood that he sent word to you this eve., and I think C. understood that M. had done so both for himself and C. I told him I did not so understand him. He said to write you to-day that C. was *all right in every way.* That he spent the entire evening with him on Friday, and that among other things he talked with him about going to see you. That C. said he had agreed to go to N. Y. and listen to those who wanted to talk to him, and that he should go Feb. 1, or within a day or so of it, one way or the other. That he should simply hear what they had to say, and should make no committals in any way; and that after he had heard them, he and M. should go to you. C. told M. that was his idea of the best way to do it—if agreeable to you. I think he said that C. insisted upon his going to N. Y. with him. They therefore will visit you the last of the first week in Feb'y—if nothing happens. I had a very hasty talk with M., as I had but five minutes before my train started. I think I ought to say that C. has considerable *dread* of A. H. G. (Andrew H. Green). He said G. abused every one and found fault with everything, and evidently had an idea that G. represented to some extent your views. I undeceived him about that. I found M. feared that G. would get hold of his letters to you also, and that, *I think*, is one reason why M. likes better to send messages than to write, although he probably learned that from you. I do not know as I should have written the above about *G.*, *but thought* you ought to know it.

"Yours very truly,
"SMITH M. WEED."

R. T. MERRICK TO TILDEN

"*Private and confidential.*

"WASHINGTON CITY, *Feb'y 1st, 1885.*

"MY DEAR MR. TILDEN,—On the day after my return to New York from Greystone, I had a conversation with Mr. Jones as to the fusing of himself and his political associates, in regard to the appointment of Mr. Manning as Secretary of the Treasury.

"Mr. Jones spoke, very decidedly, for himself and Mr. Horace White, in favor of the appointment, and was of opinion that it would meet the approval of all the leading independents, especially in view of the fact that such an appointment was, probably, the only means by which the danger—as he characterized it—of Mr. Whitney's accession to that office could be avoided. He represented that he and his friends were opposed to the appointment of the last-named gentleman to any place in Cleveland's cabinet.

"He requested me to say to you that, in his interview with Mr. Cleveland on Sunday last, he stated to him that, but for your course, in reference to him, he certainly would never have been nominated—and that he impressed upon him the extent of his obligations to you.

"In all that he said—as far as I am informed—on this subject he was right, and would have been right had he gone further and given the President-elect a broader view of the situation.

"*But for you*, and the wonderful power and wisdom with which you conducted the Democratic party up to and through the campaign of '76, the rule of the Republican party would have remained unbroken for another quarter of a century.

"You *regained*, *preserved*, and have *transmitted* a political estate to Mr. Cleveland, and from what I know of his intellectual and moral character, cannot believe that he will fail to appreciate this condition and history. I cannot believe that he will—in the great emergency which is upon him—fail to avail himself of your wise counsel and advice; or that he will, in looking back upon the events of '76 and those which followed, allow those of your friends who were with you in your triumph, and then led the forlorn hope in the desperate fight of that hour of darkness and treachery, to be pushed aside now by the unscarred sycophants around him.

"The impression seems to prevail here that, since the election of Evarts, it would be very unwise to withdraw either Bayard or Garland from the Senate.

"We will, certainly, be overmatched in debate in that body, whether the gentlemen referred to remain or not.

"Believe me, my dear Mr. Tilden, with great respect, always

Sincerely yours,
"R. T. MERRICK."

THEODORE F. SHUEY TO S. J. TILDEN

"OFFICIAL REPORTER'S OFFICE, UNITED STATES SENATE,
"WASHINGTON, D. C., *Feb'y 1, 1885.*

"DEAR SIR,—I learn, through the N. Y. *World*, that you have recently purchased for your library a 'Financial Diary' kept by Thomas Jefferson when President of the U. S. I have at my home in Virginia a similar diary kept by him in 1774, when a young lawyer at Williamsburg and a member of the House of Burgesses. It is the Virginia Kalendar for that year, well bound in leather with blank pages, on which he wrote, and is a complete diary of his 'pai^{mts},' as well as Mrs. Jefferson's. I have never offered it for sale, nor exhibited it except to friends who take an interest in such matters. You would, of course, wish to see the diary in my possession before purchasing it, if such should be your desire; and as I do not know the price recently paid by you, I have no idea as to the worth of the one for 1774. If you wish to have both diaries in your library, I hope to hear from you on the subject.

"Very truly yours,
"THEO. F. SHUEY,
"*Assistant Senate Reporter.*"

DANIEL LAMONT TO TILDEN

"ALBANY, *February 4, 1885.*

"DEAR SIR,—Governor Cleveland directs me to convey to you his thanks for your very kind invitation, and to say that he hopes soon to have the pleasure of making you a visit.

"Mr. Manning will communicate with you concerning the time.

"Very respectfully,
"DANIEL S. LAMONT,
"*Private Secretary.*"

WASHINGTON McLEAN TO TILDEN

"WASHINGTON, D. C., *Feb. 5th, 1885.*

"MY DEAR GOVERNOR,—Unless my information is sadly at fault, and I have reason to believe it is not, your old enemies, who conceived the electoral commission to cheat you out of the Presidency, are making both active and insidious efforts to install themselves in President Cleveland's cabinet. To be frank, Mr. Bayard and Mr. Thurman, who were your rivals for the Presidential nomination, and who originated the infamous tribunal which defrauded not only yourself but the American people of their just rights, are both using tremendous forces to gain cabinet places. Mr. Bayard wants the Treasury portfolio, in which desire I have reason to believe he will fail. In such case, he will take the State Department. Thurman will be content with any designation. His candidacy is covertly in the interest of Pendleton. This you may know and doubtless do.

"I have reason to believe you will have the opportunity, quite soon, to give your well-matured views as to public men and public policy to the President-elect. I know too well that our mutual friend, Mr. Bigelow, holds justly your highest appreciation. So he does mine. Still, the purpose of my letter, without detracting at all from Mr. Bigelow's merits, is to call your attention to an old and tried friend of your own and myself. Governor Robert McLane, of Maryland, I have in my mind's eye. He is an old friend of thirty years' standing. He is a radical Democrat. I know he has always been your conscientious and personal friend and admirer. He has had large and ripe public experience, both as a diplomat, a legislator, and the executive of his State. His grandfather was an officer in the war of the Revolution. His father was distinguished for all those traits which make true Democracy illustrious. He was a member of Congress, a U. S. Senator from Delaware, Minister to England, Secretary of the Treasury, and Secretary of State. For ten years he was the president of the Baltimore & Ohio Railroad Co.

"To go back to the son. You know as well as I his public service. Jackson appointed him to West Point. In the Florida war he served with credit; also under General Scott in the Cherokee country. In 1847 he began his Congressional term, representing a Maryland district, and subsequently in 1849. President Pierce, in 1853, appointed him a commissioner to China with full powers plenipotentiary. In 1859 President Buchanan appointed him Minister to Mexico. He was again elected to Congress in 1879 and 1881, and is now the Governor of Maryland, being elected by 12,000 majority.

"Don't you think, Governor, it would be only fair to Cleveland to give him the choice between two of your friends: Mr. John Bigelow and Gov. Robt. McLane?

"Your cordial friend,
"WASHINGTON MCLEAN.

"No. 8 La Fayette Square, Washington, D. C.
"*Gov. Samuel J. Tilden.*

"P. S.—I had forgotten to add that I have conferred on this subject with Hon. Samuel Randall and other of our old friends, who concur with me in the endorsement of Gov. McLane.

"W. McL."

S. J. RANDALL TO GROVER CLEVELAND

"NEW YORK, *February 8, 1885.*

"HON. GROVER CLEVELAND.

"DEAR SIR,—The wisdom and public necessity of a discontinuance of compulsory coinage of bullion into standard silver dollars as authorized by the act of February 28, 1878, is under discussion in most of our commercial and trade organizations.

"There is a wide-spread apprehension that the continued coinage of standard silver dollars may bring about financial and trade embarrassment. Under these circumstances, I do not consider it inappropriate that I should ask an expression of your judgment in relation to this subject.

"I have the honor to enclose a copy of an amendment, which I propose to have inserted in the bill for the legislative, executive and judicial appropriations.

"Yours very truly."[32]

GROVER CLEVELAND TO S. J. RANDALL

"NEW YORK, *February 9, 1885.*

"MY DEAR SIR,—I have received your letter containing a copy of an amendment in relation to the coinage of silver, which it is proposed should be inserted in a bill now pending in Congress, and asking my judgment upon the subject.

"I have some delicacy in saying a word that may be construed by anybody as interfering with the legislation of the present Congress. But so grave do I deem the public emergency that I am willing as a private citizen to say that I think some legislation of the character suggested is eminently desirable.

Very respectfully yours,
"GROVER CLEVELAND."

DRAFT OF A LETTER TO THE HONORABLE HUGH MCCULLOCH, SECRETARY OF THE TREASURY

"GREYSTONE, YONKERS, N. Y., *February 11, 1885.*

"DEAR MR. MCCULLOCH,—I am much obliged for the kind attention you gave to my inquiries. I have been delayed in writing to you my acknowledgments, from the lack of leisure to add some observations which I desired to make. And if compelled to differ with you in any respect, I need not say that it is with a high and respectful appreciation of your opinions and abilities in finance.

"I agree that a currency strictly limited in amount so as not to exceed, but rather to be less, than the effective demand for necessary public use, may be kept in circulation at a rate higher than its intrinsic value. But that is true only on very stringent conditions.

"As to making a market for silver coin by withdrawing bank-notes and treasury notes of less denomination than five dollars—and ultimately of less denomination than ten dollars—there are grave difficulties. In your letter it is remarked:

> "'You say that fifty millions of silver is about all that the country can absorb. This is true; and it is true simply because we keep in circulation upwards of fifty millions of one and two dollar notes. If these notes were withdrawn, their place would immediately be filled with silver and gold. If the five-dollar notes were also retired, all of the silver dollars now in the Treasury vaults would be in circulation, as they ought to be. On this point, permit me to call your attention to page 34 of my report. I wish you could see your way clear to use your great influence in favor of the retiring of the one and two dollar United States notes, to be followed in due time by the retirement of all notes below ten dollars.'

"The habits of the people, and their unanimous and strong preference for the portable currency of paper over the cumbrous currency of silver, interpose an almost insurmountable obstacle to such a measure. Borrowing the idea from the practice of England, and supported by most economical writers, that measure has been often advocated, and sometimes attempted to be put in practice. But the expedient has never made much progress, and it has been resisted and rejected by the people at every opportunity.

"About fifty years ago a law was passed, by the State of New York, suppressing bank-notes of a less denomination than five dollars. Although in my general views friendly to free banking, I justified myself in supporting the measures on the ground that it was legitimate to apply an artificial restraint to an artificial system. Enclosed is a copy of the resolutions drawn by myself, opposing the repeal of that law.

"On that issue, more than on any other single question, the party of Jackson and Van Buren was overthrown in the State of New York in the election of 1838. William L. Marcy was defeated as a candidate for re-election as Governor, and 'Small-Bill' Seward was elected in his place. The law was immediately repealed. The question had some special disadvantages at that time; but the indications of the popular wishes were unquestionable.

"I understand from members of my family, that ladies shopping at retail stores in New York city almost universally refuse to take silver dollars. Even one silver dollar is considered an incumbrance, is, in fact, too large to be carried in a ladies *porte-monnaie*, while several of them are quite out of the question.

"I understand, also, that our small notes are very popular in Canada, and in the Bahama Island, being preferred to silver coin.

"I think that the best way of making a market for silver through the small circulation, is for the government to receive the silver at its intrinsic value, and to issue certificates against it dollar for dollar.

"Among your observations on the question of the expediency of making the nominal value of the silver dollar correspond to its intrinsic value, it is suggested:

> "'Another objection might be that the adoption of this standard would probably operate to prevent joint action, by the leading commercial nations, in fixing a ratio of silver to gold which would be concurred in by all nations; and, perhaps, thus delay or frustrate that which would seem to be very desirable. No legislation by the United States alone, would be effectual in fixing the rules of silver outside of its own boundaries. Joint action of the principal powers appears to be the only mode through which a satisfactory solution of the question can be reached.
>
> "'If there is no hope that such an arrangement can be made, it would be desirable that the intrinsic value of the

silver dollar should be brought so nearly as possible to its nominal value.'

"After looking over the discussions of the last two International Conferences, I cannot avoid the conclusion that it is hopeless to make any further attempt to obtain the co-operation of the leading commercial powers in fixing a ratio between gold and silver coins, and that the contingency in which you would deem it 'desirable that the intrinsic value of the silver dollar shall be brought as nearly as possible to its nominal value,' has already occurred.

"The statement of the Treasurer accompanying your letter for January 26, 1885, is as follows:

Gold coin	$172,439,478
Gold bullion	64,195,150
Total gold assets	$236,634,628
Gold certificates outstanding	107,917,890
Amount of gold actually owned	$128,716,738

By the statement of the Treasurer for January 31st, it appears that United States notes on hand were $43,958,468 83, against which were certificates of deposit, $30,130,000, leaving a balance of	$13,818,468 83
National bank notes	13,880,647 67
Deposits in nat. banks	13,491,186 39
Gold actually owned	128,716,738 00
Total gold assets	$169,917,040 89

Trust Funds:

Five per cent. nat. bank	$12,980,825 43

Fund for redemption of notes of nat. banks "failed in

liquidation" and reducing circulation	39,671,925 54
Undistributed assets of failed nat. bank	416,131 41
Amount forward	53,068,882 38

Brought forward		$53,068,882 38
Agency for paying D. C. bonds		444,161 55
Treasury transfer checks and drafts outstanding		2,490,273 13
Interest due and unpaid		1,966,923 86
Matured bonds and interest		250,148 90
Called bonds and interest		5,203,077 78
Old debt		756,188 31
P. O. Department acct		2,712,968 02
Disbursing officers' balances		25,298,865 44
Fund for redemption of nat. gold notes		146,774 09
Miscellaneous		86,681 64
		$92,424,945 10
	$169,917,040 89	
	92,424,945 10	
Balance gold assets	$77,492,095 79	

"These two statements are for different periods. The results, therefore, are not exact. They afford, however, the basis of a conjecture as to the actual condition of the Treasury. Although the amount really belonging to the Treasury, and over which it has permanent control, is very much reduced, I presume it ventures to use, for temporary purposes, temporary balances liable to be drawn at the will of other parties and trust funds, upon the assumption that the balances are likely to remain about the same, as a bank uses its deposits.

"Renewing the assurance of my high consideration and best wishes, I remain,

"Very truly yours."

TILDEN TO SMITH M. WEED

"*Confidential.*

"*Feby. 13/85.*

"DEAR MR. WEED,—I understand from you that Mr. Manning hesitates about accepting the Treasury. You may tell him for me that I do not think he is quite a free agent in the matter.

"Mr. Manning will recollect before the State convention, and when he wanted my aid in carrying the delegation, he went to New York, and got Mr. Bigelow and came up to see me. He stated to me and to Mr. Bigelow that he came at the request of Mr. Cleveland, and was authorized to give to me any assurance which he might deem necessary. He said that in case of Mr. Cleveland's election, I should have a practical influence in the selection of the cabinet, and particularly should name a member from the State of New York. The only qualification was that the men should be of good cabinet material, and he instanced Mr. Bigelow as a specimen and type of the sort of man to be recommended.[33]

"My friends had particularly wished that I should not publish my letter of declension until after my name had been presented by the State convention; they wished this as a matter of delicacy, and also as a matter of feeling. My letter had been written with that view. Mr. Manning stated that Mr. Cleveland thought it would do him good to have my letter published in advance. I had no personal interest in the nomination, but a desire for the success of the Democratic party and for Mr. Cleveland's administration; that his success would be of real value to the country, and that the local chieftains who had reorganized the Democratic party on a reform basis, and renovated its moral power before the country, should be cherished and continued as instruments of public good. I acceded to Mr. Cleveland's wish, sacrificed the preference and pride of my friends, and gave my letter to the press immediately. I also aided what I could at so late a period, in selecting delegates to the State convention.

"Mr. Manning came again to me prior to the national convention, and asked for authority to communicate my judgment and wishes to friends from other States. It is well known that most of the delegates had been elected either with express instructions, or with the understanding that they were to vote for my nomination, and it was not doubted that if I did nothing, the nomination would have been conferred on me without dissent.

"The circumstances lent weight to my advice as to who should be nominated. I authorized Mr. Manning to communicate to my friends from other States that, while I could not assume to dictate to the Democratic party, my judgment was in favor of nominating Mr. Cleveland. Mr. Manning said this intimation would be sufficient.

"He communicated it to many of my friends among the delegates from other States. In addition to this, he gave assurances, in behalf of Mr. Cleveland to the delegates from several States, that the administration should be made up from those who had been my supporters, and who transferred their adhesion to Mr. Cleveland.

"If now the cabinet should be made up largely, and almost exclusively, from men who were hostile to Mr. Cleveland's nomination, and unfriendly to the veterans in all the localities who had created a new success for the Democratic party a cabinet of rivals of Mr. Cleveland, self-seekers who would be devoted to their own schemes instead of building up Mr. Cleveland's administration, it would not only weaken the administration, but chill the masses with a sense that their leaders had turned their back upon their followers to whom they were indebted for everything.

"Mr. Manning cannot afford, by any act of omission or commission, to be responsible for such a result. Unless he accepts the Treasury, I am not mistaken in the belief that the veterans will have no true and reliable friend among the advisers of Mr. Cleveland.

"On public ground, also, the Secretary of the Treasury ought to be taken from the State of New York. He ought to be in communication with the most intelligent and experienced men in the centre of finance and commerce. He ought to be a man who can command ready access to, and have confidential relations not with speculators and gamblers, but with the solid men of property and business.

"Next to Mr. Manning, if he should refuse—which, I think, he has no right to do—Mr. Bigelow is the best substitute. He is an accomplished man, accustomed to deal with great public questions, utterly unselfish and unambitious, without any tendency to inferior associations, and would command the confidence and support of the financial classes.

"But I still adhere to the opinion that Mr. Manning cannot avoid accepting the trust which sacrifice, duty, and honor toward the Democratic masses demands at his hands.

"In discussing thus frankly this subject, I serve no interest personal to myself. My career is completely ended. If the new administration should drift out of relations to those who have given me special support during the last ten years, I should be liberated from all care and trouble, should escape generating discontent among any portion of the Democracy, and should preserve the almost unanimous favor enjoyed by me when I retired from public life. To invite the antagonisms of active politics without the power to submerge them by shaping a policy which should appeal overwhelmingly to the people, would be to impair the repose and comfort for which I have surrendered all public honors. I cannot be induced to meddle at all, even in the way of private advice or opinion, except under the influence of patriotic and friendly motives.

"You may read this letter to Mr. Manning, but keep it and return it to me.

"Yours truly."

DANIEL MANNING TO TILDEN

"*Confidential.*

"ALBANY, *Febry. 13, 1885.*

"MY DEAR GOVERNOR,—You must release me. The place has been offered, but I have no heart for it. The very thought of it has made me ill for two days. The sacrifice will be too great, and I constantly feel that if I make it, I may as well bid good-by, forever, to comfort and happiness. I am so contented now, and I will always, there, be miserable. Telegraph me, to-morrow, one word—'Released.'

"Most sincerely yours,
"DANIEL MANNING."

SMITH M. WEED TO TILDEN

"Confidential.

"Feby. 16, 1885.

"MY DEAR GOVERNOR,—I had but a moment to write you from A. (Albany). C. (Cleveland), as you know, had offered the (State Department) to Bayard, and he had become convinced that it was wise to offer a place to Lamar. We relied upon him and upon Manning until we got that fixed with both—that left three places. We all agreed that Frank Jones was our best man in New England, and we got that to a practical point, the only question being, where would he go? I wanted him to have the Navy, but C. seemed disposed to give him the P. O. That left two places open. Scott and Gorman both agreed with me that, on the free-trade question, Vilas was not a good appointment. Cleveland, on the other hand, wants him, and I think, in the end, will select him for War or P. O. Then came McD. (as he would not appoint Dr. Miller, for reasons that I will tell you when I see you, and which are personal to M., and in no way show any indisposition to go back on his backers), and Scott, G. (Gorman), M. (Manning), and myself all urged Converse for a place instead of McD. He almost consented to it. I did it upon the ground that if Vilas went in, he had to put in some one who stood with Randall on the tariff, or the consequences would be bad in this State and New Jersey and Connecticut. When we left him last night, he was apparently of our mind. This A.M. he wanted to know of me if I did not think that Whitney, in McDonald's or Converse's places, would be a good change. I told him that W. was infinitely preferable to McD., but I thought W. and C. were much better than V. and McD., as all the rest were inclined to free trade except Manning. He has an idea that he should not put any M. C. in who has taken strong grounds on tariff either way; but I told him Lamar had, and Vilas was an out and out free-trader, and Bayard was like Lamar.

"Gorman, who really wants Jones instead of Lamar, says that there will be no trouble with Lamar; that it is his nature to go with his chief, and he will be loyal. That Bayard is so constituted that he will not try to influence Lamar, and that he will not set up for himself, while Garland will always be true to you and your friends. As I wrote you, Cleveland wants Whitney, and I think it will be a good thing for your friends that he should go in with Manning.

"This is just as the matter stands to-day. I told him this A.M. that I will, if desired, come down again, etc., and as he did not ask me to stay, I am going home. I would have gone to New York had not Mrs. Weed been quite ill and really needs me; and, again, I did not care to have C. (Cleveland) get the idea that I was taking the result of the conference to you. He has, by our advice, gone seriously into the preparation of his Inaugural Address. I am delighted that M. (Manning) has consented to go in. Some able, bright man should be selected for his solicitor, and at least two others for his assistants. I infer you will see M. (Manning) ere long.

"I am writing on the train to send back by to-day's mail.

"Very truly yours,
"SMITH M. WEED."

SAM. J. RANDALL TO TILDEN

"HOUSE OF REPRESENTATIVES, U. S.,
"WASHINGTON, D. C., *Feb. 17, 1885.*

"HON. SAML. J. TILDEN,—Your letter received this morning. The silver interest is much more aggressive than I anticipated it would be. I was not able to carry the amendment to the Sundry Civil bill in the subcommittee. So I did not introduce it there; but I mean to discuss it, and have a vote upon it in the full committee. Messrs. Scott and Barnum, when they left me, promised to return to-morrow; and if there are any points which they can attend to, I will indicate them to those gentlemen.

"I learn that Mr. Warner, of Ohio, and Judge Keagan, of Texas, and others have sent to Mr. Cleveland a petition with about a hundred signatures, asking him not to say anything on that subject in his Inaugural.

"I will keep you further advised as the matter proceeds.

"Yours truly,
"SAM. J. RANDALL."

TILDEN TO DANIEL MANNING

"*Strictly confidential.*

"GREYSTONE, *March 1, 1885.*

"DEAR MR. MANNING,—1. I have advised Mr. Jordan that he must not assume to advise you as to government policy. He can be useful in doing particular things under direction, and in furnishing such information as he may have, or as he shall be specially delegated to obtain, but must not undertake to advise on important matters. He must not expect to be appointed to a confidential position in your department. You can recompense his service in some other way. He has some knowledge which is capable of being made useful, but his talk is cloudy and confused.

"2. I think you must move very slowly in changing important subordinates. The impression seems to exist that French must go sooner or later. I do not think Coon should be changed right away, if at all.

"3. Mr. Fairchild is rather technical, but is entirely trustworthy. You might put him in French's place, and let him get the run of the department, which is a very large and complicated concern, while the other officers, who are experienced, will be there to give information and to carry on the routine. Both yourself and Mr. Fairchild can judge better what changes are desirable after you have got acquainted with the men and their capabilities, and with the functions of their several offices, and shall have ascertained your own wants in respect to assistance.

"4. I hear a Mr. Gilfillen highly spoken of, but I have no personal knowledge of him.

"5. I send you a letter of Senator Gibson, who is entitled to consideration. Please return it to me when you have read it.

"6. I think it would be well for you to ask Mr. Marble about men—what he knows about the existing officers, and what he knows about any experts with whom he is acquainted."

A. M. GIBSON TO S. J. TILDEN

"Private and confidential.

"17 DUPONT CIRCLE, WASHINGTON, D. C., *Mch. 8/85.*

"MY DEAR SIR,—I am dreadfully embarrassed financially, and, although very reluctant, seek employment in the government, since I see no other way open to me as a means of livelihood. I have rendered the Democratic party some service. You, perhaps more than any one else, know and appreciate the work I have done during the past ten or twelve years. I came to Washington comparatively unknown to all the public men of the country save Judge Black. Grant's first term was just closing, and jobbery and fraud were rioting in every department of the government. At considerable personal peril, and with inevitable social ostracism to myself and family, I began the work of exposing rogues and roguery, rascals and rascality. You signalized your life by overthrowing the Tweed ring, and destroying those who organized it and profited by its robberies. You exposed and broke up the canal frauds. You were rich and powerful politically, but you know how potent those whom you brought to grief were to do you injury.

"My first work in Washington was to assail the Navy ring, and to make known the jobs and frauds by which the Navy had been ruined, and millions of dollars stolen from the public treasury to enrich contractors. I followed this work systematically for years, and I do not exaggerate when I say that the country would not have a realizing sense to-day of the way its Navy has been destroyed and its Treasury robbed of hundreds of millions if my work had not been done.

"The first Democratic House of Representatives after the war was elected chiefly because of the exposure of the Credit Mobilier fraud and other disclosures of jobbery which resulted from my work. I broke up the Shepherd ring in this city and drove out the robbers. For eight years I labored without intermission to destroy the Star Mail-route ring, and finally made it possible to bring the guilty to punishment. That the result was a scandal upon, and a perversion of, justice was no fault of mine. That I was deprived of the credit due me for exposing the frauds never grieved me, because I was not working for glory, but to make good government possible. What I did to bring to just punishment the authors and abettors of the great fraud of 1876, and to make forever odious that great crime, you know.

"That I have incurred the hostility of many and excited the envy of still more is but the natural sequence of the work I have done. Politicians are not prone to remember those who made their success possible, unless you are a present potential factor. Of course, in all that I did I had a fearless newspaper with a great circulation as an engine to work with. But I created, in no small degree, the power I used and the influence I exerted. When I began my work here the *Sun* had only a *local* circulation and a *local* reputation. It secured, largely through my work, a *national* circulation and reputation. It profited largely by my work, while I received only a modest salary and fell heir to all the enmities provoked.

"Pardon me for wearying you with this long letter, but of all the Democrats I know you are the only one upon whom I feel that I can rely for some appreciative exertion in my behalf, now that the party, in whose faith I was born, and for which the best years of my life, and the best energies of my poor abilities have been exerted, is in power. I know I am not egotistical when I say that I know more of the inner workings of the government than any man in Washington. I have, for nearly fourteen years, made every department of the Federal government a close study. I know where and how the jobs and frauds have been worked, and how the rottenness can be exposed, and, moreover, can point out the defects of the Treasury system which made many of these possible. I could be invaluable in many ways here, but I would prefer a quiet place abroad. I confess that I am not *en rapport* with many of those who are likely to be most influential with the administration. My tastes are naturally literary, and I have been at work for several years upon the history of the last four months of Buchanan's administration. I have a book of 600 pages nearly ready for the press, the principal data for which I got from Judge Black. The preparation for this work naturally led me to study closely and carefully the political history of the United States, so I could succinctly and graphically deal with the course which led to the Civil War. Becoming deeply interested in the subject, I began writing *The Political History of the United States.* I have nearly completed the first draft of the first volume of this work, and I want the means and leisure to complete it. The place of all others which I would like, and which would enable me to have the resources at hand, would be the Consul Generalship to London; but I presume that it is useless to aspire to that. Some one with more social and political influence than I can command will get it. But I think that I might aspire to be Consul at Liverpool. That place was given to Packard, of Louisiana, as the price of his yielding gracefully to the Hayes Commission, which, in pursuance of the *bargain* made with Southern Democrats in 1876, went to Louisiana to install the Nichols government. Inasmuch as I contributed largely to make the work of that commission odious, and to have the Returning Board indicted and convicted, I think it would not be presumptuous to claim Packard's place.

"May I not ask you to take more than an ordinary interest in my behalf? My lifelong friend, who knew me from childhood, and who always took the deepest interest in my welfare, is no more. You esteemed him at his true worth. You know how emphatic he always spoke in my behalf. If Judge Black was alive, he would join heartily in any effort to secure me the place I seek. But I know no one now, save yourself, to whom I can appeal. There are possibly a *few* who would damn me with faint praise.

"I know how many there are who will importune you, and that there are others with more and better claims upon you; but I am sure that none *needs* your good offices more, and that none will appreciate them higher than

"Yours truly,
"A. M. GIBSON."

TILDEN TO GOVERNOR D. B. HILL

(THE BROADWAY RAILROAD BILL)

"GREYSTONE, *April 21, 1885.*

"DEAR GOV. HILL,—1. The bill entitled 'An act to annul and dissolve the Broadway Surface Railroad Company' is a very proper and necessary bill.

"2. The bill entitled 'An act to provide for the winding up of corporations which have been annulled and dissolved by legislative enactment' does not seem to me to contain any deceptive or dangerous promises, and may be deemed unobjectionable.

"3. The bill entitled 'An act in relation to the consents of property-owners, order of the general term confirming reports of commissioners, and the consents of local authorities,' &c., preserves, notwithstanding the repeal of the charter: *first*, the consent of the property-owners abutting on the street to be occupied by the railroad; *secondly*, the consent of the local authorities having control of the street or highway to be occupied by the railroad; *thirdly*, the order of the general term confirming the report of any commissioners that such railroad ought to be constructed or operated.

"This bill fails to protect the public from dangerous abuses, with the experience of them in the case of the Broadway Railroad before our eyes.

"It is known that the consent of the local authorities was obtained by bribery. Yet this bill provides that that consent shall be valid and effectual.

"It is known that the general term appointed improper persons as commissioners to decide whether or not the Broadway Railroad ought to be built.

"It is known that the general term confirmed the report of those commissioners in favor of having the road built by the grantees without regard to the fact that the compensation to the city from the grantees was grossly inadequate.

"In the case of the Cable Railroad grant, the same general term refused to confirm the report of the commissioners on the express ground that the compensation to the city from the grantees was inadequate.

"Yet this bill adopts, by legislative act, the consent of the local authorities obtained by bribery.

"It also adopts the action of the general term which was at least improvident and unjustifiable in face of its later action in the cable case.

The appointment of commissioners, and the confirmation of their report, was a substituted consent in behalf of the property-owners. The direct consent of the property-owners could probably not have been obtained.

"The substituted consent was obtained only by the abusive action of the general term.

"Again, the effect of this bill is to deny to the people, to the local authorities, and the property-owners interested any opportunity to pass fairly upon the question, whether or not Broadway should be occupied by a surface railroad; it practically determines that there shall be a surface railroad in Broadway.

"The only question which it leaves open is, Who shall own and operate that railroad?

"In my judgment, this bill ought to be held under advisement, after the two former bills have been acted upon.

"You will thus have opportunity for mature consideration, and for manifesting your vigilance in protecting the public interest.

"It is very possible that you will come to the conclusion to withhold from it your approval.

"That is my judgment of what ought to be done.

"I have dictated this letter, after reading, this evening, the newspapers, and finding out as well as I could what has been done to-day. I will endeavor to write about the remaining bill to-morrow.

Very truly yours,
"S. J. TILDEN."

TILDEN TO BIGELOW

"GREYSTONE, *May 2, 1885.*

"DEAR MR. BIGELOW,—I send you the two addresses. Do not cut them. Carefully preserve them. If lost, I probably could not replace them.

"1. The address to which I referred in the account, I gave of it to you, is entitled 'Address of the Democratic Members of the Legislature of the State of New York.'

"The first part of it contained on the first and second pages, and a part of the third page was, I think, drawn by John Van Buren, and prefixed after the preparation of the main body of the document.

"One of the passages written in by me while revising a part of the address will be found on pages 11 and 12. It is marked.

"2. On the subject of adapting a colonial system, or entering into a partnership with mixed races, you will find a declaration in the address of February 16, 1848, pp. 8 and 9, and also in a resolution on p. 16. They are marked.

"I should like to know of exactly what use you propose to make of them. After you have read both papers, I should like it if you could run up here for half an hour and talk it over.

"Very truly yours."

TILDEN TO DANIEL MANNING

"GREYSTONE, YONKERS, N. Y., *June 9, 1885.*

"DEAR MR. MANNING,—I am sorry to hear that the President has been unwell. Having invoked Mrs. Manning's influence in favor, in your case, of a reform of the excessive and destructive sway of the 'interview' evil, I regret that there is no Mrs. Cleveland to co-operate in this reform in the case of the President. He starts with an admirable constitution, but there is a limit to what even he can endure.

"Paper recommendations are a poor reliance at best. A regular trial on a paper basis, of fourth-class postmasters, is beyond the strength of any one man.

"It is necessary that the appointing power should find out friends in every locality, who can be trusted to give accurate information and conscientious advice, and put the responsibility on them, and then accept their judgment.

"It is a mistake to suppose that the party leaders are not capable of being extremely useful as means of intelligence. A party is a living being, having all the organs of eyes, ears, and feeling. No man can rise to leadership without having some qualities of value. The appointing power should not be governed absolutely by local leaders; but should hear them in important cases, cross-examine them, derive all the benefits they are capable of rendering, and not be ambitious of displaying a disregard of them. Distrust of one's friends will generally result in misplaced confidence in inferior persons or in ill-advised action.

"The importance of the little postmasters is very great. In many of the purely rural districts there is one to every hundred voters. They are centres of political activity. They act as agents and canvassers for the newspapers of their party, and as local organizers.

"The immense power of this influence is now wholly on the side of the Republicans. To allow this state of things to continue is infidelity to the principles and cause of the administration. The wrong should be gradually corrected.

"I send herewith some extracts from the letters of Mr. Jefferson, both because the view taken by him is sound, and because he had a felicitous mode of statement, which is a good example to his successors when they have occasion to discuss the same subject.

Very truly yours."

FRANK McCOPPIN TO S. J. TILDEN

"THE PACIFIC CLUB, SAN FRANCISCO, *June 9, 1885.*

"DEAR SIR,—The Chinese question has again disturbed the people, or some of them, upon this coast; but this time it came to us in a new form, as the printed matter enclosed will explain.

"At one time the President intended to appoint a Californian Minister to China (he offered it to Mr. S. M. Wilson of this city), but changed his mind later; hence the present disturbance.

"In this so-called interview I mention the names of all the members of the cabinet save one, and that one I do not admire. A very witty friend of mine, the late John B. Fetton, once said, in regard to very old case cited by opposite counsel, that it was like ox-tail soup—it came from too far back. And so it appears to be with Mr. Secretary, judging by his late performance in Kansas; he comes from too far back. You will, I hope, pardon me for addressing you in this apparently flippant manner; but, though new to you as a correspondent, I am a very old friend of yours, and served on the national committee (Democratic) from 1872 until 1879, when I resigned in consequence of having to go to the Sandwich Islands. Therefore, I served through the campaign of 1876, when this State was lost to us, and the Presidency to you, by a stupendous fraud committed in this city.

"Mrs. McCoppin is a New-Yorker, was a Van Ness, and a niece of the late Mrs. Roosevelt, 836 Broadway.

"Before leaving Washington, I wrote Mr. Manning, who, I suppose, will pay no heed to me, pointing to the fact that our Southern friends in California are pressing forward, to the exclusion of all other classes, for *all* the Federal patronage upon this coast. In this city we have 51,000 registered voters, 2400 of whom are from the South; and yet the 2400 want *all* the offices, and I suppose they will get them.

"The Gwin clique alone have more than enough to fill every place.

Very respectfully yours,
"FRANK MCCOPPIN."

MANNING TO GEORGE W. SMITH

"MR. GEORGE W. SMITH, GREYSTONE, YONKERS.
"WASHINGTON, D. C., *July 2nd, 1885.*

"DEAR SIR,—I made inquiry, to-day, as to the appointment of Mr. Noyes as government director of the Union Pacific Railway Company,[34] and received the copy, which I append.

"I had previously advised the appointment of Mr. Canda.

"Faithfully yours,
"DANIEL MANNING."

"*Tuesday, 2.*

"DEAR MR. MANNING,—Noyes was appointed at the suggestion of Governor Hoadley, who was here when the President and Secretary of the Interior were considering the matter.

"D. S. LAMONT."

G. W. SMITH TO MR. MANNING

"*July 3, 1885.*

"HON. DANIEL MANNING, WASHINGTON, D. C.—Letter received. Such an appointment would be the greatest possible mistake. If commission is not issued, better defer its issue until we can communicate.

"G. W. SMITH."

MANNING TO G. W. SMITH

"WASHINGTON, D. C., *July 3rd, 1885.*

"DEAR MR. SMITH,—Immediately upon receipt of your telegram this morning, I made the necessary inquiry, and received the reply, which I append.

"Faithfully yours,
"DANIEL MANNING."

"EXECUTIVE MANSION, WASHINGTON, *July 3, 1885.*

"DEAR MR. MANNING,—The commissions for the appointment of Union Pacific Railroad directors were issued on the 1st, and are now beyond recall.

"Sincerely yours,
"D. S. LAMONT."

D. MANNING TO GEORGE W. SMITH

"WASHINGTON, D. C., *July 4, 1885.*

"MY DEAR MR. SMITH,—No one can regret much more than I do the composition of that railroad list of officers. I had supposed that in view of what I said as to Mr. Canda that I would hear more of the case before final action, but in this I was disappointed. Two, and possibly three, of the number certainly have no good qualification for the offices given them. Hoadley, it appears (I did not see him), was over here on some business of his own, just in the nick of time to be consulted, and the result was what might have been expected from so good a man—thoughtless and injudicious advice.

"It is not possible that there was any viciousness in the purposes of the two, who may be said to have been the appointing power. I shall have further conversation with them, but without expecting any practical result.

"I cannot, in a letter, write just as fully on this subject as I should like, and shall reserve this, and some other matters of more or less consequence themselves, for the conversation with you, that I promise myself later on in the summer.

"Faithfully yours,
"DANIEL MANNING."

DANIEL MANNING TO TILDEN

"ALBANY, *July 13th, 1885.*

"MY DEAR GOVERNOR,—I send you herewith a copy of a letter received to-day. I send it because it may serve to amuse, and because it enables one to measure the sizes of certain men who are playing their best on the Washington stage. My correspondent is a truthful writer, and is well entitled to my confidence.

"Faithfully yours,
"DANIEL MANNING,
"M. F. M."

The following is the letter mentioned in the above note:

—— TO DANIEL MANNING

"WASHINGTON, *July 12th, 1885.*

"DEAR MR. SECRETARY,—I have a piece of news for you, which I can only hope will not annoy you as much as it has some of us here. You will remember that on one of my visits to the Hot Springs, I told you that some of the gentlemen of the department had organized a social club, and out of respect and admiration for you had named it 'The Manning Club.' Well, the organization seemed to be a vigorous and thriving one, and we had in it almost every Democratic chief of bureau and chief of division in the department. We had rented a fine house for a year, had partly furnished it, and were rapidly getting into good shape when a bomb-shell fell among us in the shape of a notification of the displeasure of the President, and now the organization is completely disorganized and about ready to disband.

"So far as we can learn, the President was misinformed of the objects of the club; he was told that it was a political organization; but even when its real purpose, that of promoting good feeling and good fellowship among Democratic officers of the Treasury Department, was explained to him by Judge Maynard, he insisted upon continuing his disapproval; and intimated that if the organization were continued, he would write a letter for publication, denouncing it and kindred organizations. This I learn from persons who talked with him about it.

"Of course, under the circumstances, there is nothing for us to do but disband. The president of the club wrote Mr. Cleveland, asking for an interview at which he might explain to him its purposes. This was on Friday last. To-day (the 12th) he received a note from Colonel Lamont saying that the President referred the writer of the letter to Mr. Fairchild, to whom he (the President) had spoken on the subject.

"I had a talk with Mr. Fairchild the other day, and found that he had been misinformed as to the objects of the club; but even after I had explained its purpose to him, and while he acknowledged the legitimacy of that purpose, he expressed disapproval of it as liable to misconstruction, and apt to become a source of embarrassment to the administration because of the political qualification for membership.

"The matter is all the more annoying, because there is treachery at the bottom of it. Mr. Fairchild tells me that on Wednesday evening last he heard of it and went to the President about it, and that he found the President already knew of and disapproved of it, as he then understood it. Judge Maynard, who saw the President on Friday, and explained the real purposes of the club to him, tells me that on Wednesday morning he was informed by Colonel Youmans that the club was disapproved of by the President. Youmans thus appears to have been the first person in the Treasury to know that the club met with disfavor at the White House. He knew of it Wednesday morning. On Tuesday night his name was proposed for membership in the club, and the person who proposed his name said he had talked with the chief clerk about the organization that day (Tuesday). It is hard to think it possible, but almost every member of the club believes that Youmans carried the information he had concerning the club and his own impressions of its purposes to the White House.

"However, the club is now a thing of the past; or will be as soon as we can close up its affairs and dispose of our house and furniture, and that part of the incident is at an end; but what puzzles all of us is that a social club of Democratic officials should be vetoed, while State Democratic associations, with purposes assuredly partisan, continue to flourish in Washington.

"I do hope, Mr. Secretary, that the matter may not annoy you or cause you any embarrassment, but I am fearful that it will. I did not write you on Friday, because I wanted to wait and see how it would turn out. It is proper that I should write you about it, now that the President has refused to have the matter explained to him by our officers, and that we have determined to disband."

Shortly before the receipt of the letter which follows, Mr. Manning, one day on leaving the cabinet, experienced an apoplectic attack which compelled him to be transported to his home, and was destined, I believe, to prevent his ever placing his feet again in the Treasury Department. As soon as he was able to travel, he repaired to Albany, where he was accustomed to find the comforts and consolations of home, and expected in seeking them again to be speedily restored to health. In this, however, both he and his friends were disappointed; and though he survived until December of '87, he early realized that his illness was incurable, and that his public career, so full of promise, was ended. In the latter part of July he was invited by Mr. Tilden to join him at the Kaaterskill House in the Catskills, where Mr. Tilden himself was temporarily sojourning. To this invitation the following was Mr. Manning's reply:

DANIEL MANNING TO S. J. TILDEN

"153 WASHINGTON AVENUE,
"ALBANY, N. Y., *July 26th* (*1885.*)

"MY DEAR GOVERNOR,—I have read and carefully thought over your letter of the 16th inst. Dr. Hun and Dr. Simons are agreed as to the heart, the examination of the urine, and the necessity for careful attention to diet.

"I think that I should much like to go to the Catskill Mountains, but I doubt if I would be comfortable there without the company of some cheery friends. I am now under engagement to go to the Watch Hill House, Watch Hill, R. I., next Thursday. Chancellor Pierson, a gentleman of great good-humor, talkative, and a jolly disposition, undertakes to go along. We may spend a couple of weeks there, and then I shall be at the end of my rope.

"I want to see you very much to talk about my proposed communication to the President. I feel more and more, daily, that I need your assistance. Have you thought over the matter? Have you prepared a form for me? Do you know when our friend will return from Europe? I should feel much more at ease if everything was ready in advance. I do not know when I can get to see you. It occupies a day to go from Watch Hill to New York or Yonkers, and for me the trip will be a long one. Kindly clear my mind on this point. I do so much want to decide on my action before the vacation closes. That done, I should feel comparatively free.

"My health is improving daily. My physician talks encouragingly, and I feel that I am better, stronger, than I was when I left Greystone.

"Faithfully yours,
"DANIEL MANNING,
"M. F. M."

DANIEL MANNING TO TILDEN

"*Personal.*

"WASHINGTON, D. C., *July 29, 1885.*

"MY DEAR GOVERNOR,—Will you be at Greystone on the 7th of August? I want to see you, and perhaps I cannot find a better time than that day. I expect to leave here with Mrs. Manning and Miss Mary on the 6th or 7th, and will be compelled to remain in New York over the 8th. I am booked for Watch Hill for the 10th, to remain there two or three weeks.

"I have many things to say, and I need your help and advice.

"Faithfully yours,
"DANIEL MANNING."

C. A. DANA TO A. H. GREEN

"'THE SUN,' NEW YORK, *Aug. 28, 1885.*

"MY DEAR MR. GREEN,—If Mr. Tilden would add to the papers you gave me, the other day, some memoranda on the following questions, it would help me out a great deal.

"1. Would not the expense of deepening the canal, so as to add two feet to the depth of water, be very great? I understand that now, for a great part of its course, the bottom of the canal is composed, for about a foot depth, of clay and hydraulic cement packed closely, so as to prevent leakage; and would not the expense of taking this up and replacing it, after the bottom was dug up, be more serious than any calculation has yet allowed?

"2. How far does the fact that the lake transportation has almost entirely passed into the hands of railroad people, affect the probability of increasing the business of the canal, in case it should be deepened?

"3. Can the canal be maintained in the face of the increasing railroad competition?

"I do not want to trouble Mr. Tilden for any elaborate answers to these questions, but only for hints, such as his knowledge and experience can easily supply, and that I can make useful in discussing the points.

"Yours sincerely,
"C. A. DANA."

D. MANNING TO GEORGE W. SMITH

"215 STATE STREET, ALBANY, N. Y., *Aug. 30, 1885.*

"DEAR MR. SMITH,—I am just back from Watch Hill. I want to see you, and will take the early train Wednesday morning, stopping off at Yonkers at 10.30 A.M. I expect to return to Washington next Thursday evening or Friday morning, and as I do not think I can come over again for some months, I will be glad of a chance for a long 'talk' with you. Please advise me by telegraph if it will be agreeable to see me about the hour named; or if some other hour on Wednesday or Thursday will be more convenient.

"Faithfully yours,
"DANIEL MANNING.

"*Geo. W. Smith, Esq.*

"How the papers do lie!"

GEORGE W. SMITH TO DANIEL MANNING

"*Telegram.*

"The time you name will be agreeable.

"G. W. SMITH.

"Aug. 30/85. (Sat. 2.36 P.M.)."

S. J. TILDEN, JR., TO S. J. TILDEN

"NEW LEBANON, N. Y., *Sept. 2nd, 1885.*

"DEAR UNCLE SAMUEL,—Yours of yesterday received this morning. In reply, would say that I am sorry you had gained the impression that I was intending to seek a position on the State ticket this fall, for such a thing was far from any intention of mine. When this matter was first brought to my notice, by an article which appeared in the N. Y. *Graphic*, some time since, I immediately requested a friend of mine, who is connected with that paper, not to refer to the matter again, as I was not a candidate, and would not accept a place upon the State ticket. This same answer I have always given whether spoken to upon the subject, and had so thoroughly dismissed it from my mind that it did not occur to me to speak of it when I saw you two weeks ago. I have always made our business here of first importance and politics secondary, working at the latter when time would permit. I appreciate only too fully the position in which one is placed who has only a political life before him with all its uncertainties to desire such a one, having seen so many in this position.

"Had I thought of such a step I certainly should not for one moment have entertained it until I had spoken to you upon the subject, for I have appreciated and can easily understand the complications which would arise. Will come up to Greystone the first opportunity I have, and explain more fully than I can write. With many kind regards, I remain,

Yours very truly,
"S. J. TILDEN, JR."

NOTES ON THE CANAL

[*Written by Mr. Tilden on September 4-5, 1885, in Answer to Queries on the Subject by Mr. Dana.*]

"*Q. 1.* Would not the expense of deepening the canal, so as to add two feet to the depth of water, be very great? I understand that now, for a great part of its course, the bottom of the canal is composed, for about a foot depth, of clay and hydraulic cement packed closely, so as to prevent leakage; and would not the expense of taking this up and replacing it, after the bottom was dug up, be more serious than any calculation has yet allowed?

"*A.* The idea of increasing the depth of the canal two feet is a gross exaggeration of what is possible or proper to do.

"To build up the banks two feet would necessitate building up the locks. To excavate the bottom two feet would be impracticable.

"At page 23 of my Message for 1873 it was stated: 'The waterway was practically never excavated in every part to its proper dimensions. Time, the action of the elements, and neglect of administration all tend to fill it by deposits.' There is no doubt that the sides of the waterway have been changed, and the slope filled in with silt, narrowing the bottom of the canal, so that it is only in the middle that the proper depth is approached, and inconvenience is felt in one boat passing another.

"My suggestion was to bring up the canal to an honest seven feet. All the structures of the canal were adapted to that. 'Bring it up to seven feet—honest seven feet—and on all the levels, wherever you can, bottom it out; throw the excavation upon the banks; increase that seven feet toward eight feet, as you can do so progressively and economically. You may also take out the bench-walls.'

"This suggestion looked to gaining on the long levels, when it was found practicable, some inches increasing seven feet '*toward*' eight feet. The suggestion was carefully limited, because in many places you cannot change the bottom without interfering with culverts, or carrying the excavation below the mitre sills of the locks."

As to the Capacity of the Erie

"The lockages at Frankfort, during the season of 1884, were 20,800.

"The lockages in 1873 were stated on page 22 of my Message of 1875 to have been 24,960.

"'The theoretical capacity of the canal will be three or four times the largest tonnage it has ever reached. There is no doubt it can conveniently and easily do double the business which has ever existed, even though the locks be not manned and worked with the highest efficiency.'

"If that was true when the lockages were 25,000, how much more so is it when the lockages have fallen to 20,800 as in 1884?

"*Q. 2.* How far does the fact that the lake transportation has almost entirely passed into the hands of railroad people, affect the probability of increasing the business of the canal, in case it should be deepened?

"*Q. 3.* Can the canal be maintained in the face of the increasing railroad competition?

"*A.* Total tons of each class of articles which came to the Hudson River from Erie and Champlain Canal:

[From the Annual Report of the Superintendent of Public Works upon the trade and tonnage of the Canals for the year 1884, page 100.]

	1874	1884
Products of the forest	1,192,681	1,097,450
Agriculture	1,470,872	1,054,041
Manufactures	49,426	56,899
Merchandise	12,905	45,538
Other articles	497,228	377,259
Total	3,223,112	2,631,187

"Tonnage of the canal, and of the Central and Erie railroads:

[From the Annual Report of the Superintendent of Public Works upon trade and tonnage of the Canals for the year 1884, pages 94-95.]

	1874	1884
New York Canals	5,804,588	5,009,488

New York Central R. R.	6,114,678	10,212,418
Erie Railway	6,364,276	[35]16,219,598
	18,283,542	31,441,504

"The railroads have competed successfully with the Erie Canal, and have carried off all the increase in the tonnage. Notwithstanding the State has ceased to charge tolls, and has imposed an annual tax of $700,000 upon the taxpayers to maintain the canals. The Erie Canal has failed to keep up its business. It holds on to a portion of the lumber, and of the grain.

"There seems to be no probability that the Erie Canal will regain any portion of the business it has lost.

"None of the grand schemes by which it is proposed to enlarge or improve it can, to any appreciable extent, cheapen the transportation. They will simply waste the money of the taxpayer, and revive the system of contracting, jobbery, and fraud.

"The advantage of lengthening the locks so as to pass two boats at once, when there is plenty of time to pass four times the boats which the tonnage requires, is doubtful, and is at least inconsiderable. It can only pretend to save five minutes in a lockage, if, in fact, it will save any time.

"Unless some effectual expedient be adopted to prevent the waste of water in locking through a single boat, it would consume three times as much water in the long lock as in the short lock. I understand that the superintendent thinks that ruinous mischief can be avoided, but I have had no means of testing how the thing would work in practice.

"In 1867, when I examined the subject, I found that on the Delaware and Raritan they used boats of about the same dimensions as the boats in use on the Erie, notwithstanding the locks were capable of passing two boats at a time.

"I send my Message of 1875; my speech in the Constitutional Convention in 1867, which contains a fuller discussion of the subject. I send, also, the last report of the Superintendent of Public Works on the canals.

"The statistical tables are so changed from the ancient forms that it is difficult to get the materials for a satisfactory comparison of the present with the former business.

"A certain portion of the business naturally belongs to the railroads. The principles which govern this division are set forth in the beginning of my speech in 1867. The business would naturally be divided, and the share of the railroads would be increased as the network of the railroads is perfected, and more and more points are touched.

"Besides, the railroads will compete for additional business at less than cost, charging the loss upon the paying portion of their traffic.

"On the whole, it must be observed:

"Within the last ten years the cost of transportation by railroad has been reduced one-half. All the improvements tending to cheapen transportation are made by the railroads.

"As to the clamor about diverting traffic to the Canadian lines, it is senseless. The great mass of grain brought from the West is for local consumption. Two millions and a half of people residing in the city of New York and its suburbs are not going to bring the grain for their own consumption by way of Montreal. A large share of the flour and grain carried by the New York Central is for local consumption in New England. Formerly it came to New York city, and was distributed from that point. It is now carried direct. For instance, flour and grain, for consumption at Springfield and Worcester, are carried from the point of shipment in the West direct to those places without change of cars. They cannot be diverted.

"The Erie Canal still has a certain utility. It should be nursed along, but without any expectation of regaining the place it once occupied in the transportation of the country. The taxpayers of this State will not always consent to pay a bonus of $700,000 per year in order to get tonnage for the Erie Canal."

HORATIO SEYMOUR TO TILDEN

"UTICA, *Sept. 25, 1857* (*1885*).

"DEAR SIR,—I have received your letter of the 22d inst. I wrote the note to the Rochester paper, not because you would care for it, but because I felt it was due to myself to correct any such statement. I am aware that you are used to and indifferent to such attacks.

"I am seventy-five years old, and suffer from nervous attacks. I had *a sunstroke* in 1876, from which I never recovered. It has progressed until it has weakened my body and my memory in many respects. I have not been away from Utica during the past two years, except to visit my sister at Coquemen. I have a man in constant attendance. I leave my farm to drive over to Utica about once in a week. If I get into your section of the State I shall be happy to call upon you. I do not keep track of current events. I went to the convention about our canals. I was nominally its chairman; but I presided only a few minutes, as I was too deaf to hear. My attendance harmed me. I have not been as well since. As I can take no exercise, I grow in weight, which makes me look better and feel worse. I hope I may live to see you again, but it is doubtful.

"Truly yours, &c.,
"HORATIO SEYMOUR."

HORATIO SEYMOUR TO S. J. TILDEN

"UTICA, *October 7, 1885.*

"MY DEAR SIR,—A few days since I received with my mail a letter from you. I glanced at it, and laid it aside with a view of reading it with attention. Since then I have been unable to find it amongst my papers. I find my memory is so much impaired that I am apt to forget what I do when I put aside with care. I cannot, therefore, write you a responsive reply. I am mortified by such mistakes, which multiply as memory fails.

"During the past eight years my memory and health have been impaired by a sunstroke.

"I am obliged to live in a quiet way at my farm; all excitements are hurtful. I have not been away from home, save to make a short journey to see one of my sisters in Madison County. I know but little about current events. I think over the past or speculate about the future.

"Now and then a reporter calls. As my views upon public [sic] are vague and vaguely expressed, they give such interpretation as they wish, so that I am frequently surprised by my opinions as they are given in the press.

"I wish I could visit New York again, but I fear I am too weak to do so. With my wishes for your health and welfare,

"I am, truly yours,
"HORATIO SEYMOUR.

"*Hon. S. J. Tilden.*"

GEORGE BANCROFT TO TILDEN

"NEWPORT, ON THE WING FOR WASHINGTON, D. C.,
"*18 Oct., '85.*

"MY DEAR MR. TILDEN,—I thank you very much for the volumes of your writings, which you have been thoughtful enough of me to send me. I am one of those who have always held and constantly avowed the opinion that you were duly elected President of the United States; it would be instructive if some one well versed in our public law would look through the laws enacted in the period for which you were chosen, and mark such of them as would have encountered your veto. That should be done while you live to confirm the result of the inquiry.

"I remain, dear Mr. Tilden,

"Yours very truly,
"GEO. BANCROFT."

S. J. TILDEN TO BANCROFT

"GREYSTONE, YONKERS, N. Y., *Oct. 21, '85.*

"DEAR MR. BANCROFT,—I have received, through Mr. Bigelow, your note acknowledging a copy of my *Writings and Speeches* edited by him.

"I observe that in your note to him, you mention that the copy sent you does not contain my autograph.

"If the idea that you would desire it had occurred to me, I should have been particular to add every homage of esteem and regard for you in my power.

"Very truly yours,
"S. J. TILDEN."

TILDEN TO PRESIDENT CLEVELAND

"GREYSTONE, YONKERS, NEW YORK, *Oct. 21, '85.*

"To His Excellency, GROVER CLEVELAND.

"MY DEAR SIR,—Mr. D. A. McKnight, the law clerk in the Patent Office, is the author of a book of great ability entitled *The Electoral System of the United States.*

"Without adopting all of his views, his independence, integrity, and conscientiousness are shown by the fact that his masterly analysis of the doings of the electoral commission, in which he exposes the inconsistencies of their decisions, and condemns them as illegal and unconstitutional, was published in a volume printed in 1878, with a preface dated March 10, 1877. At that time Mr. McKnight was holding his present office under the administration of Mr. Hayes.

"I understand that his resignation has recently been requested, in order to give the appointment to some other person.

"Mr. McKnight is confessedly an excellent officer, serving the government with fidelity and skill; and is personally free from every objection.

"Under these circumstances, I take the liberty of appealing to you for an intimation in favor of the retention of Mr. McKnight, or his promotion to a higher grade in the service.

"The Democratic party of the United States have beheld, with indignation, the chief agents in the frauds, perjuries, and forgeries by which a pretext of documentary evidence was furnished on which to base a false count, rewarded by their appointment in numerous cases to most important civil trusts.

"It would scarcely be anticipated that a Democratic administration should have so little sympathy with, or respect for the popular feeling on this subject as to discard a meritorious officer having the peculiar claim to its recognition which the facts I have narrated show Mr. McKnight to possess.

"I have no personal interest in the matter, but consider it my duty to represent the cause of public justice, to the end that the crime against the people consummated in 1876, and again meditated in 1884, shall never be repeated.

"I trust that you will excuse me for calling your attention to what might otherwise escape your observation.

"Very truly yours."

D. A. McKNIGHT TO S. J. TILDEN

"UNITED STATES PATENT OFFICE,
"WASHINGTON, *October 24, 1885.*

"HON. SAML. J. TILDEN.

"MY DEAR SIR,—A few moments ago I received the two letters which you were good enough to write at my request. I am, as you may surmise, very highly gratified with them. They contain all (and more than all) that I had hoped for, and must certainly accomplish their purpose. And I assure you that I am full of gratitude to you for an interest in my affairs which gives me fresh courage, and which shows me again the great heart that inspired these letters. I only wish that I could thank you in adequate terms, or that I could again *do something* to exhibit the warm personal regard for you into which my original esteem has developed. If the day ever comes that I can be of service to you, command me.

"With my kindest regards and warmest wishes for your health and happiness, I am,

"Very respectfully and truly,
"Your obedient servant,
"D. A. MCKNIGHT."

MARSHALL PARKS TO S. J. TILDEN

"NORFOLK, VA., *14 Dec., '85.*

"HON. S. J. TILDEN, GREYSTONE, N. Y.

"MY DEAR SIR,—Your letter to Hon. Mr. Carlisle on the subject of our coast defences has been published in our papers, and I can assure you were read with great interest.

"The change in the mode of warfare has rendered a number of our forts almost useless. I would call your attention to those near this city—Fortress Monroe and Fort Wool (formerly Fort Calhoun). The former is said to be the largest for defence in the world, and the latter on an artificial island, one mile distant, not yet completed; both designed to protect Hampton Roads, James River, Norfolk, and the U. S. Navy-Yard here. As they are only one mile apart, I presume it was about the range of guns at the time they were designed. Modern ordnance renders this structure of *no value*, and it is likely it never will be completed, and I write to suggest the importance of its removal to another location, which will, I think, make it a defence for the capital as well as Baltimore, Norfolk, Richmond, and other cities. By reference to the map of Chesapeake Bay, you will observe there is a shoal between Cape Henry and Cape Charles called the *Middle Ground* on which a modern fort could be erected from the material now useless at Fort Wool. This fort is built on an artificial island having a base of fourteen acres, in water from twelve to fifty feet deep, entirely of rough granite. This could be removed at little cost, and a modern structure of iron or steel erected on it, with necessary fixtures for torpedo service.

"Just inside Cape Henry is Lynn Haven Bay and river. The river would make an admirable station for torpedo-boats, as it is a safe harbor, completely landlocked, and may be connected by a few short and inexpensive canals with Back Bay, Currituck, Albemarle, and Pamlico sounds which may extend the inland route to Florida at little cost.

"Several years ago I made the voyage from New Berne, North Carolina, to Oswego, New York, *in the same steamer, going inland the entire way*! I have spent many years on this inland project. By the construction of two short canals (only fourteen miles) we have opened up to commerce 1800 miles of navigable waters. I am now about to open a canal from Neuse River to Beaufort Harbor, North Carolina, which will be a continuation of the inland navigation. It would cost but little to make an inland water route to Florida, as a few short canals would unite the natural waterways existing, and the inland route would then be complete from the Great Lakes to Florida, passing by all our great seaboard cities.

"As we have now no defence to our national capital, I have thought a line from you at this time would bring it to the favorable consideration of Congress.

"If you have not the charts convenient, I would be pleased to furnish them and any further information desired.

"Very resp'y, y'r obt. st.,
"MARSHALL PARKS."

DANIEL MANNING TO S. J. TILDEN

"WASHINGTON, D. C., *Dec. 16, 1885.*

"MY DEAR GOVERNOR,—I write a line to acknowledge receipt of your letter to the Saratoga convention in which, for the second time, you decline to be nominated for the Presidency by the Democratic party. The manuscript of that letter will, of course, always have very high value to me. It will be the most prized of the few heirlooms that I possess.

"Mrs. Manning and I are very glad that you consented to a visit to us, during the New Year week, from Miss Ruby and Miss Susie. Everything and everybody promises to be gay here, and I think they will find pleasure in the visit.

"Faithfully yours,
"DANIEL MANNING.

"*Hon. Sam. J. Tilden, Greystone.*"

S. J. TILDEN TO DANIEL MANNING

"GREYSTONE, YONKERS, N. Y., *Dec. 19, 1885.*

"DEAR MR. MANNING,—I read over your report when I first received it, and laid it aside intending to give it a second and more thorough perusal, and waited about acknowledging it until I should do so; but I have been less well than common, and have found so many things pressing upon me that I have not had a chance to execute my good intentions.

"The impression your report made on me was very favorable. I think it does you great credit, and congratulate you on the manner in which it has been received by the public.

"Very truly yours,
"S. J. TILDEN."

TILDEN TO HON. GEORGE BANCROFT

"GREYSTONE, *Feb. 12, 1886.*

"DEAR MR. BANCROFT,—I have received a copy of your *Plea for the Constitution of the United States*, which the publishers sent to me at your request.

"I note your strong impression of your sense of the importance of the theme, when you say you 'have thought it right to bestow upon it many of the few hours that may remain to you for labor.'

"To the eyes of your countrymen, those hours grow more valuable as they become fewer.

"As an argument your *Plea* is overwhelming.

"Indeed, until new lights recently dawned upon the court, and upon some others, in all our national history it had been universally considered as axiomatic that Congress had no constitutional power to make anything but gold and silver a legal-tender. That conclusion was always assumed when the subject was incidentally alluded to. Forty years ago, in a speech in the constitutional convention of the State of New York on the subject of Currency and Banking (Tilden's *Public Writings and Speeches*, Vol. I., p. 222), I recognized the disability of any government in this country, State or Federal, to make a legal-tender of anything but gold and silver.

"In all the literature of political economy, of currency and banking, this postulate was taken for granted.

"It is a long time since I have had the pleasure of seeing you or Mrs. Bancroft. I was gratified at the account of you, which I received from my nieces who recently visited Washington. I hear that you have lit up your household by the sunshine of a young lady of your kindred.

"I am passing the winter at a country home perched upon a cliff overhanging the Hudson four hundred feet above the tide. I send you a picture of the place.

"With best regards for yourself and Mrs. Bancroft,

"I remain, very truly yours,
"S. J. TILDEN.

"P. S.—Since writing you, I have received the *Evening Post* of this afternoon. It is a 'Mugwump' journal. I send a cutting from its editorial columns upon your *Plea*."

HIRAM SIBLEY TO TILDEN

"ROCHESTER, N. Y., *Feb. 6", 1886.*

"HON. SAMUEL J. TILDEN.

"MY DEAR FRIEND,—This is *my* birthday, and, as I remember, *yours*. I see in the papers they say you were born on the 9th of Feb. But I dare not place much reliance on what some newspapers say of you.

"Seventy-nine is not eighty. Eighty is considered *old.* While it is unsafe for us at this age to make plans for the future, we may contemplate the past, and that is what I am doing to-day.

"Among those who took active part in the *Free-soil* movement of 1848, you were an able leader. Your associates, *Wright*, *Gardner*, *Van Buren*, and many others from whom I took counsel, are gone. You among the larger, myself among the less important of that band of noble patriots, are left to enjoy the consolation of doing what we could at that early day to check the growth and extension of slavery.

"The *present* I regard with fear and apprehension, and I have recently written to, and received an answer from, our *inaugurated* President, whose administration I heartily approve, and I now address the *uninaugurated* President to say one word of approval to him also.

"You should encourage, by word and deed, our President to hold fast to the pledges in the Democratic platform, to *Civil Service* especially.

"The times are trying the metal of our President. The army on whom the people rely for defence are greatly demoralized.

"The *veterans* are nearly all *dead*, the *regulars* are *skirmishing* for votes, and recruits are *few*.

"Pardon me for this rambling letter. Don't trouble yourself to answer me.

"The times, the time (Feb. 6"), all conspired to move me to write you.

"May you live to see many a birthday, as I hope to.

"With great respect, I am,

"Your friend and obt. svt.,
"HIRAM SIBLEY."

TILDEN TO JOHN F. SEYMOUR

"*Telegram.*

"GREYSTONE, *Feb. 13, 1886.*

"HON. JOHN F. SEYMOUR,—I learn this morning the sorrowful intelligence that the mortal career of your illustrious brother is closed. Convey to his relatives, and when a suitable occasion arises, to Mrs. Seymour, my warm sympathies at their loss. We have the consolation of knowing that he passed away without suffering, in the fulness of years, and amid the largest homage of public esteem.

"S. J. TILDEN."

GEORGE BANCROFT TO TILDEN

"1623 H STREET,
"WASHINGTON, D. C., *February 15th, 1886.*

"MY DEAR MR. TILDEN,—I thank you very much for your note of the 12th. We old men must keep up the good tradition which we received from the fathers, and which you defended in the constitutional convention of New York.

"I am also alive, as you undoubtedly are, to the dangers that overhang the country by a legislative measure, designed to throw gold out of circulation, and to depreciate the currency fully twenty per cent. By this measure, among infinite evils, all contracts now in force between the employer and the laborer will be depreciated twenty per cent., to the injury of the poor; and every one of our newspapers will be compelled to stop its publication or to raise its price.

"Wishing you perfect health and long life,

"I am, very sincerely yours,
"GEO. BANCROFT.

"Pray recall me to the kind recollection of your nieces, whom I had great pleasure in meeting a few weeks ago."

TILDEN TO HIRAM SIBLEY

"GREYSTONE, *Feb. 27, 1886.*

"DEAR MR. SIBLEY,—I have received your interesting letter. The newspapers are correct in saying that the 9th of February is my birthday, but some of them are quite astray in saying that I am seventy-nine years old. I was born the 9th of February, 1814, and was seventy-two years old on my last birthday. Although seven years younger than you are, I can readily believe that you are practically younger than I. You have not done so much as I to exhaust the vital powers, and have not so large a debt to pay for strength borrowed and consumed in advance. My eyes are extremely good, and enable me to pass most of my time in reading; my ears are both of them much more acute than those of most people. The doctors tell me that every vital organ is in strong and sound condition. But I have been for some years greatly annoyed by a mysterious malady of some of the nerves of motion, which imparts a tremor to my hands, and impairs my voice so that I lose most of the pleasures of conversation.

"I have also read the brief biography of your life and doings which you were kind enough to send me. It illustrates an example of an active, useful, and successful career.

"Wishing you every blessing of continued health, and prolonged years of happiness and prosperity,

"I am, very truly yours,
"S. J. TILDEN."

"ACCOUNTABILITY OF CORPORATIONS[36]

"The governmental policy of the State of New York has been a long while established, that charters of corporations within its jurisdiction, carrying on business for profit, should be subject to alteration or repeal in the discretion of the Legislature.

"The Revised Statutes of 1830 applied that rule to corporations thereafter to be created. A reservation of that power had been previously inserted in the special charters which had latterly been granted. The origin of this reservation was ascribed in an article asserting the repealability of corporate charters, written by Mr. Tilden for the *Democratic Review* of August, 1841 (Tilden's *Writings and Speeches*, Vol. I., p. 171), to Silas Wright, who procured the insertion of such a reservation in a charter granted in 1822.

"In the convention of 1846, which formed the present Constitution of the State of New York, Mr. Tilden, from the select committee to whom was referred the report of the standing committee on the subject of corporations, made the following report:

> "'Section 1. Corporations may be formed under general laws, but shall not be created by special act, except for municipal purposes, and in cases where, in the judgment of the Legislature, the objects of the corporation cannot be attained under general laws. All general laws and special acts passed pursuant to this section may be altered from time to time or repealed.

> "'Section 3. The term corporations as used in this article shall be construed to include all associations and joint stock companies having any of the powers of corporations not possessed by individuals or partnerships.'

"At the afternoon session on the same day the first section was adopted unanimously, and the above clause of the third section was adopted without considerable opposition.

"The discussion in the convention shows that those clauses were understood to apply to all corporations then existing or thereafter to be created.

"Those provisions stand in the Constitution of the State of New York. They are referred to in a speech on canals and railroads made by Mr. Tilden in the constitutional convention of 1867. The passage is as follows:

> "'The convention of 1846, by provisions which it fell to my lot to report, provided, first, in favor of a system of incorporation under general laws, and, secondly, for a supervisory legislative control over the chartered power and privileges of all corporate bodies.
>
> "'In my judgment, those two provisions were, and are, perfectly adequate to secure every public object, however freely we may grant to private enterprise all the powers necessary to enable it to create these great machines of travel and transportation, and to the management of them by corporate bodies, which can serve the public with more skill and economy than the State can. The authority thus reserved to the State is doubtless capable of being perverted by it to private injury and oppression; but it seemed to be necessary to the public safety, and is a trust to be exercised with wisdom and justice.'

"The general Railroad act, chapter 140 of the Statute Laws of 1850, passed April 2 of that year, faithfully executed the mandate of the Constitution. The forty-eighth section of that act is as follows:

> "'The Legislature may at any time annul or dissolve any incorporation formed under this act; but such dissolution shall not take away or impair any remedy given against any such corporation, its stockholders, or officers, for any liability which shall have been previously incurred."

"The Broadway Railroad charter was formed under chapter 252 of the laws of 1884, entitled 'An act to provide for the construction, extension, maintenance, and operation of street surface railroads and branches thereof in cities, towns, and villages.'

"The first section of that act expressly provides that every corporation formed under it 'shall also have all the powers and privileges granted, and be subject to all the liabilities imposed by this act, or by the act entitled "An act to authorize the formation of railroad corporations, and to regulate the same," passed April 2, 1850, and the several acts amendatory thereof, except as the said acts are herein modified.'

"In the case of 'The People of the State of New York against Dispensary and Hospital Society of the Women's Institute of the city of New York' (7 Lansing, page 304), a corporation formed 'under an act of the Legislature of the State of New York, entitled "An act for the incorporation of benevolent, charitable, scientific, and missionary societies, passed April 12, 1848, and the acts amendatory thereof,"' was judicially determined to have forfeited its charter by reason of the payment of money as a reward for the use of influence in obtaining an appropriation from the State, and the corporation was dissolved by judgment of the court.

"The authority of the Legislature to repeal a charter is much broader than the judicial authority. It is expressly declared by the Constitution and by the law to be in the discretion of the Legislature. It may be done on moral evidence of wrong-doing on the part of the corporation, while a court could only act on judicial proof. It may be done on grounds of public policy or expediency.

"The bill pending in the Senate for repealing the charter of the Broadway Company and annulling its franchise may do well enough if a Broadway railroad is to exist.

"Whether any holders of Broadway Railroad stock or bonds can be shown to be innocent and entitled to special indulgence, can be better judged of when the investigations are concluded.

"One thing is quite clear. The corruption of public officers in order to obtain possession of valuable franchises at much less than their real worth, can only be stopped by making such schemes impossible to result in any profit.

"A general law should be passed requiring every such franchise to be disposed of at public auction.

"If proofs cannot be found to bring the wrong-doers to criminal punishment, the confiscation of their investment will be a salutary warning to them and to the public generally."

D. MANNING TO TILDEN

"WASHINGTON, D. C., *Mch. 5, 1886.*

"MY DEAR GOVERNOR,—One of the first copies from the press, of the reply to the House resolution, was duly mailed to you, from here, addressed, 'George W. Smith, Esq., Greystone, Yonkers, N. Y.' I sent you another copy to-day, addressed to you personally, which I hope won't miss fire.

"There is 'a squall on,' hereabouts, concerning financial matters, and it may grow to the size of a heavy storm, but I doubt. At any rate, I think we are in waters deep enough for safety, and the record isn't a half bad one.

"I have plenty of work and worry, and no day passes that I do not wish I were near enough to you to get the benefit of your safe judgment and advice. There is none here to whom I can go with such confidence and sure dependence.

"Faithfully yours,
"DANIEL MANNING."

TILDEN TO PRESIDENT CLEVELAND

"*Confidential.*

"GREYSTONE, YONKERS, N. Y., *March 12, 1886.*

"DEAR MR. PRESIDENT,—I read in the public journals that the name of Brigadier-General Newton, Chief of Engineers in the United States army, is before you for promotion to a Major-Generalship.

"I have had occasion, in the course of his duties near the city of New York, although having no personal acquaintance with him, to form an opinion as to his character and capacities; and have otherwise acquired information concerning him.

"I believe him to be a very able and accomplished officer. I understand that his commission as lieutenant antedates that of all other officers now in active service; that he entered West Point at the same time with General Pope, and graduated higher in his class; that he graduated twelve years prior to General Howard.

"Although a Virginian by birth, he greatly distinguished himself on the Union side—commanding the First Army Corps at Gettysburg, and taking an important part in other battles.

"At his age, and to be retired more than six years sooner than General Howard, unless he is now restored to the priority to which he is entitled, he probably will be denied altogether the promotion which his services, his character, and capacity merit.

"Another consideration seems worthy of attention. The highest honors of the army ought not to be confined exclusively to Republicans, so long as Democrats not inferior, not to say superior in services and professional capacity, older soldiers if not better, remain to be chosen. General Hancock's death made a vacancy which, though well filled, was not filled by a successor of General Hancock's political faith. General Newton's selection now would for the time redress the balance.

"With assurances of cordial regard, I remain,

"Very truly yours,
"S. J. TILDEN."

S. J. TILDEN TO DANIEL MANNING

"*Confidential.*

"GREYSTONE, *March 14, 1885.*

"DEAR MR. MANNING,—1. I hear a rumor that there is a movement to turn out Mr. Nimmo, who is the head of the Bureau of Statistics. I have examined his reports. They make the impression on me that he is a valuable officer and should be retained.

"2. I have received a letter from Mr. R. H. Henry, of the *State Ledger*, Jackson, Mississippi, saying that, at the suggestion of Mr. Lamar, he has become a candidate for appointment as Register of the Treasury. I infer from his letter that some other appointment would satisfy him.

"I know nothing about his qualifications, or to what appointment he would be adapted. He was chairman of the committee deputed by the Chicago convention to wait upon me with its complimentary resolutions. He is a man whose appearance makes a favorable impression. He has co-operated with us for twelve years, and went early and strongly for Mr. Cleveland. I bespeak your good-will and kindness towards him, without assuming to judge what you wish to do with the Registry of the Treasury, or what you are able to do for Mr. Henry.

Very truly yours,
"S. J. TILDEN."

MRS. MANNING TO S. J. TILDEN

"1501 18TH ST., WASHINGTON, *March 25th (1886).*

"MY DEAR GOVERNOR,—There has not been an unfavorable symptom so far in Mr. Manning's case since he was taken ill.[37] He is a sick man, but we believe that good nursing will bring him out all right. He takes very light nourishment, is kept very quiet, and the physicians prescribe very little medicine. I could not deny myself the comfort of writing to you myself. I thank you for your helpful letter; such words and sympathy help me to behave.

"I will keep you informed of his condition.

"With high regards,

Sincerely yours,
"MARGARETTA F. MANNING.

"*Hon. Saml. J. Tilden.*"

W. E. SMITH TO TILDEN

(THE SECRETARY OF THE TREASURY'S FATAL ILLNESS)

"TREASURY DEPARTMENT, WASHINGTON.

"HON. S. J. TILDEN.

"MY DEAR SIR,—Mr. Manning was, as you know, struck down a few days ago. A small blood-vessel burst at the base of the brain. It was impossible to tell at the time how serious the attack would prove, but this morning his physicians say that the chances are that he cannot recover, although the case is not entirely hopeless. At best, they say it will be months before he can attend to any business. The worst may be expected at any moment.

Y'rs truly,
"W. E. SMITH.

"*Mch. 26/86, 11 A.M.*"

C. JORDAN TO TILDEN

"TREASURY DEPARTMENT, WASHINGTON, *March 27, '86.*

"HON. SAML. J. TILDEN.

"DEAR SIR,—You, as a matter of course, have heard of our loss, and will regret it as much, or more, than I do, if such a thing be possible. I am about to take a liberty that, I think, the situation will justify—that is, suggest that you tender to the Secretary the use of your yacht. He is fond of the water, and if he recovers will need rest and recreation. He can obtain it nowhere so well as on the water. I feel that I have taken a great liberty, but my desire to serve Mr. Manning is very great. He deserves all the affection and esteem of his friends, and now their air and sympathy.

"Yours very respectfully,
"C. N. JORDAN."

S. J. TILDEN TO GOVERNOR HILL

"15 GRAMERCY PARK, NEW YORK, *March 28, 1886.*

"DEAR GOVERNOR HILL,—I feel that Mr. Husted[38] is permitting the resolution on coast defences to slumber too long, and that New York is failing to take the position which is necessary to the safety of the whole country, and especially to her own safety.

"I think it is highly desirable that you should call his attention to the subject.

"Very truly yours,
"S. J. TILDEN.

"I am here until Monday afternoon."

"SEA-COAST DEFENCES

"In considering the state of the public revenues, the subject involves the question whether we shall extinguish the surplus by reducing the revenue; or, whether we shall apply the surplus to payments on the public debt; or, whether we shall seize the occasion to provide for our sea-coast defences, which have been too long neglected. The Secretary is of the opinion that the latter is a paramount necessity, which ought to precede the reduction of the revenue; and ought, also, to precede an excessive rapidity in the payment of the public debt.

"The property exposed to destruction in the nine seaports—Portland, Portsmouth, Boston, Newport, New York, Philadelphia, Baltimore, New Orleans, and San Francisco—cannot be less in value than five thousand millions of dollars. To this must be added a vast amount of property dependent for its use on three seaports. Nor does this statement afford a true measure of the damage which might be carried to the property and business of the country by a failure to protect these seaports from hostile naval attacks.

"They are the centres, not only of foreign commerce, but of most of the internal trade and exchanges of domestic productions. To this state of things the machinery of transportation of the whole country has become adapted.

"The interruptions of the currents of traffic by the occupation of one of our principal seaports by a foreign enemy, or the destruction of them by bombardment, or by the holding over them the menace of destruction for the purpose of exacting contribution or ransom, would inflict upon the property and business of the country an injury which can neither be foreseen nor measured.

"The elaborate and costly fortifications, which were constructed with the greatest engineering skill, are now practically useless. They are not capable of resisting the attacks of modern artillery.

"A still greater defect exists in our coast defences. The range of the best modern artillery has become so extended that our present fortifications, designed to protect the harbor of New York, where two-thirds of the import trade and more than one-half of the export trade of the whole United States is carried on, are too near to the great populations of New York city, Jersey City, and Brooklyn to be of any value as a protection.

"To provide effectual defences would be the work of years. It would take much time to construct permanent fortifications. A small provision of the best modern guns would take several years. Neither of these works can be extemporized in presence of emergent danger. A million of soldiers with the best equipments on the heights surrounding the harbor of New York, in our present state of preparation, or, rather, in our total want of preparation, would be powerless to resist a small squadron of war-steamers.

"This state of things is discreditable to our foresight and to our prudence.

"The best guarantee against aggression—the best assurance that our diplomacy will be successful and pacific, and that our rights and honor will be respected by other nations, is in their knowledge that we are in a situation to vindicate our reputation and interests. While we may afford to be deficient in the means of defence, we cannot afford to be defenceless. The notoriety of the fact that we have neglected the ordinary precautions of defence invites want of consideration in our diplomacy, injustice, arrogance, and insult at the hands of foreign nations.

"It is now more than sixty years since we announced to the world that we should resist any attempts, from whatever quarter they might come, to make any new colonizations on any part of the American continent—that while we should respect the *status quo*, we should protect the people of the different nations inhabiting this continent from every attempt to subject them to the dominion of any European power, or to interfere with their undisturbed exercise of the rights of self-government.

"This announcement was formally made by President Monroe, after consultation with Mr. Madison and Mr. Jefferson. It was formulated by John Quincy Adams. Our government has firmly adhered to the Monroe Doctrine, and even so late as 1865 it warned Napoleon III. out of Mexico.

"It is impossible to foresee, in the recent scramble of the European powers for the acquisition of colonies, how soon an occasion may arise for our putting in practice the Monroe Doctrine. It is clear that there ought to be some relation between our assertion of this doctrine, and our preparation to maintain it.

"It is not intended to recommend any attempt to rival the great European powers in the creation of a powerful navy. The changes which have rapidly occurred by the diminution of the relative resisting power of the defensive armor of ironclads, and by the increased efficiency of modern artillery—which, on the whole, has gained in the competition—suggest that we should not, at present, enter largely into the creation of armored vessels.

"In the questions that beset this subject until they shall have reached a solution, we can content ourselves with adding but sparingly to our navy.

But what we can add should be the very best that experience and science can indicate. This prudential view is reinforced by the consideration that the annual charge of maintaining a war-vessel bears an important proportion to the original cost of construction.

"In constructing permanent fortifications, and in providing an ample supply of the best modern artillery, the annual cost of maintenance is inconsiderable. Nearly the whole expenditure is in the original outlay for construction.

"If we do not make this expenditure necessary to provide for our sea-coast defences when we have a surplus, and have no need to levy taxes, we certainly will not make those expenditures when we have no longer a surplus in the Treasury.

"To leave our vast interests defenceless, in order to reduce the cost of whiskey to its consumers, would be a solecism.

"The present time is peculiarly favorable for providing for this great national necessity too long neglected. Not only does the surplus in the Treasury supply ample means to enable us to meet this great public want, without laying new burdens upon the people, but the work can now be done at a much lower cost than has ever before been possible. The defensive works would consist almost entirely of steel and iron. Those materials can now be had at an unprecedentedly low price. A vast supply of machinery, and of labor, called into existence by a great vicissitude in the steel and iron industries, offers itself to our service. We should have the satisfaction of knowing that while we were availing ourselves of these supplies, which would ordinarily be unattainable, we were setting in motion important industries, and giving employment to labor in a period of depression. With encouragement by the guarantee of work, or, perhaps, by the government itself furnishing the plant, the inventive genius of our people would be applied to the creation of new means and improved machinery, and establishments would spring into existence capable of supplying all of the national wants, and rendering us completely independent of all other countries in respect to the means of national defence."

TILDEN TO C. JORDAN

"15 GRAMERCY PARK, NEW YORK, *March 30, 1886.*

"DEAR MR. JORDAN,—You need have no hesitation in suggesting to me anything in my power which you think would be beneficial to Mr. Manning.

"The *Viking* is laid up for the winter, and has to undergo some refitting before she can be brought into service.

"But I do not think Mr. Manning could, by any possibility, use her with advantage, unless his present situation should be greatly changed.

"It is too late in the season to go South. I do not believe that Mr. Manning could bear the motion of the largest ocean steamer, still less the greater motion of a small steamer, or the gas and noise of the machinery. A great deal of strength and health is required by the roughing incident to a sea voyage of any considerable duration. I have myself to limit my excursions in the *Viking* to a few hours at a time. Nor would it be easy to take on board a man weighing 280 pounds who cannot walk, and more difficult still to convey him down the narrow gangway.

"The medical treatment, as I understand, prescribes absolute quiet; this is incompatible with yachting. I am here for a few days, and shall then return to Greystone. I receive frequent information in regard to Mr. Manning, but should be glad of anything which you may be able to communicate.

"I should be delighted if Mr. Manning should become able to use the *Viking* with benefit.

"Very truly yours,
S. J. TILDEN."

WILLIAM E. SMITH TO TILDEN

"*Personal.*

"TREASURY DEPARTMENT,
"WASHINGTON, D. C., *March 31, 1886.*

"MY DEAR SIR,—Mr. Manning's condition is apparently about the same, but he is now believed to be out of danger, although it will probably be many months before he can attend to any business whatever. His case is complicated by disease of the kidneys, but the physicians say they do not fear any serious trouble from this cause. It is very difficult to obtain any reliable information as to his actual condition.

"Yours truly,
"W. E. SMITH."

C. N. JORDAN TO TILDEN

"TREASURY OF THE UNITED STATES,
"WASHINGTON, *April 1st, 1886.*

"HON. SAMUEL J. TILDEN,—Many thanks for your kind answer. My own opinion is that Mr. Manning is sorely hurt, if he ever wholly recovers. He is a shy man, who does not like to be made a spectacle of, and is fond of the water, so that my idea was and is that a boat would suit him best, as the place where he would be most secluded. How he is to be replaced I can't see; there isn't a member of the cabinet who has made the impression he has, either on Congress or the people with whom he has been brought in contact. 'The only Democrat' in the cabinet is the name he goes by, and it called forth, when his sickness became known, both from Democrats and Republicans, a general expression of regret. He is said to be better to-day. I hope so, but am afraid.

"Yours very respectfully,
"C. N. JORDAN."

GEORGE W. SMITH TO GENERAL BARLOW

"GREYSTONE, *April 2nd, 1886.*

"DEAR GENERAL BARLOW,—The petition sent by you has at last arrived. Mr. Tilden requests me to say that it is a very long paper, and would require much investigation before he could adopt it. The delicate state of his health forbids his undertaking to examine the questions which it raises.

"Even if he should come to the same conclusion which the authors of the paper have reached, Mr. Tilden is in no condition to carry on the controversy which it would involve, and he would be unwilling to initiate, or to become responsible for, a movement to which he could not give the personal attention and effort which could alone conduct it to a useful result.

"Mr. Tilden knows better than anybody else the burden which the proceedings of 1871-2 entailed, and the prolonged efforts and sacrifices through which success was achieved.

"Without them the mere use of a name, or, indeed, of any number of names, would be utterly futile. Mr. Tilden, therefore, does not think it necessary or useful to examine the preliminary questions.

"Very truly yours,
"GEO. W. SMITH."

F. B. GOWEN TO TILDEN

"CREISHEIM, MOUNT AIRY, PHILADELPHIA, *April 22, 1886.*

"DEAR MR. TILDEN,—It is so long since I have had the pleasure of seeing you that I fear you may have forgotten me, unless the newspapers have kept you advised of the struggle I am now making to rescue my old company, the Philadelphia & Reading Railroad Company, from the receivership and syndicate that now environ it.

"In this attempt I should, above all things, be delighted to have your aid and counsel, and if you would give me a half-hour of your time whenever and wherever most convenient to yourself, it would give me very great pleasure to bring to your attention, and ask your aid in favor of, the scheme I have now prepared for the relief of the company.

"Believe me, my dear sir,

"Very sincerely yours,
"FRANKLIN B. GOWEN.

"*Hon. Samuel J. Tilden.*"

TILDEN TO GOVERNOR HILL

"GREYSTONE, YONKERS, N. Y., *April 23, 1886.*

"DEAR GOVERNOR HILL,—In submitting suggestions to you, I should have great delicacy if I did not offer them as mere suggestions which you, who have the public responsibility, must pass upon according to your own judgment, and not according to mine.

"In addition to the objections to the Consent bill, which I mentioned in my letter of night before last, there is another difficulty. That act does not provide any mode by which railroads not now connecting with the Broadway Railroad at Fourteenth Street can make such connections. This would give great advantage to the Seventh Avenue Railroad in competing at auction for the Broadway franchise. If in consequence that company should succeed in getting the franchise at a low price, such a result would be likely to create a reaction against the reform movement.

"I adhere to the opinion that the Repeal bill and the Winding-up bill should be acted upon promptly; that the Consent bill should be retained for fuller consideration and, eventually, be rejected.

"About the remaining bill of the four reported by the Senate Investigating Committee, I cannot find, by the newspapers, that it has passed.

"It seems to me better than the original Cantor bill, which is now a law, but it still has serious defects.

"1. It leaves the present law standing whereby the general term, appointing commissioners, and rectifying their action, will dispense with the consent of the abutting property-holders.

"2. It allows the Aldermen to pass over the veto of the Mayor a resolution granting a railroad franchise, provided the consent of one-half of the abutting property-owners be obtained.

"The first defect is the most serious. Perhaps the second may be risked, though I do not think it quite safe to dispense with any restrictions upon these grants.

"I do not know whether it is intended to pass this bill, or whether it can be amended.

"In discussing these bills, I am not advised how far, if at all, any of them have been changed by amendment.

"Very truly yours,
S. J. TILDEN."

TILDEN TO F. B. GOWEN

"GREYSTONE, *April 29, 1886.*

"DEAR MR. GOWEN,—I have received your letter of April 22d. I have not found an earlier opportunity of answering it.

"I have a pleasing memory of you when you were in the profession. Since that time, I have known you only through the public journals.

"My esteem for you would make it a pleasure to shake you by the hand.

"But I cannot see how I can be of any use to you in the matter of which you speak. The delicacy of my health, and the necessity of my avoiding fatigue as far as possible, render it inexpedient for me to undertake anything more than the unavoidable attention to my personal affairs compels me to do.

"I therefore cannot engage in the work of considering any scheme for the reorganization of the great interests involved in the Reading Railroad, or make the investigations which would be necessary to give any real value to my opinion on the subject.

"Assuring you of my high regard,

"I am, very truly yours,
"S. J. TILDEN.

"*Franklin B. Gowen, Esq., Philadelphia, Pa.*"

E. B. YOUMANS TO TILDEN

"TREASURY DEPARTMENT, OFFICE OF THE CHIEF CLERK,
"WASHINGTON, D. C., *May 4th, 1886.*

"HON. SAMUEL J. TILDEN, Greystone, Yonkers, N. Y.

"DEAR GOVERNOR,—Agreeable to my promise, I write you regarding the present condition of the Secretary. He is recovering quite rapidly. He takes an interest in the affairs of the department; makes inquiries regarding the same; has interviews with various departmental officers. He seems to have retained his full mental vigor. He is not able as yet to walk freely, but it is expected that within a short time he will regain sufficient strength to enable him to go out upon the street without the aid of an attendant. It is proposed that as soon as he is able to walk that he visit some of the springs—White Sulphur Springs, if you please—and take a course of treatment, bathing, &c., after which, it is thought, that he will be able to take his vacation.

"In an interview I had with him, I stated what you had said regarding the yachting cruise, and what you would be pleased to do, &c., &c. He seemed very much delighted with the idea; said he was very fond of yachting, and thought he would enjoy it very much indeed. He said he had thought of taking a little cruise inspecting the light-houses along the Potomac, &c. I did not state to him what you said to me regarding the unhealthy condition of the Potomac, regarding which I agree with you. I think it would be much better for him if he could take the Hudson River and Sound, going as far east as New Bedford and Martha's Vineyard.

"With great respect, I remain,

"Very respectfully yours,
"E. B. YOUMANS."

TILDEN TO MAYOR GRACE

"GREYSTONE, YONKERS, N. Y., *May 7th, 1886.*

"DEAR MAYOR GRACE,—I have from the beginning taken great interest in the welfare of the Central Park. I had much to do in enlarging it from the northern limit, which originally was a straight line across the hill and the ravine.

"This is my excuse for writing to you now. It is my judgment, and the judgment of many of the original friends of the Park, that the filling in of a portion of the ravine is a great wrong. It is probably the beginning of a series of measures which will be the desecration and ruin of the natural beauties of the great pleasure-ground of the people. It matters not whether these results come from incompetency or from jobbery. A change in the administration of the Park seems to be absolutely necessary.

"Gentlemen well acquainted with the subject, and with the individual, recommend the appointment of Mr. C. H. Woodman in the vacancy which you are about to fill.

"I am satisfied of his competency and integrity; and join my entreaty with those of the public, that you will rescue that imperilled work by his selection. After the mischief is done to the Park, and the people realize it, there will be a storm of indignation. All this can be averted by you now.

"Very truly yours,
"S. J. TILDEN."

D. MANNING TO TILDEN

"WASHINGTON, D. C., *June 4, 1886.*

"DEAR GOVERNOR,—I send you herewith a printed slip of correspondence that has recently occurred between two of your acquaintances. You will learn from it that I want to leave Washington and go home, and that the President is loath to have me go. He prefers to give me leave of absence, and at the outset named the 1st of August as the limit. To this I demurred, because the 1st of August marks the middle of every sensible person's vacation, and brings to us extreme hot weather. I could not bring myself to think it would be right for me to return here at that early day, and in the mean time my mind would be worried by thoughts of returning to the old tread-mill, in the hottest part of Washington's hot season. So the President changed it to the 1st of Oct., which certainly is a more proper date.

"I trust that what I have done, or rather what I have let be done, will have your approval.

"We are making arrangements for me to go to the Hot Springs of West Virginia within the next two or three days. I think we shall remain there about a month. After that, I hope I may be permitted by my physician to go North, in which event I want to visit you at Greystone, if only for an hour. That, I know, will do me great good.

"Your sincere friend,
"D. MANNING."

TILDEN TO GOVERNOR HILL

"GREYSTONE, YONKERS, N. Y., *June 5, 1886.*

"DEAR GOV. HILL,—There are two bills before you which ought to be rejected.

"1. The bill pretending to abolish imprisonment for debt. Your inquiry as to its effect upon Tweed's case, if this bill had been a law in Tweed's time, shows that you see one of the important points.

"If there are cases where the present law ought to be ameliorated, they should be specified. The present bill is not fit to be passed.

"If you will compare the bill with the existing law, you will see that the bill is deceptive and fraudulent.

"2. The bill appropriating $200,000 towards doubling the line of the locks on the Erie Canal will not be of the least utility to the navigation. Some time ago, I sent you some papers on this subject.

"If you have lost or mislaid them, I will send you duplicates.

"I have but a few minutes at my command this morning.

"Very truly yours,
S. J. TILDEN."

TILDEN TO JOSEPH R. HAWLEY

"GREYSTONE, YONKERS, N. Y., *June 9th, 1886.*

"MY DEAR SIR,—I am obliged by your courtesy in allowing Lieutenant Jaques to read to me a copy of your report on Coast Defences.

"I approve it highly, and think it does you great credit.

"I will thank you to send me a printed copy of this document.

"The apathy of Congress on this subject would be incredible, if it did not confront us.

"It contrasts with the rivalry which is so conspicuous to insist on our taking a high tone towards foreign nations on every occasion of difference between them and us.

"It contrasts, also, with the favor which is shown to schemes of prodigality, and schemes to waste the public resources on things known to be absolutely useless.

"Among the people, the desire for liberal appropriations towards the means of public defence, is well-nigh unanimous.

"I am well informed as to the popular feeling from the circumstance that more than seven hundred newspapers from all parts of the country, and representing all political parties, containing expressions upon the subject, have been sent to me.

"Very truly yours,
"S. J. TILDEN."

TILDEN TO MANNING

"GREYSTONE, *June 10, 1886.*

"DEAR MR. MANNING,—I received your letter enclosing the correspondence between the Secretary of the Treasury and the President.

"Your resignation will be a misfortune for the country, and a calamity to the Democratic party. To yourself it presents nothing but advantages.

"It is probably absolutely necessary to the restoration of your health, which ought to be a first consideration with you. You could not increase your reputation if you were to be Secretary a thousand years, and there are many chances that it might be diminished.

"Your letter is excellent; the only doubt I have is whether the remarks on the tariff are sufficiently guarded to prevent misrepresentation.

"I shall be glad to see you and Mrs. Manning at Greystone whenever you come North, but do not assent to so brief a call as you speak of.

"I hope the Hot Springs may be beneficial to you.

"Very truly yours,
"S. J. TILDEN."

JAMES C. CARTER TO TILDEN

"66 WALL ST., NEW YORK, *June 10th, 1886.*

"MY DEAR SIR,—Mr. D. D. Field has succeeded in getting through the Legislature a bill purporting to be a codification of the Law of Evidence.

"It is as bad as, or worse than, any of his schemes for bedevilling the law under the pretence of simplifying it.

"No one man in twenty of the members even read it, as I am assured. It is replete with gross errors, and in many ways changes the existing law not only in respect to evidence, but other topics.

"The chairman of the Judiciary Committee of the Assembly, who was mainly instrumental in working it through both houses, confessed before the Governor last Thursday in my presence that in its present shape it is unfit to go into operation.

"He urges the executive approval on the ground that it contains a clause authorizing the Governor to appoint a commission for the purpose of amending it, and postponing the time of its taking effect until after the next session.

"This very provision seems to me to be abundantly sufficient to call for a veto. There can be no more shocking fallacy than that it is safe to pass bad laws merely because they may be amended.

"I write this to the end that, should the Governor consult you about this measure, you may have such assurance as my opinion, whatever that may amount to, may afford that it is an unwise one.

"Mr. Field's abominable tinkering of our law has already brought about measureless mischief, and I am doing all I can to prevent the further progress of it.

"Very truly yours,
"JAMES C. CARTER.

"*Hon. S. J. Tilden.*"

D. MANNING TO TILDEN

"HOT SPRINGS, BATH CO., VA., *June 24, '86.*

"MY DEAR GOVERNOR,—Your very kind letter of the 10th inst. came duly to hand. I have been here taking the hot-spout baths daily for two weeks, and I feel pretty certain that I have been benefited by them.

"From the beginning much rain has fallen, and the mountain air, instead of being dry, crisp, and invigorating, has been moist, cool, and depressing; nevertheless, the stimulating effect of the baths are health-restoring, and I am satisfied it was wise to come here, because of the helps to my strength that I have gathered.

"I suffer somewhat from an old complaint characteristic of most invalids—viz., homesickness, and I am promising myself to start for New York early in July. There are several subjects about which I am anxious to consult you, and I propose to accept for Mrs. Manning, myself, and daughter your invitation to visit you at Greystone soon after we reach New York.

"I have heard from our friends in England, and they sent me information and matter that I want to bring to your attention.

"If you have occasion to write me before July 1st, address me here; anything sent to Washington should be sent to the care of my stenographer, Thos. J. Brennen, or to the care of Mr. Jordan.

"Very respectfully yours,
"DANIEL MANNING, "M. F. M."

D. MANNING TO S. J. TILDEN

"HOT SPRINGS, BATH CO., VA., *June 25, 1886.*

"MY DEAR GOVERNOR,—I have been offered, and I have accepted, the use of a special car from here over to New York for Saturday, July 3d. This, I understand, will get me to the city on the 4th—always a wearisome day to those who have to pass it there. May I venture, with Mrs. Manning and our daughter, to call on you at Greystone, say Monday, the 5th prox.? I do not expect to leave here before the morning of the 3d.

"My health is mending and improving, and I begin to feel somewhat like my old self again.

"Do not be much surprised if you see in the papers something like an interview with me on the Irish Home Rule question.

Faithfully yours,
"DANIEL MANNING."

TILDEN TO DANIEL MANNING

"*Telegram.*

"*June 29, 1886.*

"Letter received. Shall expect you and wife and daughter early on the morning of the 5th, unless you prefer to come on the 4th. Advise me as to train.

"S. J. TILDEN."

DANIEL MANNING TO TILDEN

"153 WASHINGTON ST., ALBANY, *July 11th* (*1886*).

"MY DEAR GOVERNOR,—We arrived home safely and comparatively well. The railroad ride did not tire me much; indeed, I stand railroading quite as well as I did two or three years ago.

"I have consulted with Dr. Hun, and because of a certain shortness of breath that troubles me now and again, his conclusions is that high, rarefied mountain air would not be beneficial, but that the sea air along the coast is desirable and would be helpful; therefore, under the advice of Dr. Hun, it is better that I keep away from the Catskill Mountains. What do you think and say?

"We are still feeling the good effects of our visit to Greystone. I am feeling better and more hopeful, and I realize that good has come to be because of my visit to you, and the healthful air that surrounds your very pleasant home.

"Your faithful friend,
"DANIEL MANNING,
"M. F. M."

D. MANNING TO TILDEN

"ALBANY, *July 21, 1886.*

"MY DEAR GOVERNOR,—Your note of the 16th inst. came to me in due course of mail, and was comforting.

"Like Dr. Simmons, Dr. Hun does not think there is any serious difficulty of the heart, but because of shortness of breath advises caution. I feel that I would like to go to the Catskill Mountains, but because Dr. Hun shows preference for the sea air, I have communicated with the Watch Hill House landlord, and hear that he will give me desirable quarters on the 29th of this month. I think we shall go there. No doubt I can get there all the exercise that I may need.

"Mrs. Manning had the pleasure of meeting, at the railroad station yesterday, Miss Ruby *en route* to Lebanon, and says she was looking well and happy.

"A letter from Fairchild tells me that the N. Y. collector had communicated with him concerning the proposition that I be given the use of the revenue-cutter *Grant.* You will conclude, of course, that this means much. I replied that if I concluded I should like to use that boat, I would communicate thereon with the President and himself. It is better so, but I have determined to give up the idea. I cannot place myself under such obligations. Nothing of the kind has been suggested or offered to me.

"I am almost constantly thinking of the 1st October letter. I suppose it must be written. I shrink from it, but I need your help and advice. What should I say?

"I am resting nicely here in Albany. There is excitement over bicentennial celebration, and I always find something of interest in what is daily occurring.

"The President and two or three of his secretaries are to be here to-morrow. Can I serve you in any way?

"I have a fierce and somewhat threatening [letter] from Thompson about the Custom-house. He says the President authorized Stetson to ask Hedden for his resignation, and he (T) consequently intimates his intention of opening a warfare on Cleveland, who, he writes, 'Tilden, you, and I nominated.' Evidently he is feeling very ugly, for he characterizes this step as 'base ingratitude,' and a 'dastardly outrage.' There is very noisy music near at hand.

"Respectfully and faithfully yours,
"DANIEL MANNING,
"M. F. M."

TILDEN TO DANIEL MANNING

"GREYSTONE, *July 27—86.*

"DEAR MR. MANNING,—Your letter of the 26th is received.

"I have thought much of the nature of the communication which you wish to make, but have written nothing. Do you wish to say anything further than to announce your final purpose, and your reasons for it? The letter, it seems to me, will be short.

"I will try my hand on a draft and send it to you.

"No further intelligence has been received from our friend in Europe.

"I have been busy all the morning answering a letter from Mr. Fairchild.

"By what route do you intend to go to Watch Hill—across the country or by way of New York?

"Very truly yours,
"S. J. TILDEN."

On the 4th day of August, and only eight days after the date of the preceding letter, I received the following telegram from George W. Smith, then Mr. Tilden's private secretary, and by his will to become one of his executors and Trustees:

"GREYSTONE, *Aug. 4, 1886.*

"Mr. Tilden died this morning at 8."

S. J. T.

(GREYSTONE, August 4, 1886.)

Once more, O all-adjusting Death!
The nation's Pantheon opens wide;
Once more a common sorrow saith
A strong, wise man has died.

Faults doubtless had he. Had we not
Our own, to question and asperse

The worth we doubted or forgot,
Until we stood beside his hearse?

Ambitious, cautious, yet the man
To strike down fraud with resolute hand;
A patriot, if a partisan,
He loved his native land.

So let the mourning bells be rung,
The banner droop its folds half-way,
And let the public pen and tongue
Their fitting tribute pay.

Then let us vow above his bier
To set our feet on party lies,
And wound no more a living ear
With words that Death denies.

John G. Whittier.

BIGELOW TO WHITTIER

"21 GRAMERCY PARK, NEW YORK, *Aug. 14, 1886.*

"VENERABLE AND DEAR SIR,—I am impatient to thank you for your admirably just and graceful tribute to the memory of my friend, the late Mr. Tilden.

"Though a prince of peace by training and self-discipline, Mr. Tilden, like all men of large moral proportions, came not to bring peace into the world, but the sword, and like all such men was much misunderstood and misrepresented; in many cases by those who at heart were entirely in sympathy with his aims. Of these latter, I venture to think you have made yourself the faithful and acceptable interpreter. You are right in thinking Mr. Tilden was ambitious, but his was not the kind of ambition by which angels fell. He sought power as a means, not as an end. To the mere pomp and circumstance of official eminence, no man could be more indifferent. His ideal of a State was a very exalted one, and he thought, in 1876, that he needed the *pou sto* of the Presidency to realize it. A majority of his countrymen were apparently of the same opinion. It was ordained, however, that he should never attain that eminence, as it was ordained that Moses should never enter into the Promised Land. If he ever murmured at his fate, it was as a citizen, and not as a candidate; as a victim of a wrong to the Republic, not to himself. He accumulated a large fortune in the prosecution of an honorable profession; but in his professional, as in his political, career, he was always accomplishing more for others than for himself. The acquisition of his own fortune was but incidental to the enrichment of a multitude.

"Had he been 'perfect,' he would, of course, have 'sold what he had, and given it to the poor.' He was not perfect. But few, however, have come much nearer to this divine standard than Mr. Tilden has done, in consecrating the greater part of the fruits of a laborious life to the welfare of his fellow creatures.

"Your verses encourage me to hope that death has lifted the veil which concealed from the world many of my friend's virtues, and much of his greatness.

"Respectfully and gratefully yours,
"JOHN BIGELOW."

FOOTNOTES:

[1] The cost of the war being practically packed away in loans.

[2] "In my opinion, any other than a *very slow* contraction of the excess of credit issue will be followed by a general dislocation of existing contracts. They are essentially 'nine-pins,' and if you knock over a few they will most likely bring down all the rest."

[3] The previous reports of which this is a synopsis were made to the Legislature.

[4] A striking illustration of this may be found in the first report of this commission to the Governor, on the Port Schuyler and lower Mohawk aqueduct contract.

[5] See statement of Professors Michie and Wheeler, of the United States Military Academy at West Point, on page 12 of first report of this commission to the Governor.

[6] Cost of extraordinary repairs made since the year 1867, including the year 1875:

Erie and Champlain	$6,602,858 60
Oswego	583,555 22
Cayuga and Seneca	163,480 76
Chemung	220,328 34
Crooked Lake	74,145 93
Chenango	255,073 77
Black River	120,410 22
Genesee Valley	369,478 20
Oneida Lake	50,063 60
Baldwinsville	5,432 70

Total $8,444,827 34

[7] See Exhibits D, E, F.

[8] See first report to the Executive, pages 15, 16, and 17.

[9] Mr. Sperry was Mr. Henderson's son-in-law, and at the time managing editor of the *Evening Post.*

[10] Charles Francis Adams, our minister to England during the Civil War.

[11] Mr. Horatio Seymour having refused to accept a nomination for Governor to succeed Governor Tilden, Mr. Hand, a leading barrister at Albany, was urged by Mr. Tilden and his friends to accept such nomination.

[12] "Under the Constitution three copies of the certificate of the Louisiana vote were necessary, one of which had to be forwarded to the president of the Senate by mail, another delivered to him by hand, and the third deposited with the United States district judge—all of which had to be accomplished within a certain number of days. When the Republican messenger—one T. C. Anderson—arrived in Washington and delivered the package containing one of those three certificates to Mr. Ferry, the president of the Senate, that gentleman called his attention to an irregularity in the form of the endorsement on the envelope and suggested that he consider its legal effect. Anderson therefore retained the package, and secretly opened it to ascertain if the error had been repeated in the certificate itself. To his consternation he discovered far more vital defects in the document, and flying back to New Orleans consulted with the party leaders, who agreed that the instrument must be redrawn, and the electors were hastily resumed. Then, to the managers' horror, it was discovered that two of the necessary officials were absent, and could not possibly be reached within the time limited by law for the delivery of the paper in Washington. 'Heroic' measures were therefore deemed essential, and after all the available signatures had been obtained the others were forged, and the doctored certificates, which, of course, were obviously different from the one previously forwarded by mail, were rushed back to Washington just in the nick of time. All these facts were subsequently unearthed, but those who actually committed the forgeries were never detected."—H. R. R., No. 140, 45th Cong., 3d Session, pp. 50-63 and 89-91.

[13] Mr. Barlow did not overestimate the good sense of the American people, but he underestimated the depravity of the Republican leaders in Washington, as he afterwards discovered to his sorrow.

[14] It was probably William E. Chandler, of New Hampshire, who is here referred to.

[15] When Mr. Pierrepont evidently expected him to be inaugurated as President.

[16] New York *Sun*, Wednesday, November 22, 1876.

[17] New York *Sun*, September 21, 1876.

[18] At the date of this note a judge of the Court of Appeals of the State of New York had been nominated and was running for the Presidency.

[19] For a copy of the protest referred to in the preceding letter, see Bigelow's *Life of Tilden*, Vol. II., Appendix A.

[20] The testimony of Kennedy referred to by Mr. Cottman follows:

WASHINGTON, February 21.—Patrick J. Kennedy, of Jefferson Parish, testified to-day to an interview with Governor Wells, in which the latter said that he thought he had done wrong in throwing out 1,100 votes in New Orleans and 1,400 votes in the Parish of East Baton Rouge. He also asked what guarantee Kennedy supposed would be given him if he so arranged the returns as to protect him and secure him his property and standing among the people of the State of Louisiana.

[21] Judge Bradley's peculiar if not exclusive responsibility for counting Mr. Hayes instead of the candidate chosen by the people into the Presidency is more clearly set forth in a communication of the writer entitled, "The Supreme Court and the Electoral Commission: An Open Letter to the Hon. Joseph H. Choate," first published in the New York *Sun*, on the 19th July, 1903, and later in a pamphlet by G. P. Putnam's Sons, New York.

[22] This remark was confirmed to me by a very competent authority. In June of 1877 Mr. James G. Blaine was one of the Inspectors of the United States Military Academy at West Point. He spent an afternoon with me at my residence in the immediate neighborhood, and the action of the Electoral Tribunal, among other things, became naturally enough a topic of conversation. He said, with some emphasis, "I was surprised at the time that the Democrats consented to the Electoral Tribunal," and added in substance—I cannot pretend to recall his exact words—that if they had remained firm it could not have succeeded.

[23] This I afterwards learned from Mr. O'Conor's own lips was his invariable practice. He never asked pay for his professional services until he had earned it.

[24] The italics are the editor's.

[25] A daughter of S. F. B. Morse, who is credited with having established the first telegraphic line of communication in America.

[26] This was in reply to a note of the 9th September, 1881, from Mr. Purcell, the editor of the Rochester *Union and Advertiser*, stating that he had been "mentioned" as a candidate for the office of Secretary of State, and wishing to know if the nomination would be disagreeable to him and be discountenanced by him: in which case he would prefer not to be considered a candidate.

[27] See *Tilden's Public Writings and Speeches*, Vol. I., p. 348.

[28] Mr. Tilden was aware that I wrote the biography of him which is here referred to, and which first appeared in the Louisville *Courier-Journal* during the campaign of 1876.

[29] Present Chief Justice of the United States; appointed in April, 1888.

[30] That would have meant rather an end of Samuel Randall's career as the agent of the protectionists in Congress.—*Editor.*

[31] Mr. Tilden's private secretary, and, for intimate correspondence, his synonyme.

[32] This is the draft of a letter doubtless emanating from Mr. Tilden, as it is in the handwriting of one of his secretaries.

[33] While knowing nothing of this correspondence, Mr. Tilden asked me one day while it proves to have been going on, "how the office of Secretary of Treasury would suit me, or rather how I would like it." I replied very promptly that I would not like it at all, nor would I accept it under any imaginable conditions; that I was principled against accepting any station, private or public, that I did not believe I could fill creditably, and that I did not feel competent to fill that office creditably; nor would I take it if I did, for its duties would be, from the beginning to the end, absolutely uncongenial to me.

[34] As Mr. Noyes had been one of the conspicuous Republican emissaries from Washington to corrupt the electoral vote in the South in 1876, Mr. Tilden regarded his appointment by Mr. Cleveland to any public office as not only a personal indignity to him but as an outrage to the country.

[35] Of this amount, 5,147,660 tons is the tonnage for twelve months of the N. Y. P. & O. R. R. Co., leased by the Erie.

[36] Originally printed in the New York *Sun* of March 4, 1886.

[37] On withdrawing from a cabinet meeting a day or two before the date of this letter, Mr. Manning experienced a burst of a blood-vessel at the base of his brain, from which he never entirely recovered.

[38] Mr. Husted, then Republican leader in the Assembly at Albany, had charge of some resolutions urging the New York members in Congress to push Mr. Tilden's policy of strengthening our coast defences. The paper that immediately follows this letter, entitled "Sea-coast Defences," is a contribution which Mr. Tilden made to Mr. Manning, with a view of its being made a part of the annual report.

CPSIA information can be obtained
at www.ICGtesting.com
Printed in the USA
LVHW050310311222
736049LV00002B/510

9 789356 718708